Reviews of the first edition:

'Mulhall's philosophical discussion of each film is highly stimulating. A provocative and engaging book which makes for stimulating reading for anyone interested in both film and philosophy.'

Matthew Kieran, Philosophical Books

'The themes he identifies as central – most crucially, a concern with human embodiment and thus, with both human generativity and mortality – are explored convincingly, even brilliantly at times. ... Despite the amount of closely argued material which is packed into a relatively short book, the clarity and precision of the writing make it something of a page-turner.'

Deborah Thomas, European Journal of Communication

ON FILM

In this significantly expanded new edition of his acclaimed exploration of the relation between philosophy and film, Stephen Mulhall broadens the focus of his work from science fiction to the espionage thriller and beyond.

The first part of the book discusses the four *Alien* movies. Mulhall argues that the sexual significance of the aliens themselves, and of Ripley's resistance to them, takes us deep into the question of what it is to be human. These four chapters develop a highly original and controversial argument that films themselves can philosophize – a claim Mulhall expands upon and defends in part two of this book, before applying his interpretative model to another sequence of contemporary Hollywood movies: the *Mission: Impossible* series.

A new chapter is devoted to each of the three films in that series, discussing them in the context of other films by the relevant directors. In this discussion, the nature of television becomes as central a concern as the nature of cinema; and this shift in genre also makes room for a detailed reading of Spielberg's *Minority Report*.

On Film, Second Edition is essential reading for anyone interested in philosophy, film theory and cultural studies, and in the way philosophy can enrich our understanding of cinema.

Stephen Mulhall is Fellow and Tutor in Philosophy at New College, Oxford, and author of *Heidegger and Being and Time* (Routledge) and *The Conversation of Humanity*.

ON FILM

Second edition

Stephen Mulhall

Routledge
Taylor & Francis Group

LONDON AND NEW YORK

First published 2001 by Routledge
2 Milton Park Square, Milton Park, Abingdon, Oxon OX14 4RN

Simultaneously published in the USA and Canada
by Routledge
270 Madison Ave, New York, NY 10016

Reprinted 2004, 2004
Second edition published 2008
Routledge is an imprint of the Taylor & Francis Group, an informa business

Typeset in Joanna by Taylor & Francis Books
Printed and bound in Great Britain by Antony Rowe Ltd,
Chippenham, Wiltshire

British Library Cataloguing in Publication Data
A catalogue record for this book is available from the British Library

Library of Congress Cataloging in Publication Data
Mulhall, Stephen, 1962-
On film / Stephen Mulhall. – 2nd ed.
p. cm.
Includes bibliographical references and index.
1. Alien (Motion picture) 2. Science fiction films–History and
criticism. I. Title.
PN1997.A32253M85 2008
791.43'72–dc22
2007050592

ISBN10: 0-415-44153-6 (pbk)
ISBN10: 0-203-92852-0 (ebk)

ISBN13: 978-0-415-44153-7 (pbk)
ISBN13: 978-0-203-92852-3 (ebk)

FOR ELEANOR (ONCE AGAIN), AND FOR
MATTHEW – WHO LIKED THE
MOTOR-BIKE CHASE

CONTENTS

PREFACE TO THE SECOND EDITION

I'm grateful that Routledge have made it possible for me to produce a second edition of this little book, and so given me the
chance to recall and redouble the pleasure I took in its original
composition. Since, however, this new version of that original
subverts in various ways the expectations a reader might reasonably have of 'a second edition', some initial words of orientation
seem called for.

In order to achieve all the goals that I set myself for this edition, it needed to be far longer than the original; and since this
forced me to contravene one of the central principles of the
Thinking in Action series to which the first edition belonged, this
second edition can no longer claim to be part of it (although I
hope that it continues to conform to another of its principles –
that of accessibility to a non-academic readership).

I have made use of the additional space in ways which are
reflected in the division of this new book into three parts. Part I
reproduces in its entirety the text of the five chapters that made
up the first edition. The introduction is essentially unaltered, and
the four following chapters have been slightly expanded to
include brief new discussions either of other films by the relevant
director or of films that at least appear to constitute additions to
series whose earlier members were discussed in the original
chapter. So, Chapter 1 now includes remarks on Scott's *Gladiator*,
Black Hawk Down and *Kingdom of Heaven*; Chapter 2 discusses *Terminator
3*; Chapter 3 looks at Fincher's *The Game*, *Fight Club*, *Panic Room* and
Zodiac; and Chapter 4 addresses Jeunet's *Amelie*, as well as *Alien vs*

Predator. Otherwise, everything that originally appeared in these five chapters reappears here.

Parts II and III, by contrast, both consist of new material. Part II is conceived of as transitional, and so its two chapters look, respectively, backward and forward. Chapter 5 aims to respond to the main objections raised by critics of the first edition, and so to clarify the conception of film's relation to philosophy that underlies both editions. Chapter 6 is intended to return the reader to the book's primary emphasis on reading specific films, by offering a detailed interpretation of Spielberg's *Minority Report*. In so doing, it looks forward to the work of Part III, by exemplifying a shift of generic focus (from science fiction to thrillers pivoting around conflict between upholders and violators of the law) and a switch of attention from Sigourney Weaver to Tom Cruise (taken as exemplars of stardom).

Part III aims further to test the plausibility of the original interpretative model advanced in the first edition. It does so by retaining my original focus on a specific series of Hollywood movies (a set of interlinked sequels each of which exemplifies the work of a different director, and so simultaneously invites consideration of its relation to other films by the same hand or eye, and an evaluation of its way of inheriting the cinematic universe established by his predecessors), but varying other parameters established in that earlier discussion. For the three *Mission: Impossible* films operate in a different genre to that of the *Alien* series; the directors involved (De Palma, Woo and Abrams) have either no established cinematic body of work, or one which has raised unremitting questions about its superficiality or fascination with mere appearance; and the series as a whole is indebted from the outset to work in another medium entirely – that of television – whose differences from the medium of cinema thereby become a matter of compelling interest. This series accordingly engenders a range of questions about modernism (as opposed to postmodernism or modernizing) in cinema that were less explicitly addressed in the *Alien* series; although, in doing so, surprisingly similar questions to those posed in and by the *Alien* films – questions about identity and embodiment, and about film's capacity to reflect on its distinctive powers – turn out to recur in this new context.

Accordingly, the three chapters that make up Part III reproduce the general, Janus-faced template of the four substantial chapters in Part I. They each look both at an individual director's contribution to the series that is my central concern and at other related work by that same director; but they follow the specific issues that arise as a result of reapplying that template wherever they happen to lead, and so broach some questions that remain largely untouched in Part I.

In effect, then, significantly more than half of this second edition consists of entirely new material, and almost all of that is contained in new chapters covering new films rather than in expanding or qualifying my original treatment of the films I originally chose to discuss. Since, however, this new edition contains an extended defence of the procedures of the old, and its new material otherwise amounts to a further extension of those procedures, it seems to me nevertheless to form a single, unified text, even if its new claims and readings are not exactly predictable in either structure or content from the old material that it retains. I hope that those familiar with the first edition will feel that the range of reference of the second (both philosophically and cinematically) has expanded in a way that merits their renewed attention.

Whilst this edition contains much material not contained in the first edition, some of that new material first appeared in other contexts (even if in very different forms). Earlier and much shorter versions of Chapter 5 appeared in *Film and Philosophy*, vol. 9 (2005) – under the title 'Ways of Thinking' – and in *Proceedings of the Aristotelian Society*, Volume CVII, part 3 (2007) – under the title 'Film as Philosophy: The Very Idea'. An earlier and much shorter version of the material that here appears as Chapters 7 and 8 was first published in Smith and Wartenberg (eds), *Thinking through Cinema: Film as Philosophy* (Blackwell: Oxford, 2006) under the title 'The Impersonation of Personality: Film as Philosophy in *Mission: Impossible*'. I would like to thank all those involved in these publications for giving me the opportunity to begin thinking about this new material, as well as the three anonymous readers commissioned by Routledge to offer critical suggestions on the idea of a second edition by way of critical comments on the first (and, of course, those who published critical comments on the first edition in various fora).

I would also like to thank Alison Baker, for reading and offering comments on Parts II and III in manuscript, and for making it possible to compose this second edition without being either overwhelmed by or deprived of Eleanor's and Matthew's companionable interruptions.

Part I

INTRODUCTION

The four members of the *Alien* series (*Alien* [1979]; *Aliens* [1986]; *Alien*³ [1992]; *Alien Resurrection* [1997]) managed to combine popular success and critical interest in a way matched by very few films produced in the last two decades of the twentieth century.[1] They focus on Flight Lieutenant Ellen Ripley (played by Sigourney Weaver) as she confronts the threat posed to herself, her companions and the human race by the spread of a hostile alien species. But this description hardly begins to capture their peculiar economy of simplicity and power – the charismatic force of Weaver's incarnation of Ripley's despairing but indomitable courage, the uncanny otherness of the aliens, and of course the alien universe itself, stripped of the clutter of social particularity to reveal receding horizons of mythic significance. It now seems as if it was clear from the outset that it would take more than one film to explore those horizons, and thereby to unfold the full meaning of Ripley's intimate loathing of her foes.

But there are, of course, more specific reasons for choosing to focus on this series of films in a philosophical book on film – reasons having to do with what one might call the underlying logic of the alien universe they depict. For these movies are preoccupied, even obsessed, with a variety of inter-related anxieties about human identity – about the troubled and troubling question of individual integrity and its relation to the body, sexual difference and nature. What exactly is my place in nature? How far does the (natural) human ability to develop technology alienate us from the natural world? Am I (or am I in) my body? How

3

sharply does my gender define me? How vulnerable does my body make me? Is sexual reproduction a threat to my integrity, and, if so, does the reality and nature of that threat depend on whether I am a man or a woman? These are themes that emerge with quasi-mathematical elegance from the series' original conception of an alien species which involves human beings in the furtherance of its own reproductive cycle, and which thereby confronts its human protagonists with the flesh-and-blood basis of their existence. This issue – call it the relation of human identity to embodiment – has been central to philosophical reflection in the modern period since Descartes; but the sophistication and self-awareness with which these films deploy and develop that issue, together with a number of related issues also familiar to philosophers, suggest to me that they should themselves be taken as making real contributions to these intellectual debates. In other words, I do not look to these films as handy or popular illustrations of views and arguments properly developed by philosophers; I see them rather as themselves reflecting on and evaluating such views and arguments, as thinking seriously and systematically about them in just the ways that philosophers do. Such films are not philosophy's raw material, nor a source for its ornamentation; they are philosophical exercises, philosophy in action – film as philosophizing.

Furthermore, the *Alien* series' interest in the bodily basis of human identity inexorably raises a number of inter-related questions about the conditions of cinema as such. For the medium is itself dependent upon the photographic reproduction (or, better, transcription) of human beings, the projection of moving images of embodied human individuals presented to a camera. In one sense, in one frame of mind, this phenomenon can appear utterly banal; in another, it can seem utterly mysterious – as fascinating as the fact that a human being can be portrayed in paint, or that ink-marks on paper can express a thought. One might say that cinematic projections, with their unpredictable but undeniable capacity to translate (and to fail to translate) certain individual physiognomies into movie stardom, are one of the necessary possibilities to which embodied creatures such as ourselves are subject; and we cannot understand that subjection without understanding the nature of photographic transcription as such, hence without understanding what becomes of anything and everything on film.

These questions, about the nature of the cinematic medium, are perhaps those which we might expect any philosophical book on film to address – they are what is typically referred to when philosophers refer to 'the philosophy of film'; and this book does indeed find itself addressing such questions in a number of places. But it does so because it finds that these films themselves address such questions – because it finds that, in their reflections on human embodiment, they find themselves reflecting upon what makes it possible for them to engage in such reflections, upon the conditions for the possibility of film. In other words, a fundamental part of the philosophical work of these films is best understood as philosophy of film.

But the series has developed in such a way that its individual members have ineluctably been forced to grapple with a range of other conditions for their own possibility. To begin with, each film sits more or less uneasily within the genre of science fiction, with more or less strong ties in any individual case with the adjacent genres of horror, thriller, action, war and fantasy movies; and, although each film can be regarded as self-contained or self-sufficient, hence capable of being understood on its own terms, each succeeding film has also been created in clear awareness of its relation to its forebears. The distinctive character of each new episode in the series is thus in part a consequence of the increasingly complex nature of its thematic and narrative inheritance; but primarily it results from a commitment on the part of the series producers (Gordon Carroll, David Giler and Walter Hill) to find a new director for each episode, and preferably one with great potential rather than with an established cinematic track record. The series so far has used the talents, and helped to make or to consolidate the reputation, of Ridley Scott, James Cameron, David Fincher and Jean-Pierre Jeunet. Each episode can therefore be seen as an early step in the development of a highly influential and acclaimed cinematic career, and hence as internally related to such original and substantial films as *Blade Runner*, *Gladiator* and *Black Hawk Down*, *Terminator* and *Terminator 2*, *Se7en*, *The Game*, *Fight Club* and *Panic Room*, and *The City of Lost Children* and *Amelie*.

This unusual conjunction of circumstances means that a detailed study of the *Alien* series will allow us, first, to examine the ways in which the specific conventions of traditional film genres, and the more general conditions of movie-making in Hollywood (as opposed, say, to those in the independent sector or in Europe), can both support and resist the achievement of artistic excellence. Here, what emerges in the coming chapters will confirm that, if we have not already done so, we can and should move beyond the disabling thought (a thought that can only disable genuine thoughtfulness about cinema) that artistic excellence is necessarily unobtainable in even the most unpromising of Hollywood contexts. Second, such a study also allows an investigation into the condition of sequeldom – a mode of movie-making that has appeared to dominate in Hollywood since the late 1990s, as if American commercial cinema had returned to one of its most influential early forms of the 1930s and 1940s, but in a much more self-conscious (sometimes serious, sometimes merely exploitative) way. An important issue here is the way in which a 'franchise' can renew itself over time, in part by explicitly reflecting upon what is involved in inheriting a particular set of characters in a particular narrative universe – the constraints and opportunities internal to (what, as a philosopher, I am inclined to call the logic of) that inheritance.

A third reason for studying this series is that each individual member of it is also an individual film in the series of a particularly gifted director's work. Each such movie can thus be studied as a point of intersection between a director's talents and artistic vision, and the narrative and thematic potential inherent in the alien universe; each film simultaneously unfolds more of the identity or individuality of its director and of its universe, as if each is made more itself in and through the complementarities and contrasts generated by their intense mutual engagement. In this way, we might be able to make some progress in understanding the general significance of (the insights made available, as well as the confusions engendered, by) our desire to talk of a film's director as its author, and hence to regard a film director's *oeuvre* as possessed of a particular thematic and artistic unity.

If, then, the developments of plot and character that make up the individual substance of these films can be thought of as generated by a reflective engagement with their own status as sequels, and hence with questions of inheritance and originality, then we could say that the series as a whole makes progress by reflecting upon the conditions of its own possibility. We might think of this kind of reflection as particularly demanded of any art in the condition of modernism – in which its own history (its inheritance of conventions, techniques and resources) has become an undismissable problem for it, something it can neither simply accept nor simply reject. But to make progress by reflecting upon the conditions of its own possibility is also as good a characterization as could be desired of the way in which any truly rigorous philosophy must proceed; for any philosophy that failed to engage in such reflection would fail to demand of itself what it makes its business to demand of any and every other discipline with which it presumes to engage. Hence, as well as thinking of the *Alien* series as an exemplary instance of cinematic modernism, we might also consider it as exemplary of cinema that finds itself in the condition of philosophy – of film as philosophy.

It is because I believe that these movies can be thought of in this way – as at once film as philosophizing, philosophy of film, and film in the condition of philosophy – that I regard myself as having written a philosophy book on film rather than a book about some films which happens to have some philosophy in it. And it is this same belief that leads me to regard the films under discussion in the following chapters in ways that differ fundamentally from the work of most of the film theorists I came across in preparing to write them. In the course of that preparation, it became clear to me that such theorists exhibit a strong tendency to treat the films they discuss as objects to which specific theoretical edifices (originating elsewhere, in such domains as psychoanalysis or political theory) could be applied. Even the most useful of these discussions would usually begin with a long explanation of the relevant theory and turn to the specific film only at the end, and only as a cultural product whose specific features served to illustrate the truth of that theory – as one more phenomenon the theory rendered comprehensible. Of course, I have no objection to anyone making use of whatever intellectual resources they find pertinent in coming to understand a film's power and interest – I will be doing so myself, here and there, in the chapters to come.[2] However, the approaches I encountered seemed to me to lack any sense that the films themselves might have anything to contribute to our understanding of them – that they might contain a particular account of themselves, of why they are as they are, an account that might contribute to an intellectual exploration of the issues to which these pre-established bodies of theory also contribute, or even serve critically to evaluate those theories, to put their accuracy or exhaustiveness in question.

In short, such film theory as I have encountered tends to see in films only further confirmation of the truth of the theoretical machinery to which the theorist is already committed; the film itself has no say in what we are to make of it, no voice in the history of its own reception or comprehension. One of the reasons this book approaches questions about film through a detailed reading of specific films is precisely to put this tendency in question – to suggest that such films are in fact as capable of putting in question our prior faith in our general theories as they are of confirming that faith. This is, of course, just another way of saying that films can be seen to engage in systematic and sophisticated thinking about their themes and about themselves – that films can philosophize.

Reiterating such a claim about these films, these products of a lucrative Hollywood franchise in a popular commercial genre, might bring to the surface an anxiety that is very likely to emerge whenever a philosopher finds philosophizing going on in places where we tend not to expect it – isn't such an interpretation of these movies just a matter of over-interpretation, of reading things into them that simply aren't there? There is, of course, no general way of allaying such anxieties; whether or not a particular reading of a film in fact reads things into it as opposed to reading things out of it is not something that can be settled apart from a specific assessment of that reading against one's own assessment of the given film (and vice versa). Certainly, to think that my readings must be over-interpretations simply because they quickly find themselves grappling with questions that are of interest to philosophers would suggest a rather impoverished conception of the intellectual powers of film and of the pervasiveness of matters of philosophical interest in human life.

Nevertheless, this anxiety does accurately register something specific to these particular films – the fact that (in a manner I think of as bequeathed to them by one of their producers, Walter Hill) they appear to demand interpretation, and interpretation of a certain kind. From beginning to end, the *Alien* films present us with small, isolated groups of human beings framed most immediately against the infinity of the cosmos. Each individual's inhabitation of the universe appears unmediated by the more complex interweavings of culture and society, those systems of signification which always already determine the meaning of any actions and events encompassed by them; their only carapace or exoskeleton is the bare minimum of technology necessary for their survival (whether an ore-carrying ship, an atmosphere-processing facility, a waste refinery or a covert military/scientific research station). This cosmic backdrop makes it all but impossible to avoid grasping the narrative and thematic structure of the films in metaphysical or existential terms – as if the alien universe could not but concern itself with the human condition as such (as opposed to some specific inflection of that condition, some particular way in which a given human society has adapted, and adapted to, its environment, some individual way of making sense of its circumstances).

In choosing, as my disciplinary bent would anyway incline me, to meet these films' demand to be understood metaphysically, I do not take myself to be endorsing every element of that understanding (or even endorsing the understanding of philosophy as inherently metaphysical – as opposed, say, to thinking of it as aiming to diagnose or overcome the metaphysical). Neither do I take myself to be overlooking (or denying) the fact that any narrative universe designed to depict humanity *sub specie aeternitatis* will always exemplify a particular human way of making sense of ourselves and our circumstances – that any given metaphysics is culturally and socially specific, and hence that much of interest might emerge by asking how these films' metaphysical ambitions relate to the particular historical circumstances of their production.

But, of course, choosing to plot those relations does not negate but rather presupposes a grasp of the relevant metaphysical ambitions; and, by the same token, choosing to focus exclusively upon their metaphysical register does not at all commit me to the view that any other focus is misplaced or otiose. On the contrary, whilst I have attempted to provide a full or complete reading of the series' underlying (call it metaphysical) logic, in that I have aimed to establish a coherent perspective from which these films do genuinely form a series (a sequence in which each member appears as generated by its predecessor, and generative of its successor), I do not regard that reading as exhaustive or exclusive – as if its validity entails the invalidity of any alternative readings or approaches to reading, of any claims to identify another (metaphysical or non-metaphysical) kind of coherence in their individual and collective identity. The validity of any such claims rather turns, to say it once again, on specific assessments of their bearing on our specific experiences of the films themselves (and vice versa).

All that this book implicitly claims is that philosophy has something distinctive to contribute to the ongoing conversations about particular films and the medium of cinema that play such an important role in contemporary public culture. Philosophy's voice has a specific register, one that distinguishes it even from that of film theory and cultural studies; but in making itself heard it has (and needs to have) no desire to render other voices mute.

The overall structure of (what is now Part I of) this little book takes the form of four chapters. Each is concerned with one episode in the *Alien* series, but each also looks in detail at other work by the director of that episode. Chapter 1 develops at some length my understanding of the basic logic of the alien universe; the other three are more preoccupied with the artistic problems and possibilities they pose, as well as the incitements and resistances they generate, for the directors who follow Ridley Scott. Chapter 4, on *Alien Resurrection*, functions as a conclusion that is also a prologue, since this episode in the series is itself most knowingly constructed as a meditation upon the degree to which any such series can successfully renew itself, and thus places the further continuation of the series in question whilst at the same time suggesting that its potential for continuation can survive the most thoroughgoing attempts (as, for example, in *Alien*[3]) to exhaust or foreclose its narrative possibilities.

I would like to thank Simon Critchley and Richard Kearney for inviting me to contribute a volume to their Thinking in Action series, Tony Bruce at Routledge for helping to develop and support such a worthwhile publishing venture, Philip Wheatley and Alison Baker for reading and offering comments on the book in manuscript form, and a number of anonymous readers for Routledge whose responses also helped to improve the text. The portion of Chapter 1 devoted to *Blade Runner* is a much-revised version of an article that first appeared in *Film and Philosophy*, vol. 1, 1994.

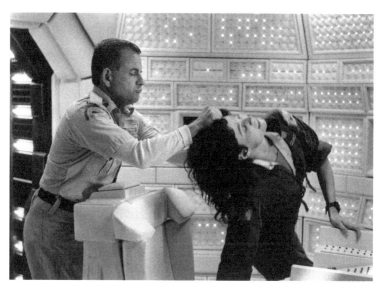

Source: 20th Century Fox courtesy the Kobal Collection

1

KANE'S SON, CAIN'S DAUGHTER

Ridley Scott's *Alien*

Above the sparse opening credits, as the camera pans slowly from the outer rim of a planet's Saturnian rings across the pitch black of its surface and back out to the opposite rim of those rings, the title of this film is indicated in a slowly emerging sequence of vertical strokes. It thus appears to emerge from the surface of the planet itself, the place from which the alien creature after which the film is named emerges; and it is indicated rather than spelt out, because some of its constituent letters (not being wholly composed of (near-)vertical strokes) are rather implied or suggested, their precise identity left for the viewer to determine in her imagination – just as this film's director will leave implicit the overall appearance and exact nature of the alien creature itself until (and in some respects beyond) its end. Perhaps, then, we should not expect the exact nature of this film to be any less alien to us than its eponymous protagonist – any less unpredictable from what we think we know that a science fiction or horror movie must be, any less unaccommodated by our existing sense of what the medium of film as such can allow or achieve.

Next, the camera watches the enormous expanse of the *Nostromo* approach and pass by, with its substantial command module utterly dwarfed by the industrial landscape of domed cylinders and stackpipes (containing 20 million tonnes of mineral ore) in tow behind it. We cut to the interior of the ship: the camera reveals an octagonal corridor, neither spacious nor oppressive, then turns to look down its junction with another corridor; it pans unhurriedly across a table in a communal area, then down another corridor to a space cluttered with monitor screens and banks of instruments. There is movement – the flutter of paper in a draught, the dipping head of a toy bird – but it is mechanical, devoid of human significance. Then one of the display screens lights up as a computer begins to chatter; we see downscrolling symbols reflected in the visor of a helmet. As the ship absorbs and reacts to this burst of activity, we cut to a doorway: coats flutter in the draught induced by the doors as they open, and the camera takes us into a blindingly white, sterile room, dominated by an array of glass-lidded coffin-shaped modules, each oriented towards a central stem, like the petals of a flower. The lids rise, to reveal a number of human bodies: in a series of stately but fluid dissolves, we see one of them sit up, remove a monitor pad and stand up. He is wearing a loincloth or a pair of shorts, the whiteness of the material combining with that of the room to accentuate the pallor of his skin; his eyes are closed, he rubs his face, as if unwillingly acceding to consciousness. His face – deeply lined and weary, marked by some kind of suffering from which it has not yet escaped – is instantly recognizable as that of John Hurt, whose name was perhaps the most famous of those which appeared during the film's opening credits. We think we have finally arrived at the human centre of the film that is about to begin.

And we are wrong (as we are wrong in taking Janet Leigh's character to be the protagonist of Psycho). But we have been shown a great deal in this prologue that is true to what will follow, true both to this director and to his tale (as written by Dan O'Bannon). The slow, calm, controlled movements of the camera have established the basic rhythm of the direction – unhurried but supremely confident that what we will eventually be shown is worthy of our investment of interest. We can also see Scott's confidence in his sets and special effects, even in the wake of 2001 and Star Wars: they can bear up under close scrutiny in the absence of human activity, and thus make more credible the normalcy or everydayness of that activity when it finally begins. This is not a cartoon or fantasy of space technology and interstellar travel; it is a working ship in the real world of the human future – a world quickly shown to have inherited our predilection for social hierarchy and salary disputes, whose bickering inhabitants can barely summon an interest in their fellows or themselves.

Beyond this, the camera's unhurried scrutiny of the *Nostromo*'s empty spaces points up the imperturbable self-sufficiency of the ship, its ability to guide itself safely across interstellar distances in the complete absence of conscious human control. This subtly inflects our sense of the relative dependence of human beings and their technological tools. When the crew finally emerge from their ship's hibernation pods so that they might respond to the unidentified radio beacon, the ship's need for them in these unusual circumstances only emphasizes their superfluity in normal circumstances. They appear as useful creatures for the ship's purposes, as if a kind of pet or parasite, and the significance of their own purposes and fate is correspondingly diminished. Indeed, when we come to realize that the planet and the ship of the prologue constitute the entirety of the coming narrative's locations, and hence that we have been shown the terrain of the film as a whole before its inhabitation by character and narrative, as if demonstrating the world's continuation beyond our participation in or knowledge of it, this prologue underlines the essential belatedness and relativity of human concerns, their insignificance in the face of the universe which makes them possible.

Most important of all, however, is the complex manner of the crew's entry into consciousness, and into their own story. On one level, the suddenly deadened soundtrack and sequence of overlapping dissolves that chart Hurt's emergence into conscious awareness seem to mimic the mode of that emergence – as disorganized and disorienting as his first perceptions appear to be to him, as if he were awaking from a dream. But it could, of course, equally well characterize the process of beginning to dream, of being translated from consciousness to that mode of awareness in which nightmares come; and we have already been shown that nightmare landscape, the source and context of their coming trials. On another level, the crew appears to be undergoing a kind of rebirth.[1] They emerge like seeds from a pod, as if extruded by the ship itself, almost as naked as the day they were born; and Hurt's dazed face registers the impact of the world on his senses as if for the first time. However, his umbilical cord is a monitor pad and line, the pallor of his body is barely distinguishable from the sterile whiteness of his technological womb, and his sexual organs are covered over; and the presentation of these details through a silenced soundtrack and overlapping dissolves, with their subversion of the conditions of ordinary perceptual experience, now suggest a displacement of reality not by dream but by fantasy. We are being given a picture of human origination that represses its creatureliness, that represents parturition as an automated function of technology rather than of flesh emerging noisily and painfully from flesh – as essentially devoid of blood, trauma and sexuality.

Does this fantasy originate in the director, or in the characters themselves, or in the society to which they are returning? Does it represent a consummation devoutly to be wished, or (given the scene's conjunction of this fantasy's realization with the onset of nightmare) are we rather meant to see that the monstrousness of life is not so easily to be avoided? It is, at any rate, umbilically linked to the nightmare that is about to penetrate and overwhelm the Nostromo.

The alien cycle of life

How is it that Alien transforms itself slowly but surely from a pure science fiction film into a horror movie, or rather into a highly original hybrid of the two? Why is it that the alien inspires – in the Nostromo's crew and in us – not only fear and terror, but horror? Stanley Cavell has suggested one way of discriminating between these responses, by discriminating between those aspects of the world to which they respond:

> Fear is of danger; terror is of violence, of the violence I might do or that might be done me. I can be terrified of thunder, but not horrified by it. And isn't it the case that not the human horrifies me, but the inhuman, the monstrous? Very well. But only what is human can be inhuman. – Can only the human be monstrous? If something is monstrous, and we do not believe that there are monsters, then only the human is a candidate for the monstrous.

If only humans feel horror (if the capacity to feel horror is a development of the specifically human biological inheritance), then maybe it is a response specifically to being human. To what, specifically, about being human? Horror is the title I am giving to the perception of the precariousness of human identity, to the perception that it may be lost or invaded, that we may be, or may become, something other than we are, or take ourselves for; that our origins as human beings need accounting for, and are unaccountable.[2]

This is why the monster in horror movies is so often a zombie or one of the living dead, a vampire, a botched creation, construction or reconstruction of the human – this is why Frankenstein's monster is prototypical of the genre. As well as threatening to inflict a peculiarly intimate, distorting or rending violence upon vulnerable human flesh and blood (a threat repeatedly carried out in this film and its successors), these creatures are themselves mutations or distortions of the human. What, then, of Ridley Scott's alien; what precisely is it about the precariousness of our own human identity that we see in the monstrosity of this monster?

Beyond the threat of violence that this dragon, as big as a man, represents (and to which terror rather than horror is the primary response), there stands first the alien's motive for inflicting that violence upon the human beings who encounter it. For it harbours no general or specific malice against the human race as such, or against the crew of the *Nostromo*. It attaches itself to, and exits from, Kane's body because this is dictated by its mode of reproduction: it can grow only within another living being. And it attacks the rest of the crew because they threaten its survival (hence, at least initially, that of its species) and because they represent the only available means for the continued existence of that species. It is, in short, just doing what comes naturally to any species – following the imperatives of nature.

However, the alien species appears not so much to follow nature's imperatives as to incarnate them. This is not because it is driven to survive and reproduce, but rather because it is so purely driven, because it appears to have no other drives – no desire to communicate, no culture, no modes of play or pleasure or industry other than those necessitated by its own continuation as a species. The alien's form of life is (just, merely, simply) life, life as such: it is not so much a particular species as the essence of what it means to be a species, to be a creature, a natural being – it is Nature incarnate or sublimed, a nightmare embodiment of the natural realm understood as utterly subordinate to, utterly exhausted by, the twinned Darwinian drives to survive and reproduce.

The alien's monstrosity derives further specificity from the fact that its mode of reproduction is parasitic. After seeing it burst from Kane's torso, we realize that neither the planet nor the alien ship from which the creature emerged is its true home: we recall the fossilized remains of a member of another alien species encountered within that ship (seated behind what looked like an enormous weapon) with a hole punched through its chest, and realize that the ship's cargo of eggs was no more indigenous to the ship itself than it is to the desolate planet upon which that ship crash-landed – indeed, that the crash-landing itself might well have been induced by the parasitic alien species' progressive infestation of that ship's crew. This parasitism is an extreme manifestation of the relationship any species has with the broader system of nature: it signifies at once their vulnerability to predation by the other species with which they must inhabit the natural realm and their dependence upon their environment for sustenance. Metaphysically, it represents a perception of life itself as something external to or other than the species which incarnates it – something that invades, makes use of, and then discards, any and every manifestation of itself, as if living beings are merely its vehicles, slaves or hosts. The alien's parasitism exemplifies the essential parasitism of Nature; it represents the radical lack of autonomy that is of the essence of creaturehood – its need to incorporate, and its openness to incorporation by, that which is not itself, and its victimization by the life within it.

However, perhaps the most uncanny aspect of the alien's monstrosity is determined by the specific mode of its parasitism. For, in order to reproduce, it must insert a long, flexible member into the host's body through one of that body's orifices, and deposit a version of itself within its host's torso, where it develops to the point at which it must force itself out again. In short, what happens to Kane is that he is impregnated with an alien foetus which his body then brings to term and labours to bring forth into the world; he undergoes a nightmare vision of sexual intercourse, pregnancy and birth. The heart of the alien's monstrosity is thus that it relates itself to its host species in a manner which embodies a particular fantasy of sexual relations between human males and human females. The threat stalking the corridors and ducts of the *Nostromo* is thus a vision of masculinity *and* femininity, hence of sexual difference as such, as monstrous. The monster itself is the incarnation of masculinity, understood as penetrative sexual violence; but, as such, it threatens the human race as a whole with the monstrous fate of feminization, forcing our species to occupy the sexual role (that of being violated, of playing host to a parasite and of facing death in giving birth) that women are imagined to occupy in relation to men.

This thought about the monster's uncanny parasitism is not contradicted, but is rather made more specific, if we further note its intensely oral focus. In this respect, of course, the alien's mode of parasitism reflects its general mode of being; for at every stage of its post-partum development, it presents itself to us as all mouth. From the metallic incisors of the near-blind chestburster to the teeth-within-teeth of the warrior, it is as if its nature finds its fullest expression in images of devouring insatiability (and the threat such images pose for men and for women might be taken to be as different, in nature and in depth, as are the threat of castration and that of an infant's limitless demands on its mother). But the facehugger variant of this being that is all mouth also chooses to penetrate the mouths of its victims when impregnating them; and on the assumption that its mode of reproduction is a monstrous image of the human mode of reproduction, this implies that to occupy the role of women in relation to men is to have one's mouth stopped or gagged, to be rendered mute (a muteness registered in the long wastes of silence on this film's soundtrack, and in its sense that any form of negotiation – any conversation or intercourse – with the alien species is utterly beside the point). Heterosexual masculinity here appears as aiming to silence the woman's voice, to deny her the most fundamental expression of her individuality. For the human race to be feminized is thus for human individuality as such to be threatened, as if the alien's monstrosity declares that something about the acknowledgement of individuality (in particular, acknowledging the relation of individuality to sexual difference) sticks in our throats, makes us gag.

What holds these various facets of the alien's monstrousness together is their relation to human fantasies and fears about human embodiment or animality: collectively, they give expression to an idea of ourselves as victimized by our own flesh and blood – as if it is essentially other than, alien to, what we are, as if our bodies not only made us vulnerable to suffering and death, but made our very humanness precarious. Sexual difference, the drive to survive and reproduce, dependence upon and vulnerability to the natural world: these are all aspects of our creaturely life, features brought to an unprecedented pitch of purity in the alien species but common nevertheless to both human and alien, and yet experienced as monstrous. The alien thus represents the return of the repressed human body, of our ineluctable participation in the realm of nature – of life.

A further aspect of the alien's incarnation of nature also serves to subvert one of our most familiar ways of repressing our own creaturehood, of understanding our humanness as other to our embodiment. For this alien, is, of course, uniquely well equipped to defend itself; or rather, with its leathery, indefinitely fertile eggs, its foetal teeth and tail, the molecular acid it uses for blood and its capacity to transform its own skin into polarized silicon body-armour, it is its own survival equipment. It has internalized or become its own array of defensive and offensive tools and instruments – its flesh is armour and its blood a weapon; in short, its body is its technology. The alien thereby represents a mode of evolution that is not dwarfed by or in thrall to (say, alienated from) its technology, as the crew of the *Nostromo* appear to be; and, more specifically, it undercuts our tendency to imagine that our social and cultural development, our ability to evolve beyond the limitations of the body by evolving tools and technology (to reduce our vulnerability and improve upon our

natural powers), is the means by which we transcend our naturalness rather than a further expression of it, simply the exploitation of the biological endowment that is distinctive of our
species. The alien's monstrously intimate incorporation of its
technology into its nature is a projection of our horror at the
thought that culture as such is in fact our second nature – not
something other to our naturalness in which our humanity might
safely reside, something from which we must accordingly think
of our incarnate selves as alienated, on pain of annihilating our
humanity.

Ripley and Ash

It seems clear, however, that it is the alien's monstrous representation of human sexual difference that most fundamentally
drives the plot of Scott's film. For, given the alien's threatening
incarnation of predatory masculinity and its attempt to locate the
human as such in the position of femininity, it makes perfect
sense that the heroic human protagonist of the drama that
unfolds on board the Nostromo should turn out to be a woman
rather than a man, and that, of the two female candidates for this
role, it should be Ripley rather than Lambert. Thus one of Scott's
most effective subversions of the hybrid genre in which he is
working (his association of femininity with heroism rather than
victimhood) turns out to be dictated by the logic of his monster's
monstrousness. Hence our sense that Ripley's final, isolated confrontation with the alien is not accidental or merely a generic
twist but more profoundly satisfying – something to which she
is fated.

Certainly, no other member of the crew is as sensitive as Ripley
to the risks attaching to the alien's penetration of their second,
external or technological, skin – the ship itself; only Ash's insu-
bordination (his refusal to attend to her voice over the inter-
com – as if her words were weightless, mere noise) overcomes
her rooted determination to keep the stricken Kane outside the
airlock. And in her climactic struggle with the alien once it has
entered the ship, she succeeds in ejecting it from the shuttle only
because she immediately protects herself from it by getting into a

spacesuit. The strength and orientation of Ripley's instincts here are best understood as giving expression to her instinctive familiarity with, her subconscious inhabitation of, the very conception of femininity in its relation to masculinity that underpins the alien's monstrousness. She acts consistently from the outset to preserve the physical integrity of the ship she briefly commands because she has all along understood her own femaleness in the terms that the alien seeks to impose upon the human species, and hence has always understood her body as a vessel whose integrity must at all costs be preserved.

The alien's distinctive mode of parasitic predation is profoundly shocking to the men in the crew, to whom a female subject position – one of vulnerability to rape, impregnation and giving birth – is essentially alien and traumatizing. It is no less so to the only other woman in the crew (Lambert), who – whilst sharing Ripley's innate caution – is happy to risk the integrity of the ship when she needs to re-enter it, and who is rendered powerless when that integrity is violated. The scene of her death, in which she seems hypnotized by the alien, which is there given its most explicitly sexualized repertoire of gestures (its prehensile tail shown creeping between her legs), suggests that the predatory aspect of masculinity is either too unfamiliar to her, or perhaps in a certain sense too familiar,[3] to be gainsaid. On the deepest psychic level, such male monstrosity is no surprise to Ripley at all; it is rather a confirmation of her basic view of the human world of sexual difference, and an opportunity for her to act upon her long-matured comprehension of how best to oppose its essential monstrosity – by doing whatever it might take to avoid the violation of heterosexual intercourse. In short, extending a long-familiar mythological trope, Ripley's emergence as the human hero of this tale is empowered or underwritten by her implied celibacy, her refusal to submit to the alien's advances has been long prepared by, is in a sense the apotheosis of, her resolute virginity.

On one level, of course, the purity of her resolution here is precisely what makes her a match for the pure hostility of the alien: she is as profoundly attuned to, and as psychologically well equipped for, survival as the alien itself – and this is perhaps the germ from which the developing interest of the other films in the series in presenting Ripley and her alien opponent as somehow made for one another (as if each sees the other as its equal or as itself) can be seen in retrospect to have evolved. At the same time, however, what – mythologically speaking – endows Ripley with her drive for survival is her equally resolute repression of her drive to reproduce; and, in this respect, she exists in utter opposition to the alien's incarnation of that drive. In other words, to become capable and worthy of vanquishing her opponent she must sever the connection between femaleness, heterosexual intercourse and fertility – she must, in short, deny her body's openness to maternity. This severance is tracked most explicitly by the film in its representation of Ripley's relationship to the sole embodiment of the maternal principle in the *Nostromo* – the ship's computer that the crew all refer to as 'Mother'.

Like the rest of the crew, Ripley is reborn by Mother from the ship's technological womb in order to embark on a mission to locate and bring back a member of the alien species, a goal in relation to which her life is deemed utterly expendable: it is as if Mother is prepared to sacrifice the offspring of her own fertility in order to secure the cosmic embodiment of fertility as such. When, after Kane's and Dallas' deaths, Ripley gains direct access to Mother, she uncovers this programmed malevolence – and, in so doing, she unleashes upon herself a near-lethal attack from Ash. Against this background, it can seem rather more than accidental that her final plan for bringing about the alien's destruction should involve the destruction of the ship itself, and hence of the ship's computer; and when Mother prevents her from aborting that countdown, as if refusing to attend at once to her words and her needs, Ripley herself is clear that this is more than a merely mechanical failure: her response is to scream at Mother, 'You bitch!' and attempt to smash the central computer console.

Does this description simply collude with Ripley's paranoia? Should we dismiss her sense of personal victimization by a machine as a hysterical but understandable confusion between the true villains (the Company who formulated the computer's instructions) and their unthinking instruments? But, on a Dar-winian conception of things, is it not of the essence of Mother

Nature's fecundity that its individual offspring be seen as the expendable vehicles for the survival and reproduction of the species they instantiate, and that those individual species be seen as expendable vehicles for the survival and reproduction of life as such? In this sense, fertility has only its own reproduction as a goal; hence, children must conceive of themselves as reducible to expressions of and sacrifices to the motherhood of their mothers; and women must conceive of motherhood as reducing them to a vehicle for and a sacrifice to the cosmic principle of fertility.

Hence, Ripley's extreme detestation of Mother and motherhood, and her extreme detestation of the alien and its predatory parasitism, are at root responsive to the same phenomenon. The condition of maternity involves a double parasitism, because the woman's body becomes host not just to another individual being but to the principle of fecundity as such. To be a mother means becoming a vehicle for life – sacrificing one's physical and spiritual integrity to a blind, mechanical force in relation to which nothing (no particular member of a species, and no particular species) has any intrinsic significance. In short, Mother is a bitch because life is a bitch.

It is, however, worth remembering that Scott does suggest at least a vestigial nostalgia or yearning for maternity on Ripley's part – when he presents her as risking her own safety and the destruction of the alien in order to rescue Jones, the ship's cat. This animal not only becomes the object of a displaced expression of Ripley's maternal impulse; it is also, of course, a representation of nonhuman life co-existing in fruitful symbiosis with human beings, and hence provides the shadow of a suggestion that the life of the cosmos is not utterly inimical to human flourishing. The fact that Ripley can more easily allow this impulse to find expression in relation to a nonhuman animal does not exactly subvert her hostility to her own fertility; but it does provide a vital opening for James Cameron's rewriting of Scott's broader vision of the essential monstrousness of human fertility and sexuality in *Aliens*.

Nevertheless, within that broader vision, Scott reinforces Ripley's detestation of motherhood by opposing it to Ash's uncanny attunement with Mother. Ash is, at the outset of the film, the first to respond to Mother's request to speak to Dallas; he runs his continuing task of data collation in parallel with Mother's, and is the crew member most comfortable with the computational instrumentation that Mother provides for their well-being; he is the only one who was always aware of the true purpose of their mission, and is able to attack Ripley in the computer room because he has his own private means of access to Mother.

And yet, of course, Ash is not himself the offspring of a human mother; he is an android. This constitutes his deepest mode of connection with Mother, but it makes that connection paradoxical in the sense that an essentially asexual being, whose body is composed of circuitry and silicon rather than flesh and blood, should be so intimately identified in this film with maternity, and hence with fertility and nature. This paradox is deepened by the degree of Ash's identification with the alien: he implicitly guides the expedition to locate the alien eggs, he brings about its entry into the *Nostromo*, he protects it against the crew's efforts to kill it (holding back Parker from attacking it when it gives birth to itself from Kane's chest, providing a highly unreliable set of tools to track it), and his final words to the crew give explicit expression to his admiration for its purity – for the way its structural per-fection as an organism is matched only by its hostility, unclouded by conscience or considerations of morality. Most explicitly, when he attacks Ripley, in defence of the alien and on Mother's behalf, he tries to choke her by inserting a rolled-up magazine into her mouth – thus identifying himself with the alien's violation of the human body and voice. In other words, the inorganic Ash is as deeply attracted to the alien's incarnation of the essence of the organic as he is attuned to Mother's sterile realization of fertility.

The film suggests two ways of understanding this apparent paradox. First, recalling its earlier depictions of the cosmic life principle as somehow external or other to the organic realm, we can infer that the asexual circuitry of Ash and his Mother are intended to represent life as such as not itself alive, essentially not animal or fleshly, but rather a matter of codes and programming. Life as such is the non-organic, super-mechanical, blind deter-minism that drives the organic realm – call it the codedness of the genetic code. Hence, even when it is fantasized as denuded of

animality, of flesh and blood (as in the film's opening technological phantasm of birth), its essence (as unfolded to Ripley in
Mother's indifference and Ash's murderousness) is no less death-
dealing than in its alien incarnation (that incarnation of carnality
as such, of life's code made pure flesh). Whether it is conceived
of as the alien other of flesh or as its sublime essence, life is
monstrous.

The second way of understanding the paradox turns on Ash's
primary role or function in the crew – he is the science officer,
and hence the person most thoroughly dedicated to the study and
comprehension of nature. His inorganic status here symbolizes
much that our culture imagines of the scientist – that he be
purely rational, in a way untainted by considerations of emotion,
personal opinion or prejudice, or the claims of morality; but also
that he be endowed with an overwhelming admiration or awe for
the object of his study, a sense of wonder in response to nature
and the cosmos. Hence his empathy for the alien, that incarnation
of animate matter and animality, the perfect organism. For Ash,
beyond its significance as the objective of the mission he has
been programmed to take on, the alien symbolizes the true significance of the cosmic principle of life; it signifies the essential
insignificance of human morality and culture, and indeed of the
human race as such – the fact that we are not at the centre of the
universe and its concerns. His willingness to regard the crew of
the Nostromo as expendable thus encapsulates a vision of science as
essentially amoral or inhuman, not just in that its search for the
truth about nature demands that human values be set aside in
favour of objectively establishing the facts, but also in that the
truth about nature that science reveals is that nature is itself fundamentally amoral or inhuman. Both Ash and his Mother identify
themselves with life as such, not with human life and human
concerns – after all, they are not themselves incarnations of
human life. Little wonder that we feel obscurely satisfied with this
film's presentation of the ship's science officer as an inhuman
being at one with the monster.

My account thus far leaves implicit one other suggestive
dimension of the identification of science with the alien. For when
Ash imitates the alien's distinctive parasitic violation of the human

body in forcing a rolled-up magazine down Ripley's throat, the pictures on the wall around him suggest that it is a pornographic publication; his actions thereby underline the film's equation of the alien with masculine sexual violence, but they also imply an identification of science with masculinity. The idea is that scientific approaches to nature are in effect violent, an attempt to penetrate or violate the natural realm, as if emotionally neutered and morally neutral observation of and experimentation with nature amounts to its rape. But since Ash is represented as identifying with the essence of the natural realm he is devoted to observing, his essentially masculine sexual violence further implies that the cosmic life-principle as such should be understood, for all its ambivalent externality to the organic realm, as essentially masculine – as if the drive for reproduction is rapacious, inherently violent and violating.

This vision of the cosmos as unstoppable fecundity and endless self-overcoming might be related to certain aspects of Nietzsche's early, Dionysian vision of what he later calls the will-to-power – the capacity to impose form on the formlessness of chaos, and to destroy or sacrifice any given form in the name of another, newer such form. It is an idea of life as an endless becoming, but according to which fitness for life is a matter of an individual's or a species' ability to impose itself not only on its environment but (when necessary) upon itself – for instance by reinventing itself so as to accommodate any irresistible changes in that environment, or to rescue itself from the rigor mortis of stability or stasis, from mere self-repetition. Hence the film's emphasis upon the alien's plasticity – its unceasing evolution from one phase or mode of being to another, and its capacity to adapt and defend itself against the most extreme environmental circumstances within the span of its individual life-cycle.

Of course, one might read such an identification of the scientific method and its object of study with male rapacity in another way – to suggest that a vision of nature as essentially will-to-power is not a revelation of nature's essence but rather a distorting interpretation of nature that gives expression to the masculine sexual violence implicit in the scientific approach that generates it. However, the film's presentation of Ripley's almost undeviating resistance to its central symbols of life understood as will-to-power (whether in the form of heterosexual intercourse, the attentions and intentions of Ash and Mother or the parasitism of the alien) as essentially heroic appears rather to underwrite her perception of fertility or maternity as a violation or rape of femininity, of maternity as demanding an alien inhabitation of her flesh rather than as allowing its fulfilment. It is as if life itself really is to be understood as an inherently masculine assault upon women, in which they function merely as the means for the onward transmission of something (an intrinsically penetrating and aggressive force, or drive, or will) essentially alien to them.

Ripley's unremitting drive to preserve her integrity is thus, in essence, an expression of her sense of alienation from life, nature and the cosmos, and from everything in herself that participates in – that binds her ineluctably to – that which she hates so purely. For, after all, does she not in the end succeed in imposing her will upon Ash, Mother and the alien itself? Is not her final victory over the monster in the *Narcissus* (the *Nostromo*'s shuttle), her success in creating a space from which to give voice to the mayday message that she speaks over the film's concluding frames, achieved by reshaping her environment (making it a vacuum) and herself (suiting up) so that she might bury a harpoon in the heart of her opponent and in the heart of the heartless cosmos into which her weapon dispatches it? What better exemplification of the masculine will-to-power of which her thoughts, deeds and underlying psychology declare such detestation – quite as if the alien she confronts in the *Narcissus* is a reflection of herself? (Seeing this beautifully choreographed assault, this seamless dovetailing of heart, mind and spirit in the service of vengeance, we might recall Ash's description of the alien – immediately after it has burst from Kane's chest – as 'Kane's son'. This is the film's most explicit reference to the alien's unmanning capacity to make human males pregnant; but its aural reference to the Bible's name for the first human murderer further implies that the monster's death-dealing rapacity is not essentially alien to humanity, but rather at work in the first human family, and never eradicated from the human family as such thereafter. If, then, Ripley is a sister under the skin to Kane's son, she is Cain's daughter – offspring not of God's beloved Abel but of his wrathful brother, the first violator of human solidarity, condemned by God to be a fugitive and vagabond on the earth, essentially not-at-home in the universe He created.) But if what Ripley hates is what saves her from what she hates (if it is the pure flame of the life in her that overcomes its own monstrous, externalized incarnation), must she end by hating herself, by overcoming that which she hates in herself, or by overcoming her hatred?

The education of a blade runner

Developing answers to these questions will govern the evolution of the *Alien* series in the hands of other directors; but it also governs the thematic structure and narrative development of Ridley Scott's next film – *Blade Runner* (1982). For this film (written by Hampton Fancher and David Peoples) is explicitly concerned with the question of what it is to be human; more precisely, it is obsessed with it – obsessed in the way the leader of the replicants is obsessed with his quest for life, for a life which is on a par with that of human beings. To show that Roy Baty misconceives this quest as one for *more* life – as if a replicant might become human by living longer – is the goal of the film.

Like Ash, the replicants have no flesh-and-blood mother – but, unlike Ash, they find this deeply traumatizing (a question about his feelings for his mother is what occasions the replicant Leon's opening murder of Deckard's colleague). This appears to be because (again unlike Ash) the replicants are not androids but rather products of genetic engineering destined for dangerous or dirty tasks in off-world colonies – hence are themselves composed of flesh and blood. As if to underline this, the film's relentless violence (quite apart from three 'retirements', we witness an attempted strangulation, savage beatings, an attack with an iron bar, deliberately broken fingers and a climax of concentrated physical suffering) is typically[4] directed towards replicants, as if to confront the authorities' doctrine that such embodied beings are incapable of suffering, are entities upon whom the infliction of pain is not a crime.

What these scenes instead elicit is an instinctive response to this treatment of the replicants which matches our response to such treatment of human beings; we see their behaviour as expressive of pain and suffering rather than as an empty exhibition by automata. As Roy puts it: 'We're not computers ... – we're physical'; the violence inflicted upon them establishes beyond political or philosophical debate that the replicants are capable of manifesting the essential range and potential complexity of feeling open to any human being. The empathic claim their pain-behaviour makes upon us is what grounds the film's assumption that it is this aspect of the replicants' embodiment which is pertinent to their call for human status, not that of whether anything *occupies* their bodies.

Blade Runner thus rejects any understanding of the human mind or soul as hidden behind, entirely distinct from, the human body. In presenting us with entities whose embodied life has a complexity and range comparable to that of a human being, Scott brings his viewers to apply to them the full range of psychological concepts which constitute the logical space of the mental, and thereby demonstrates that our attribution of a mind to a given creature is a response to the behavioural repertoire with which their particular embodiment endows them. Wittgenstein once remarked that 'The human body is the best picture of the human soul'; this film dramatizes and projects that insight.

If, however, we are thereby given everything we need to know – indeed, everything there is to know – about the replicants which is relevant to their claim for human status, if we (and anyone in the world of the film) can see that nothing counts against their being treated as human, how and why do most of the human beings in the film apparently fail to see this? Why, for example, does Deckard's superior, Bryant – the commander of the replicant-hunting blade runner unit – regard the replicants as skin-jobs? The film's answer is to be found in the fact that Bryant is 'the kind of lawman who used to call black men "niggers"'; for nothing counts against the replicants being treated as human except the unwillingness or refusal of other human beings to treat them as such. No accumulation of facts or testimony of the senses can compel someone to acknowledge behaviour that fulfils all the criteria of pain-behaviour as the genuine expression of another human being's pain. Bryant's failure to acknowledge the replicants as human is not based on ignorance or repression of these facts, but is rather the expression of one possible attitude towards them. It follows that the humanity of the replicants is in the hands of their fellows; their accession to human status involves their being acknowledged as human by others, and if their humanity is denied, it withers. And in this respect, of course, they once again resemble the human beings who acknowledge or fail to acknowledge them.[5]

This theme is central to the film's depiction of the relationship between Deckard and Rachel. Their first meeting takes place across a Voight-Kampff machine, the equipment used by blade runners to assess a subject's capillary dilation, blush response, fluctuation of the pupil, pheromone discharge and other physiological registers of emotional response – the theory being that replicants lack any empathic attunement with others and thereby betray their difference from human beings. As Tyrell, the designer of the replicants, points out, however, this lack of empathy and its correlative emotional immaturity are determined by the decision of the replicant's makers to restrict their lifespan to four years, and hence to constrain the range of their memories and experiences. Rachel, by contrast, has been gifted with a past that creates a cushion or pillow for the emotions, but which entails that she does not know that she is a replicant.

Deckard at first sees her failure to pass the V-K test as a simple proof of her nonhumanity, oblivious to that fact that his difficulty in detecting the usual emotional absence in her suggests rather that this lack is contingent, and a matter of degree, i.e. that the replicants might rather be seen as children in an emotional sense through no fault of their own, and thus as capable of maturity, and that some uncontroversially human beings (like Bryant) never attain such maturity.

His denial of Rachel's humanity intensifies when, in his apartment, he wrenches away the pillow of her past, reciting to her face the memories that make up her inner life and informing her of their 'true' origin (Tyrell's niece); even his attempts to back away from his brutality in the face of her pain are so clumsy as to suggest an inability to care sufficiently about her to do so with any consideration. Even after she saves him from Leon's murderous attack, his declaration that he would never personally hunt her down is based on the thought that he owes her one – that they are equals only in the way a debtor and his creditor are equals. When Rachel responds to this by asking whether Deckard has ever taken the V-K test himself, Scott invites us to acknowledge that a refusal to acknowledge another's humanity constitutes a denial of the humanity in oneself.

Deckard's redeemability is, however, revealed later in the same scene, when – after finding Rachel at the piano, playing because she cannot even trust her memory of piano lessons – he says, 'You play beautifully.' The tact and delicacy of this prepare the ground for a full acknowledgement of their feelings for one another; but Deckard again mishandles things. Aware that Rachel now feels incapable of staking her life on her emotions, and hence of acknowledging her attraction to Deckard, he aims to help her overcome this anxiety; but he does so by pushing her back against the wall and dictating her expression of her feelings ('Say "Kiss me" ... "I want you" ... Again ... '). The fact that she then goes on to improvise expressions of her own ('Put your hands on me') does not make this initial forcing of words into her mouth any less disturbing a piece of sexual violence.

Deckard's actual redemption is made plain in the film's concluding sequence, when he returns to his apartment to find Rachel lying covered in a shroud-like sheet on the couch. But when he removes that covering he finds a way of addressing her which brings her fully (back) to life. In their previous encounter, they faced one another standing, giving the scene a strong vertical patterning which emphasized Deckard's superior height, strength and aggression; now, he leans over her face from the head of the couch, creating an equally strong horizontal patterning which does away with his physical superiority and suggests that their profiles are complementary. The ensuing dialogue matches this sense of achieved equality: for Deckard now does not dictate Rachel's dialogue but asks her questions ('Do you love me? ... Do you trust me?') to which she is free to respond as she pleases, and to which she freely responds in the affirmative. Thus, by creating the terms for a conversation in which Rachel could freely acknowledge her love for him, he acknowledges his love for her, and the necessary mutuality of any such acknowledgement. These two have earned their escape from the nightmarish cityscape in which everyone's humanity is at risk.

The mortality of flesh and blood

What allows Deckard to redeem his humanity is the further step in his education that occurs between the two conversations with Rachel – the lesson that Roy Baty undertakes to deliver in the film's climactic sequence in the Bradbury Building. But what licenses Roy to deliver this lesson is his own developing education about what it is to be human, and in particular his coming to learn that acquiring a more extended span of life would go no way towards achieving or establishing his own humanity.

What does it mean to claim that human beings are mortal? Perhaps that they are not immortal, that human beings do not live forever – that a human life must end at some point. This contrast encourages the view that human beings are mortal because their lives occupy a finite quantity of time, that their days are numbered and destined to run out (soon) after three score years and ten. This is plainly the view taken by Roy Baty and his group; their dangerous return to Earth is motivated by the desire for more life – the desire to extend their allotted span of days until it matches that of a human being. One brief scene in the film dis-inters and undermines the misunderstandings upon which this project is predicated with dizzying speed and subtlety.

After Deckard has shot the replicant Zhora, he is accosted by her partner Leon – who observed the 'retirement' – and dragged into an alley, where Leon administers a savage beating to the blade runner. The dialogue here bears a great deal of weight:

LEON: How old am I?
DECKARD: I don't know.
LEON: My birthday is April 10th, 2017. How long do I live?
DECKARD: Four years.
LEON: More than you. Painful to live in fear, isn't it? Nothing is worse than having an itch you can't scratch.

DECKARD: I agree.
LEON: Wake up – time to die.

Much of our sympathy for the replicants in this film relates to what we (and they) perceive as a deprivation: their genetically engineered four-year lifespan is far shorter than that which any human being can (barring accidents) rely upon, and it entails that they know from the first moment of their existence the precise date of their death. But Leon's interrogation of Deckard puts this assumption in question: for his ability to kill the blade runner destroys the illusion that a normal human lifespan trumps one with replicant limitations – death cannot thus be kept at a Biblical arm's length. Indeed, Leon here begins to emerge as a figure of real power as he names the moment of Deckard's death; it is as if his knowledge of the specific day on which he will die allows him to master and turn to his own account our common fear of dying, whereas frail human beings can never be sure when their end will come. At just this point, however, our impression of replicant superiority is in turn exploded, for Rachel saves Deckard by shooting Leon in the head – thus proving that knowing the date on which one's death is inevitable is not the same as knowing when one will die.

The moral is clear: mortal finitude is not reducible to the fact of our finite lifespan; it is rather constituted by the fact that every moment of human life is necessarily shadowed by the possibility of its own non-existence. Death is not an abstract or distant limit to life, an indeterminate but inevitable boundary to the succession of our days, but rather a presence in every moment of our existence. This is an idea Heidegger captures in his notion of human existence as Being-towards-death, where death is understood as the possibility of our own impossibility; and its emergence reveals the irrelevance of any distinction between replicants and human beings that is grounded on the length of their lifespans or the certainty with which they can predict an end to their lives on a given day. Both are alive and both possess consciousness; hence both will die, and both are conscious of that fact. Whether either will attain a grasp of its full significance is another question, but it is one that both face – which means that replicants stand in a human relationship towards death.

Roy Baty's quest for Tyrell and his ability to extend the replicant lifespan thus appear as a denial rather than an acknowledgement of mortality; but it is only through his encounter with Tyrell that this is brought home to him. For Roy's maker quickly dismisses the topic of the biomechanical limitations to extending replicant lifespan ('All of this is academic') and instead introduces the two central notions this film will advance as integral to any authentic acknowledgement of human mortality, when he says, 'He who burns twice as brightly burns half as long. And you have burned so very very brightly, Roy. . . . Revel in your time.'

For Tyrell, the value or worth of Roy's life is determined not by its length but by the intensity with which he experiences each moment of it – in other words (and again tracing out paths followed by Heidegger), by its manifestation of a specific attitude towards the temporality of his own existence. The transience of the present moment is taken not to show its insignificance but the nature of its significance – the fact that it is a moment in transition, always having been delivered from the future and always about to be delivered over to the past, and hence that human existence is always endless becoming. All human experience is present experience or it is nothing; hence to fail to engage with the present moment is to fail to engage with one's life as such. But to engage properly with it means acknowledging that it is inextricably related to past and future; hence to live one's life authentically is to let every moment burn brightly whilst (perhaps by) still acknowledging that each such moment will pass.

Tyrell talks of this as revelling in one's time. This reference to revelry or play shows that the Nietzschean subtext of *Alien* is here re-emerging, but this time Scott is invoking Nietzsche's Zarathustra, who speaks constantly of the overman (the self-overcoming human being, the individual who understands himself as essentially transitional) as one who dances through life with lightness and grace. The Heideggerian notion of authentic Being-towards-death, of living each moment to the full whilst respecting its essential transitoriness, is here interpreted as a matter of revelling in the possibilities of act and performance that the fact of embodied, finite existence makes possible.

Roy is dimly aware of this from the outset; it is why, when Pris recites the Cartesian dictum 'I think therefore I am' in Sebastian's apartment, he responds by saying, 'Very good, Pris – now show him why.' But the Nietzschean connection Tyrell forges allows him to see that the true significance or point of the moments which make up one's life should be generated from within that life rather than from a reliance upon external guarantors. For Zarathustra, the overman's authenticity was underwritten by the doctrine of eternal recurrence: one had achieved a fully human life only if, when faced with the chance to have one's life over again, one could sincerely desire that not a single moment within it should be changed. This vision is of life as a self-contained whole, its parts hanging together in utter self-sufficiency; and such a self-authenticating life could have no need for sources of value or worth external to itself.

Hence Nietzsche's association of the overman with the death of God; for the Christian God is the traditional external guarantor of the worth of human life, and, insofar as His presence tempts us to refer the worth of our existence to him, His removal from the scene becomes an essential mark of human authenticity. Nietzsche narrates this removal as the murder of God by human beings in order to underline the need to accept full responsibility for what is involved in accepting full responsibility for our lives; and by enacting this narrative – by murdering his creator in a way which brings an anguished 'Oh my God!' from Sebastian – Roy proves that he has learnt the lesson Tyrell wished to teach him. In his final encounter with Deckard, he tries to pass on that lesson.

On one level, Roy's pursuit of Deckard through the decaying Bradbury Building is motivated by revenge – for the latter's execution of Pris and the other replicants; their memory is inscribed into Deckard's body in the form of broken fingers. However, the hunt also displays Roy's overman status – specifically in his having gone beyond what Nietzsche calls the 'slave morality' of good and evil (not beyond all morality – as Ash imagines of the alien – but beyond the specifically Christian moral code which contrasts good with evil rather than with badness). Thus, Roy characterizes Deckard as the representative of good ('aren't you the good man?') and forces him to experience 'what it is to be a slave'. The Christian imagery which collects around Roy at this point (the nail through the palm, the frieze of cruciform ventilation units on the rooftop, the dove of peace) is not something he respects but something he toys with and turns to his own purposes (as in his use of the nail to slow the advance of his own impending death); he thereby casts himself as someone whose message is at least as important for humanity as Christ's, declaring his status as the revaluator of all values.

Roy's association of slavery with living in fear, thus echoing Leon's earlier perception, also reminds us of the replicants' perception of their own status in relation to their human creators; in part, his lesson is intended to teach Deckard what he, along with all human beings, is responsible for doing to the replicants – what his denial of their humanity amounts to. But, most fundamentally, it is designed to teach Deckard a lesson about his relation to death – about his mortality. Roy brings it about that Deckard feels that every moment may be his last, and Deckard's response is to flee from this threat; he functions at the level of an injured animal, incapable of anything more than an unthinking attempt to avoid the threat of extinction. His pursuer, by contrast – who knows that his own death is equally imminent, whether by genetic determinism or by Deckard's own efforts with gun and crowbar – responds to the threat by running towards it. He toys with the very threat that paralyses Deckard; he sees that, since mortality is as internal to human existence as embodiment, genuine humanity turns on finding the right relation to it.

We are thereby presented with inauthentic and authentic ways of living a human life in the face of its mortality. Deckard's flight denies the ubiquity of this threat – as if an escape from Roy would amount to an escape from the threat he incarnates. Roy treats the same threat playfully. His mourning over Pris is transformed into a mock wolf-howl, an imitation of the huntsman's pack which signals that the game of life and death is afoot; he describes firing on an unarmed man as 'not very sporting', his response to attack is to cry, 'That's the spirit!' and, most importantly, he declares to Deckard, 'You'd better get it up, or I'm going to have to kill you. Unless you're alive, you can't play, and if you can't play … '

Like Zarathustra's disciples, Roy is dancing on the edge of the abyss, performing his version of Pris' cartwheeling enactment (in Sebastian's apartment) of her thinking, embodied existence. The lightness and grace of his life find confirmation in his ability to look at death, and the death of love, without fear or hysteria. And he wants to teach this to Deckard: if to play is to be fully alive, not to play is to be reduced to death-in-life or merely animal existence. If you can't play, you might as well be dead.

Deckard's response to death is inauthentic because it transforms his own death from an (omnipresent) possibility into an actuality: it extinguishes his humanity. So Roy teaches him the difference between possibility and actuality; he allows Deckard (and us) to spend long minutes on the edge of his existence, pushes him to the edge of a real abyss, making death seem unavoidable – and then he rescues him. And he underlines the point of that lesson by making manifest, at the moment of his own death, that he has revelled in his time:

> I've seen things you people wouldn't believe: attack-ships on fire off the shoulder of Orion; I watched c-beams glitter in the dark near the Tannhauser Gate. All those moments will be lost in time, like tears in rain. Time to die.

He has lived each moment of his life to the full without denying its transitory place in the ineluctable stream of time; and any such denial would amount to denying the essential structure of human experience as such. It would, moreover, count as a further and more profound failure of acknowledgement to wish to bequeath one's experiences and memories to others – as if one could outlive oneself, as if one's moments of consciousness were alienable, as if one's mortality could be sloughed off. Heidegger understands our relation to our own death as the clearest expression of this truth. He describes it as our ownmost, nonrelational possibility: no one can die another's death for him, just as no one can die our death for us, and that is precisely what makes our death, when it comes, our ownmost possibility. Roy's calm and moving last words manifest just this authentic understanding, and they cry out for acknowledgement as such.

It is Deckard upon whom the responsibility falls of responding to that cry. To acknowledge its significance is to acknowledge not just what it says, but the fact that these are Roy's last words – part of his last moments, a testament to his life and to life as such. Deckard blinks, as if to clear his vision, and then provides Roy with an epitaph:

> Maybe he loved life more than he ever had before. All he wanted were the same answers any of us want. .... All I could do was to sit there and watch him die.

Deckard sees not only that his tormentor's nature is precisely the same as his own, but also that the only way in which to acknowledge his human mortality at the moment of its ending is to acknowledge that Roy's death is his own – not to try hysterically to postpone it, or to try incoherently to take it upon himself, but to watch that death and watch it as the death of another human being, a human other. The authenticity of this acknowledgement shows that Deckard has learnt his lesson, about acknowledging others and about acknowledging mortality. As Inspector Gaff puts it, he has done a man's job, the task of any genuine human being; and Roy's bequest to Deckard culminates in the resurrection of Rachel. It's a pity she won't live – but, then again, who does?

Excursus: the Director's Cut

If these ideas are true to the basic tenor of *Blade Runner*'s narrative, then it must be acknowledged that the alterations to the original theatrical release version embodied in the recent 'Director's Cut' are at some distance from the deep sources of the film's power. To be sure, it is good to see the removal of the hastily created, sunlit epilogue (in which Rachel is 'revealed' to have been given an ordinary human lifespan in order to create a happy ending which contradicts the whole thrust of the film's thoughtfulness) and of the voice-over (despite its occasional touches of wit and poetry, and its overall confirmation that Scott is here once again fusing or hybridizing the science fiction genre – this time, with that of Chandleresque film noir). But the sole significant addition – the restoration of a unicorn image within Deckard's reverie at the piano – has commonly been taken as intended to answer a question whose relevance to the film's central issues is itself questionable. For this inserted memory-image ensures that Gaff's placing of an origami unicorn in Deckard's apartment signifies the availability of a means of access to Deckard's memories that (just like Deckard's access to Rachel's memories) is explicable only if Deckard is himself a replicant – thus giving a literal significance to Rachel's sarcastic question about whether he has himself ever taken a V-K test. Since, however, the film itself places replicants and humans in exactly the same position with respect to its central questions (the acknowledgement of mortality and of one another), such an apparently momentous revelation about Deckard's status makes precisely no difference to the trajectory and terminus of his education. We might therefore be better advised to think of this added scene or image as itself a test of its viewers' capacity to acknowledge the film that frames it, by testing whether they recognize that it is the film's central concern to shift our conception of its importance.

Enframing and acknowledgement

It is not, then, difficult to see *Blade Runner* as a continuation of the study that Ridley Scott began in *Alien* of the flesh-and-blood embodiedness of human beings, and of their attempts to repress (and to overcome their repression of) its conditions and consequences. In the earlier film, this study focuses on the reproductive drive of the flesh – upon its sexuality and generativity, and upon its subordination of individual integrity and autonomy to the demands of life as such. In the later film, it focuses on the internal relationship between life and death, on the body's openness to its own mortality, and on the dependence of individual human flourishing upon acknowledging that fact, and upon one individual's acknowledgement of and by others. A certain Nietzschean vision of human existence can be seen to hold this study together, as it moves from a conception of life as rapacious and devouring will-to-power, a Moloch to which the human individual is sacrificed, to a conception of what the flourishing of a human life within such an ordering of the cosmos might look like.

This same background of ideas might also account for the vestigial presence of religious, and more specifically Christian, ideas in *Alien*: for *Blade Runner* appears to declare an investment in their overcoming, and many of Scott's more recent films continue to explore variations upon that theme. *Gladiator* (2000), for example, with its resolutely pagan representation of a world in which human suffering is ultimately beyond redemption, might be seen as one culmination of Scott's desire to imagine a human form of life unpolluted by essentially Christian thought; whereas *Kingdom of Heaven* (2005) attends rather to the various ways in which medieval Christendom was always already polluted by essentially un-Christian political, moral and erotic realities, and inherently ready to impose itself (with all its corruptions) upon cultures hitherto resistant to it. *Black Hawk Down* (2001) can then be viewed as a study of the contemporary West as essentially post-Christian – a culture inexorably returning to a pagan worldview but indelibly marked by the religious perspective it appears to have abandoned. For the secular liberal humanitarian ideology underlying the military intervention it records manifests a compassion for suffering distinctive of Christian slave morality, as well as its missionary impulse to convert other cultures to its conceptions of good and evil; and the warrior ethos it depicts – with its basic structure of mutuality in the face of shattered bone and torn flesh, the irreducible minimum of the human – marries Crusader values with those of Roman stoicism, in a manner exemplified by the American armed forces' obdurate, self-defining refusal to abandon any of its soldiers to the mercies of the enemy.

As the obsessive interest shown by all three of these later films in the machinery of warfare would suggest, another central theme in Scott's specifically science-fictional universes is technology – and, more specifically, its impact on human forms of life. Indeed, the physical and spiritual landscape of *Blade Runner* is very similar to the microcosm of human life manifest in the *Nostromo*: the remnants of humanity left behind by the off-world settlers find themselves in a world without sunlight, and dwarfed by their own technological achievements. Like Ash, the replicants incarnate the threat of technology coming to control its creators; their presence on Earth demands an extremity of hostile response, as if they instantiate a threat to the very essence of what remains of humanity. And yet that feared future, of human fusion with or absorption into the technological, is already manifest in the children of Earth – in the low hiss of wheels as a swarm of them glide by on their bikes, in the jabbering city-speak arguments they have over machinery stolen from vehicles, in the distorting layers of material wrapped around their small heads and bodies.

Heidegger would recognize this as the landscape of what he called 'the age of technology'. Such an age treats the natural world as a store of resources and raw materials for human purposes (rivers as hydroelectric power sources, forests as a standing reserve of paper, the wind as currents of potential energy) – a perspective that is extended to the cosmos as a whole in Scott's vision of off-world mining and of the *Nostromo*'s general and specific purposes (to recover mineral ore from the other end of the universe, and to requisition an alien species as a weapon). Heidegger contrasted this attitude with that of acknowledging and respecting nature as a field of objects, forces and living beings each with their own specific essence or Being, to the comprehension of which the Being of human beings was uniquely attuned.

Heidegger's preferred term for the destructive grasp of nature as standing reserve is 'enframing' – a term which is likely to recall any film-maker to the fact that his own artistic medium is more dependent than any other upon technology. The material basis of film is the recording capacity of the camera – the automatic production of an image of the world exhibited before the camera, and its consequent reproduction and projection on screen.[6] Since this photographic basis of cinema seems to satisfy one of mankind's perennial fantasies – that of recording the world without the mediation of human subjectivity – it is not difficult to imagine that the technological basis of film might inherently tend towards the elimination of the human. Since, however, every film director's role is precisely to take responsibility for enframing the world, for meaning the composition and exclusion constituted by each frame in her film, her attempts to utilize the camera for artistic purposes can be seen as an attempt to find a possibility of human flourishing within the heart of the humanly threatening age of technology – to subvert that threat from within.

We might reasonably expect these issues to come to a head when the camera is directed to frame human beings. When a human being is placed before the camera, what is consequently projected on screen is plainly related to its human origin, but it is equally plainly not identical with it. A photograph of an object is not the object itself, but what we see in the photograph is surely the object photographed; certainly, it is far from easy to identify any specific respect in which the two differ (to name any feature lacked or possessed by one in comparison with the other). Hence, the question: is the humanity of the camera's subject preserved or distorted or destroyed by its cinematic transcription or transformation? What, in short, becomes of human beings on film?

It is not difficult to see that this question is internal to *Blade Runner* – that this film in part takes the condition of film as its subject. The theme is announced in its opening sequence, in which the camera's long journey over the cityscape to the Tyrell Corporation building is intercut with close-ups of an unblinking, all-seeing eye; and an eye in which what is on screen is reflected but which is identified with no character in the world of the film can only be the eye through which the viewer sees that world – the eye of the camera and its director.

A further identification between the director of this film and Deckard is established when the blade runner is shown sitting in a darkened room observing photographs of the replicants and a recording of Leon's execution of another blade runner projected on a screen before him. It is confirmed by his use of the television set in his apartment to analyse a photograph of Zhora's apartment, when he is shown calling for close-ups and tracking shots within the photographed room (quite as if he were within the room itself). It is all but declared by his professional association with the Voight-Kampff machine – an obvious surrogate for the camera. And, of course, what he gazes at through this machine's viewfinder are the faces of replicants – human replicas, humanlike beings whose humanness is under suspicion, to be discovered or deemed absent by the gaze of the camera.

Does this association suggest that the attentions of the camera are lethal to human subjects? Or does it rather suggest that the camera – perhaps precisely because of its refusal of human subjectivity – is as capable of confirming the humanity of those placed before it as of denying it? Since *Blade Runner* shows its surrogate director as viewing things along the barrel of his gun at least as often as through the V-K machine, we might say that it equates the camera with a death-dealing piece of technology. Even here, however, at the end, the film discriminates between what Deckard's gun can do and what it actually does. For all his retirements of the other replicants, when he returns to Rachel in his apartment he initiates her resurrection by removing her shroud with his gun. This tells us that – although the camera (like a gun) has an inherent capacity to deny humanity, it is capable of being used to acknowledge and affirm it. What matters is the manner in which it is used.

Just as, within the world of the film, the flourishing of any given person's humanity requires its acknowledgement by her others, so the flourishing of the humanity of anyone placed before the camera's gaze is determined not by its technological basis but by the use to which it is put by the director employing it. He can either transform subjects into what replicants are thought to be, simulacra of humanity; or he can actualize and preserve their subjectivity, as Deckard learns to do with Rachel. Hence, any failure of acknowledgement in a film is the director's responsibility, a failure of his or her own humanity; and whether or not he or she will succeed or fail in this respect cannot be predicted apart from an assessment of each film he or she makes. Even when a director succeeds, however, that success can as easily be denied as acknowledged by a film's viewers – by, for example, their assuming in advance that the film is merely a generic exercise, or just another Hollywood blockbuster.

Alien is, I would say, rather less interested in these questions about the nature of film than is *Blade Runner*. But it offers one internal representation of an issue that is central to any understanding of cinema as a medium, that is recognizably related to the reflexive issues addressed in *Blade Runner*, and that is powerfully determinative of the future development of the *Alien* universe. For one aspect of the mysterious transformative powers of the camera upon embodied human subjects is the unpredictable but ungainsayable way in which its gaze can make some actors into stars and ensure that others never attain that state – in which it allows physiognomy to become destiny. And the gradual, essentially unpredictable but obscurely satisfying emergence from the *Nostromo's* crew of Ripley as the main human protagonist and hero of *Alien* is at once the cause and a mythical representation of Sigourney Weaver's translation (by means of the complex interaction of her as yet relatively unformed but already distinctive physiognomy with her character and its vicissitudes under the gaze of Ridley Scott's camera) into stardom. The other films in the *Alien* series will become increasingly obsessed with giving an account of this unaccountable, precarious but undeniable phenomenon.

Source: 20th Century Fox courtesy the Kobal collection

2

MAKING BABIES

James Cameron's *Aliens*

Terminating maternity

James Cameron's first film, *Terminator* (1986), concerns a threat posed to the future of the human race by the unintended evolution of a species of machines which respond to a threat to their own survival from their creators (who try to unplug SkyNet, the self-aware strategic defence computer who 'fathers' this species) by trying to annihilate them – first by nuclear war, then by genocide. The machines send a cybernetic organism back through time to kill the woman who will give birth to the leader of the successful human resistance; and the film charts the ensuing struggle between this 'terminator' and a resistance soldier sent by his leader to protect that woman. By the end of the film, Sarah Connor has been transformed from an underachieving waitress and overly trusting dater of unsuitable men to a mother capable of terminating the terminator even after her protector's death. She drives off into the desert, equipped to take on the task of preparing the child now growing in her womb for his future military role.

It is not difficult to imagine the producers of the *Alien* series regarding this film as a calling card or show-reel that might have been specifically designed to demonstrate Cameron's suitability for taking charge of their planned sequel. *Terminator* shows Cameron to be imaginatively at home in the field of science fiction, whilst being comfortable with the idea of a strong female character at the centre of this traditionally male-oriented genre; he has invented a 'villain' who represents an evolutionarily superior race whose very existence threatens the future of the human species; and he has embedded the duel between these two protagonists within a thematic structure that focuses explicitly on issues of survival and reproduction, of sexual difference and female generativity. Moreover, *Terminator* has one distinctive and much-prized cinematic quality of which Ridley Scott's *Alien* had no particular need – a well-paced, driving narrative that links explosive and violent action scenes in a smoothly escalating sequence. Inviting Cameron to take the next step in the *Alien* story must have seemed like bowing to the inevitable – acknowledging that director and subject-matter were made for one another, each the other's fate or destiny.

The imaginative empathy between Cameron and Scott in fact extends beyond the latter's work in *Alien* to his further investigation of distinctively human existence in *Blade Runner*. For, of course, the peculiarly powerful dread induced by *Terminator*'s eponymous villain (both in the film's characters and in its viewers) is best understood as responsive, not to the fact that its distinctive nature (flesh-and-blood encasing a titanium-alloy combat chassis) makes it uniquely capable of dealing death and of dealing with the threat of its own death, but rather to the fact that it *is* death. The terminator is death itself, embodied and made real: its mere presence spells death, it has no other interest, emotion or purpose other than causing death, and it cannot itself be killed (Death cannot die). As the resistance soldier Kyle Reese puts it: 'It cannot be bargained with, it cannot be reasoned with, it doesn't feel pity or remorse or fear, and it absolutely will not stop until you are dead.'

Heidegger's characterization of death as one's ownmost, non-relational, not-to-be-outstripped possibility might easily have been the terminator's blueprint. It is dedicated, programmed, to seek one specific individual's death; and neither the death of those who share her name (the two other Sarah Connors that the terminator kills first) nor the death of those who try to stand between her and it (the police, Reese) can prove any kind of substitute. Hence, in the end, Sarah is deprived of any helpers and friends, and proves incapable of escaping her terminator by fleeing from it, whether intellectually or physically. The comforting but inauthentic idea that one's death is a future event, something that comes gradually and predictably towards us as our lives extend themselves in time, is annihilated by the terminator's disorienting capacity to be projected into any present moment of our lives; and once it is so projected, once its gaze fixes on its target, it cannot be out-stripped by driving, running or crawling away from it. Sarah has to confront her terminator on her own – face to face with the titanium death's head, stripped of its human guise, through the bars of the robotic metal-press. (And Cameron's sequel to his own first film will have much to say about whether her crushing of the terminator in that press should be understood as her overcoming her own death, or rather as its coming to inhabit her life, and the life of the human species as such.)

In this respect, of course, Sarah Connor is no different from any other human being: if the terminator only represented death, or human mortality as such, then we would each have our own terminator, capable of appearing at any moment of our lives to isolate us from our relatives and friends and confront us with the essential non-necessity of our individual existence. But Sarah Connor is targeted by her terminator for a more specific reason, one which picks her out as a woman, and as a particular woman: she is to be terminated because she is to give birth to the human male who will bring about the extermination of the machines, and hence ensure the survival of the human race. In other words, her death is a kind of advance (or is it retrospective?) abortion; and it is required because her generativity as a female stands for the (re)generativity of the human species as such. Her capacity to become a mother symbolizes the human capacity to reproduce itself, our possession of a future.

There is a clear sense, then, in which Sarah Connor is meant to exemplify an affirmative and empowering vision of femaleness. She is exemplary of humanity as such, and her generativity is what will keep human history open to the future; and although her reception of this knowledge is at first panic-stricken, the film charts a real growth in her character towards a kind of self-sufficiency – for in acquiring a repertoire of defensive and offensive techniques (both physical and psychological), she acquires the strength to take on the terminator by herself, and to take on her responsibilities to her future son and the human race as such. In this respect, *Terminator* observes the creation of a female warrior.

On the other hand, however, what picks Sarah out as the vital figure in this narrative is also what sidelines her as an individual. For, of course, insofar as her worth to the human race turns entirely on the man to whom she will give birth, it turns on her offspring rather than herself – and on a male child, at that. This underlying sense that her femaleness is valuable only instrumentally, as a means to reproducing maleness, is reinforced by the displacements of causality that the film's disruption of the temporal order makes possible. For it turns out that Sarah acquires Reese (and hence not only self-protection, but the education for survival and motherhood that he imparts) only because he was sent to her by the resistance leader to whom she will give birth, her son John; and since it further emerges that Reese is the destined father of her son, the film ends by conferring on John Connor the power to authorize his own birth. Not only does he provide what is required for his mother to survive long enough to give birth to him, he also chooses (and brings his mother together with) the man who will be his father. Indeed, since their conjunction brings about not only his conception but his mother's acquisition of the beliefs and skills necessary to bring him up so as to become the hero of humanity, we can say that John Connor is the author not only of his own family (the [re-] birth of Sarah and Kyle as warrior-mother and warrior-father) and his own birth, but of every aspect of his life, and hence of himself.

Within this bizarre displacement of the familiar human family structure, Sarah Connor comes to seem more and more like a counter or token in a complex relationship between men. For whilst John Connor's foreknowledge of the past is what allows him to give Kyle Reese the mission that will make him his father, from Kyle's point of view that same mission allows him to write himself into his hero's own history. He is enabled to become the father of the man he most adores in the human race's post-nuclear future; he thereby finds at once a displaced heterosexual mode of expression for his love for humanity's ultimate warrior, and a means of ensuring that the son he fathers will be exactly the son he could have wished – thus insulating paternity from its inherent openness to the contribution of female fertility and of unpredictable events, from its openness to contingency, and the loss of control that such openness entails.

Of course, Sarah's room for independent manoeuvre within this exchange between men is not entirely eliminated. She is the one who refuses to accept Kyle's (admittedly half-hearted) attempts to disown his declaration of love for her, and thus brings about the sexual intercourse through which John Connor is conceived; and, within that declaration, Kyle is insistent that he fell in love with Sarah primarily because of the expression on her face in a photograph of her. Kyle thereby seeks to present the narrative of *Terminator* as a love story, a quest across time motivated by love at first sight, and hence by the woman who elicited that love. On the other hand, he is given his first sight of Sarah in that photograph, and hence Sarah herself, by John; and the final scene of the film reveals that the photograph captures her expression just as she is thinking of Kyle himself, and of their one night of love. In other words, he sees the consummation of their love in her eyes, and hence sees himself as already beloved by her (and thereby sees the removal of any risk in his declaring his love – the removal of the possibility of refusal or non-reciproca-tion, and hence the removal of Sarah's autonomy, her otherness); and he also sees his beloved son, already alive within her. In short, what he sees in this photograph is not primarily Sarah but himself and his offspring; he sees in her the consummation of a narcissistic fantasy of male sexual potency, of paternity and patriarchal family structure.

This sense that Sarah's photograph is not so much a love token as an expression of her tokenistic role in a relationship between men is confirmed by its place in one of the most disorienting sequences of the film, in which Sarah – hiding beneath a bridge with Kyle, just after his diagnosis as paranoid has been disproved by the terminator's destruction of the police station, and just before their lovemaking – appears to dream of a future in which Kyle is killed by an infiltrating terminator. In fact, since the dream is initiated and sustained by Kyle's description of his previous life in the future, it would be more accurate to say that Sarah realizes her future lover's words, uncovering a certain range of meaning in them. And what she realizes is a vision of his death, which occurs just after he has been poring over her photograph, and which results in that photo being consumed by flames before his dying gaze. Kyle's death at such a point in the future – that is, before his return to Sarah's time – would amount to the death of John Connor's father, and hence to John himself never being born. This is a salutary reminder of Kyle's own significance in the film's story beyond that of protector and educator; but the sequence also declares that his removal from the narrative would mean that Sarah would never be reborn as John's mother, hence never be in a position to be photographed whilst thinking of her dead lover and his unborn child. The destruction of that photograph thus signals that her primary role is as Kyle's lover and John's mother; her significance goes up in flames when their existence is consumed by a terminator's lethal attentions.

It is worth noting that the spatially, temporally and emotionally displaced family structure of which this photograph is the currency is not entirely unfamiliar. Its most obvious cultural precedent lies at the heart of Christianity, in the Holy Family. There, too, we have a single male offspring, whose impending birth is announced by a guardian angel, whose initials are J.C. and whose destiny is to be the saviour of the human race; and given that this child's divinity participates in the Trinitarian structure of the Christian God, we can say that he, too, creates his own family and authors his own birth. True, Cameron's (post-, or perhaps pre-) nuclear family displaces the sign of virginity from the mother to the father of this family (Kyle's declaration of love embodies a declaration of his own previous celibacy); but even this may rather indicate that Kyle, as the merely surrogate father of this family, in this respect resembles the Holy Family's surrogate father, Joseph. Otherwise, however, Cameron's representation of Sarah as the family's mother seems quite strikingly to reproduce the combination of apparent centrality but ultimate marginality typically thought to define the place of Mary (and hence femaleness) in Christianity – the woman as temporary host, vehicle or medium for a creative transaction between or within an essentially male principle of cosmic divinity. (Here is yet another point of contact with the logic of *Alien*, as well as a pointer towards a deeply buried religious dimension in that film.)

We should not, however, overlook the fact that the photograph of Sarah – by its very nature – reminds us that the material basis of the medium of film is photographic, and hence that one range of its significance in *Terminator* might be to act as the vehicle of Cameron's reflections upon the nature of the medium in which he is beginning to work. Several lines of thought find their origins here. First, if the photograph of Sarah is a synecdoche of the film in which it appears, and which is constituted by sequences of such photographs, then the person who is ultimately responsible for it – for its framing and composition, and for its appearance as a symbol of the medium of film – is the film's director.

This is confirmed by the fact that the photograph is taken for, preserved and handed on to its most avid viewer by a character whose initials are J.C. – a character who is never seen in the film, but is presented by it as the ultimate author of the events it depicts. Indeed, just as this film records John Connor's authorization of his own birth, so we might think of the film itself as James Cameron's creation of himself as a film director, at this point someone for whom this film constitutes his entire body (of serious work). And if this interpretation (with its equation of the film's director with a character whom the film further equates with God) implies a certain hubris in Cameron, it is as well to recall that this photograph of Sarah is envisaged as having more than one future. In one, it makes possible the reality that the photograph itself depicts, and amounts to a certain kind of redemption – a re-achievement of genuine humanity, say, in a medium that is otherwise reduced to the merely commercial; in another (that of dream or nightmare), it is consumed by flames, its very existence aborted by an unforeseeable evolution of time and more particularly of the very technology without which it would not even have been conceivable as a cinematic work of art. One might even think of this dream as showing Cameron's prophetic awareness of the fundamental importance that technological advances in the medium of cinema will have in the evolution and evaluation of his future career as a director.

A second line of thought opens up from the fact that this photograph finds itself central to a dream sequence in which the film's necessary distortions of time and space find their deepest and darkest expression. Such distortions are, of course, commonplace in the genre of science fiction – the natural home of time travel; but is there any reason to think, as this film's placement of its central symbol for itself suggests, that this familiar generic resource taps into something internal to the nature of the cinematic medium itself?

Here, we return to an ontological question we encountered in Chapter 1 of this book: what exactly is the difference between an object in a photograph and the object itself? Stanley Cavell has argued that a photograph of an object is not, as a painting of it may be, a visual representation of that object (it does not stand for that object, or form a likeness of it), but rather a visual transcription of it.[1] However, it does not transcribe the sight or look or appearance of an object in the way in which a recording can be said to transcribe the sound of an object – primarily because a sight is either an extraordinary happening or an object itself (the aurora borealis or the Grand Canyon); what we see when we sight something is not the sight of an object but the object itself. Objects can be said to have or to make sounds, but not to have or to make sights; so there is nothing of the right sort for a photograph to be a photograph of short of the object itself. And yet a photograph of Linda Hamilton is not Linda Hamilton in the flesh.

Cavell's mode of resolving this apparent paradox is to suggest that we are approaching the question of this undeniable difference with a questionable assumption – that the objects in a photograph or film must differ in some specifiable respect from real objects, one having or lacking a feature that the other does not. We can distinguish real objects from one another by specifying criteria, determining specific differences between them; and we can distinguish between objects in a photograph or film using the same criteria. But we cannot distinguish real objects from objects in a photograph in such a way; there are no criteria which distinguish a photographed object from the object itself – no specific respect (eye colour, height, running style?) in which Linda Hamilton in a photograph or film differs from Linda Hamilton in the flesh. This does not mean we cannot distinguish between them; it means that the distinction must be specified not in terms of visible differences but in terms of the different relationships in which we stand to them.

A useful comparison here is our relationship to the characters in a play: according to Cavell, those characters do not differ in any specifiable respect from our fellow human beings outside the theatre, but our relationship to them differs. More precisely, whilst we can place ourselves in the same time as the play's characters (can confront each presented moment of the play's events as the present moment of its character's lives, importing neither our knowledge of its ending nor any assumption that what has already happened dictates their fate), we and they cannot occupy the same space (there is no path from our position to theirs, we are not in their presence). By contrast, the viewers of a photograph or film share neither a space nor a time with the object or person photographed; they are not in its physical presence, and the moment at which the object was captured by the camera is not made present to them and cannot be made present by them (our absence is mechanically assured, not something for which we are responsible). In short, the world of a photograph does not (and cannot) exist *now*:

> The reality in a photograph is present to me while I am not present to it; and a world I know, and see, but to which I am nevertheless not present (through no fault of my subjectivity) is a world past.
>
> In viewing a movie ... I am present not at something happening, which I must confirm, but at something that has happened, which I must absorb (like a memory). In this movies resemble novels, a fact mirrored in the sound of narration itself, whose tense is the past.[2]

If this is right, then there might appear to be a conflict between the genre of science fiction, with its projections of future social and technological arrangements, and the grain of the film medium. For is there not something temporally disordered and disorienting about being present at the projection of a narrative of something that has happened, when that story – being set in the future – is presented as not yet having happened? Would that not make the experience of viewing such films one of absorbing a memory of what is to come – and what might that be like?

In *Terminator*, this is the basic shape of the experience of both of its central human protagonists. Everything that Kyle tells Sarah is of her, his and the human future, but he describes it from memory; his key message to her from her as yet unborn son is one that he explicitly says he had to memorize, and the photograph of her that motivates his every action records a moment in her life that is yet to occur. For Sarah, when that photograph is taken and given to her, its subjects – herself, her love for Kyle and her son – immediately move into the past; but she then drives into a future whose lineaments are dictated by her memory of Kyle's and her son's memories, as embodied in that photograph. In this respect, Cameron's placing of the photograph of Sarah at the heart of his narrative's most intense displacements of space and time signifies his awareness of the fact that the film he is directing is investigating (through the time-travel narrative that creates and trades upon those displacements) a fundamental condition of the possibility of films about the future.

Sarah's condition as a character thus resembles our condition as viewers: like her, we see the future only through Kyle's memories of it, whether privately visualized (as in the wrecked car before he finds Sarah) or as described to her. Hence, like us, she is presented with, and feels compelled to inhabit, a future that is fixed or determined in the manner of the past, as if remembering her future. And what remains of the future if it is stripped of its unknownness, its openness? What damage is thereby done to our sense of ourselves as having a future, and as having some control over what that future will be like? What happens to our individuality and freedom? And what happens to the world? The film's concluding image of the impending nuclear apocalypse does not encourage optimism.

One concluding line of thought extending from the photograph should be noted. For, of course, it is a photograph of Sarah Connor at her moment of rebirth as the warrior-mother of a warrior-son, which is to say it is a photograph of Linda Hamilton at the moment of her possible birth as a star. How will the peculiar conjunction of physiognomy, character and director determine the trajectory of her cinematic transfiguration? James Cameron will return to this.

Reiterating family values: real and ideal

If we think of *Alien* as an entity whose identity was determined by the dovetailing contributions of a specific director and a specific scenario or script – the two wrapping or warping around one another to form the double-helix of its internal code or pro-gramme – then *Aliens* is what results when one helical strand from the original entity is combined with another from the director-scenario double-helix of *Terminator*. The analogy limps, of course; but its emphasis upon the combination and recombination of sequences of coding goes some way towards capturing what is distinctive about Cameron's approach to the delicate and bur-densome responsibility of writing and directing a sequel to a critically acclaimed (if not commercially lucrative) film with a highly specific style and subject-matter. For, in essence, Cameron constitutes *Aliens* from displaced re-presentations of the basic ele-ments from which *Alien* is itself constructed.

The depth and degree of this repetition are as difficult to measure as they are to credit, because of the multiplicity of levels at which the repetition occurs. At the level of basic plot structure, we see Cameron restage the crew's reawakening from hypersleep to face the alien nightmare, their trip from a mothership by shuttle to the planet of the alien wreck, their gradual elimination by their enemy, the climactic need for the nuclear destruction of a human technological edifice infested by the alien species, and of course the double-climax structure of which Cameron also made use in *Terminator*. Re-enactment is also the dominant principle at the level of individual scenes – for example the panic-stricken strategy and weapons-evaluation meeting after the first alien incursion, complete with disparaging references to the android's inadequate contribution to their cause; Ripley's encounter with a facehugger in the medical lab facilities, complete with her falling backwards to throw it off whilst armed men throw themselves across her; and the scene (restored in its entirety in the Director's Cut) in which Scott's leisurely prowling of the corridors and crevices of the *Nostromo* before the crew's rebirth is recapitulated (right down to pans across corridor intersections, dipping mechanical toys and empty helmets) by Cameron as our introduction to the crew of the *Sulaco*. And at the level of specific images or tableaux, beyond that of the various phases of the alien itself, we are presented with the same design of weaponry and related technology (flame guns, motion trackers, TV monitors), the same tangles of clanking chains (transposed from Brett's death-scene to the Marines' birth-scene), the same chaos of red lights, grilles and tunnels in the first climax, and the same second-climax vision of the last alien spiralling out into space through an airlock door. Cameron underlines this aspect of his strategy by scattering his film with the figure '2': it is stencilled on Newt's bed in the medical lab, the second drop-ship, the second elevator from the alien nest, and the airlock from which the alien queen is eventually ejected – and it might as well be stencilled on Bishop's forehead, although in fact he has to make do instead with a surname beginning with the second letter of the alphabet, following on from Ash's initial 'A'.

Why does this overwhelming repetitiveness not dilute the film's undeniable pleasures, or loosen the increasing firmness of its narrative grip on us, but rather help to intensify both? In part, of course, because such repetitions provide the fundamental pleasure of recognition, allowing us to recall the pleasure those elements gave us on their first appearance, and reassuring us of the depth of our new director's familiarity with and respect for the film, and its world, that they helped constitute. More importantly, however, they give pleasure because they are not simply repetitions: for Cameron subjects his reiterated elements to various kinds of displacement or transformation.

The most obvious variation is one of magnified scale: the nuclear explosion is bigger, the weaponry and firefights more spectacular, the second climax confronts Ripley with a far more frightening variant of the alien, and accordingly provides her with a far more substantial exoskeleton than her original spacesuit (the cargo-loader). Less obviously, Cameron can utilize repetition to encourage certain expectations determined by the first film in order to sub-vert or invert them: this is clearest in the case of Bishop, who is made to re-enact Ash's admiring dissections of the facehugger before turning out to be Ripley's saviour – an inversion Cameron underlines by having him reduced to a dismembered state akin to Ash's final appearance for his climactic rescue of Newt.

Cameron himself refers to this aspect of his work as taking seriously his audience's programming – not denying but acknowl-edging their familiarity with the first film, and their knowledge that what they are watching is a sequel to it, hence ineluctably indebted to it, the same again, but different.[3] But he encodes a further explanation of his technique of displaced repetition within the film itself – an explanation prepared for by the fact that the opening act of *Aliens* (from Ripley's rescue to her accep-tance of a role in the Marine mission) presents her as someone who must relive a nightmare if she is to overcome its traumatic effects on her life. Ripley's first apparently conscious moments, which culminate in her being revealed as another victim of the alien chestburster, turn out to be a nightmare – one which she relives every night until the Company's offer of an advisory role in an expedition to annihilate the alien species gives her a chance to (as Burke puts it) get back on the horse. Hence, the first scene on board the *Sulaco* is presented pretty much exactly as was the opening sequence of *Alien*, and Cameron's multilevel reiterations of that film move into top gear, until his duplicate double climax is resolved by a repetition of Ripley's prior ejection of the alien from her mothership. Only then can she reassure Newt that they may both dream again: only by therapeutically recalling and re-experiencing her initial traumatic encounter can she locate and disable its source.

This is, in fact, the key respect in which *Aliens* differs from its cinematic source: it takes us back to the geographical (if not the cosmic) source of the alien species, and it introduces us to two aspects of its reproductive cycle about which *Alien* is silent, but without which the alien species as such could not survive (the cocooning of living human hosts in preparation for impregnation,[4] and the mode or variant of alien life from which the eggs con-taining the impregnating facehuggers themselves come) – that is, it uncovers the biological as well as the geographical source of the alien species. And by forcing Ripley to confront what she is trying to repress, and thereby forcing the *Alien* series to confront what it has so far repressed about its eponymous protagonist, Cameron presents himself as engaged in an essentially therapeutic endeavour – one in which the reiteration of that which has been repressed will bring release or liberation. It is as if Cameron takes his own film as the necessary therapy of which his predecessor's central human character and the cinematic world in which she is introduced both stand in need. He proposes, in short, to heal both Ripley and the alien narrative universe, to cure them of that which ails them; and it is in his understanding of what this requires that Cameron makes manifest his deepest acknowledgement, and his most radical subversion, of the underlying logic of Scott's prior film.

For, of course, what Ripley achieves by the end of *Aliens* – her reward for confronting her deepest fears – is a family: Corporal Hicks becomes her husband, and Newt their child. Hicks has been demonstrating his fitness for this role throughout the movie; he combines quick thinking, courage, coolness under fire and a refusal to participate in the boastful, point-scoring emptiness of his fellow-soldiers' utterances with an instinctive and unflagging concern for the film's representative of childhood (he prevents Drake from shooting Newt accidentally when she is first spotted, and he is Ripley's best supporter as she tries to recover Newt from the bowels of the alien nest). Hicks is, however, more than just a suitable partner for Ripley: he is her other, the one who is prepared to have her words put in his mouth ('we'll nuke the planet from orbit – it's the only way') and hence to give her once again a voice in her own history (a voice whose initial doubled denial by Ash is reiterated in *Aliens* by the Company's refusal to listen when Ripley tries to recount her experiences aboard the *Nostromo*); he is the sole masculine character in the movie who is represented as developing (out of the highly macho Marine culture, with its talk of taking colonists' virginity and its combination of pornography with weaponry)[5] towards the 'nurturing warrior' ideal (an ideal that the actor, Michael Biehn, also represented in *Terminator*, as Kyle Reese) – the same ideal towards which Ripley is also moving from her side of the divide of sexual difference. It is no accident that their marriage is sealed (when he gives her a wristband location tracker, which he rather too insistently tells her 'doesn't mean we're engaged or anything') just before educating her in the complexities of Marine weapons technology. Both can overcome their anxieties in battle, both do the right thing at the right time for the right reasons, both can handle themselves without losing touch with their humanity. Their union thus represents a fusion of what is deemed best in the prevailing cultural stereotypes of masculinity and femininity – the film's answer to the question implicit in the exchange between Hudson and Vasquez on the *Sulaco*: 'Have you ever been mistaken for a man?' 'No – have you?'

Ripley's understanding of the significance of Hicks' gift of the location tracker is made clear when in the scene immediately following her 'engagement' she gives the tracker to Newt, as if binding her into the union. Her accelerating inhabitation of the role of mother to Newt is, however, central to the film's development throughout: she goes after Newt in the ducts and walkways, cleans her up, defends her in the med lab against the facehuggers, promises never to leave her and fulfils that promise against all the odds. As a consequence, when Newt welcomes her back after her climactic confrontation with the alien queen, her sigh of 'Mommy!' can seem not only deeply satisfying but also disquietingly tardy – as if Newt's expectations of anyone wishing to become her mother are savagely demanding, as if motherhood itself asks for devotion beyond any rational limit. Certainly, on the film's view of the matter, if the true warrior is nurturing, the true nurturer is a warrior: it is, after all, Ripley's devotion to her daughter that generates the film's two most thrilling images of her as a soldier – when she is arming herself in the elevator going back into the alien nest, and when she walks out in the cargoloader to confront the alien queen (and deliver the film's most famous line: 'Get away from her, you bitch!')

To conceive of Ripley's overcoming of her nightmare, her healing, as the acquisition of a family shows how deeply Cameron is attuned to the logic of sexual difference and generativity implicit in *Alien*, and to Ripley's own place within that logic – fated to heroism by virtue of her obdurate refusal of heterosexual inter-course and its reproductive consequences. But the kind of family she acquires, or more precisely the way in which she acquires it, shows that Cameron's conception of what it would be for Ripley to be healed is in fact a continuation of – essentially in complicity with – the very attitude to sexuality that locks her into her nightmare. For Ripley's family has a non-biological origin: her union with her husband is not physically consummated, and she becomes a mother to Newt without conceiving, being pregnant with or giving birth to her. In short, whilst Ripley's achievement of this film's conception of female fulfilment demands that she lay her body on the line for Hicks and Newt, it allows her to avoid any acknowledgement of her body's fertility.[6]

But that which is repressed is not annihilated – indeed it has a habit of returning in an only apparently unfamiliar guise; and we know from the first film in the series where to look for the dis-placed expression of this vision of flesh-and-blood fertility as monstrous – the alien species. To be sure, Cameron's way of representing the horror of the aliens differs significantly from that of Scott: without depriving himself of the specific modes of disgust aroused by its facehugging and chestbursting forms, he emphasizes two other aspects of its form of life.

The first (as the plural form of the film title suggests) is its multiplicity: the humans in this film face not a single alien being but hundreds of them. This has the cinematic advantage of enhanced scale for the fight sequences, and underlines their unstoppable reproductive drive; but it has the further con-sequence of allowing Cameron to represent the alien species exclusively in large numbers, and thereby to emphasize his sense of that species as itself a kind of monstrous whole, an agglom-eration or incorporation of its individual members. This comes through most clearly when Hicks looks up into the overhead ducts of their last redoubt, and sees a multi-limbed, hydra-headed tangle of alien flesh apparently dragging itself through the confined space towards them. What Cameron portrays as monstrous here is not exactly community as such, but one mode of it. For the Marines represent a human mode of communal existence whose individual members are trained to subordinate themselves to the good of the whole; but their humanity is manifested in the film as their capacity to make decisions and to establish individual loyalties for themselves, in opposition to those deemed to represent the good of the community (as when Hicks and Vasquez conceal ammunition on their first foray into the alien nest, or when Vasquez and Gorman decide to sacrifice themselves in the airducts). The aliens, by contrast (like ants), have no genuinely individual existence in their community – they are foetuses or nurses or warriors, utterly subsumed by their roles within the community that is their species. They have no interests of their own, no conception of what such expressions of individuality might be; in this respect, they are monstrous.

The other new aspect of their monstrosity resides in their queen. Ripley first confronts her when, having rescued Newt from cocoonment and imminent impregnation, the pair stumble into the heart of the nest – its nursery. The camera relays to us Ripley's horrified gaze as it moves from the ranks of alien eggs, to the arrival of a new egg from a large, trembling orifice, and then back along the enormous, semi-translucent, sagging egg-sac to its point of connection with the alien queen, who is revealed from tail to ornate head, her crown internal to her own cranial anatomy. The monstrosity of that egg-sac – supported by resinous stays fixed to the ceiling, half-hidden by steam arising from the warm, newly laid eggs, half-full of a soupy, slightly bubbling liquid (as if it represented the birth of life itself from a primeval amniotic fluid) is so extreme that it even undercuts the awesomeness of the queen's body. It is the absolute embodiment of Ripley's vision of flesh and fertility, of the biological realm, of life as such: it is everything that she and her family are not.

And yet, of course, the queen as mother is also a mirror-image of Ripley herself, as she has been transformed by Cameron's therapy – as Cameron implies even in the prologue to his film, when he introduces us to Ripley in her new apartment on Earth by focussing first on her hand as it holds a cigarette, a hand whose fingers look remarkably like the digits of the alien face-hugger; and as he further suggests by presenting Ripley with a shorter haircut, the better to reveal her distinctive high cheekbones and slightly jutting jaw, so strikingly reminiscent of the sculptured alien face (physiognomy as cinematic destiny). Both are, in essence, nurturing warriors. The queen simply incarnates the reproductive drive that is internal to any species, including the human; and her aggressive impulses are as informed by her maternity as are Ripley's – as her willingness to accept Ripley's wordless bargain ('Let us go and I won't torch your nursery') underlines. Thus far, she responds exactly as her nature demands – her motivations are as natural as they could be, and hence the monstrosity of her representation can be understood only on the assumption that nature itself (as incarnated in her) is felt to be monstrous. What transforms her from a brooding mother to a warrior is not some malevolent or gratuitous desire to destroy human beings, but rather Ripley's attack on her nursery; the queen's final pursuit of the human mother and child is driven by a desire for vengeance upon the one who slew her offspring.

This simply confirms the implicit equivalence between Ripley and the queen – since it was the same drive to protect her child that brought Ripley into the nursery in the first place. But it also suggests a certain asymmetry between the two warrior-mothers – and one rather to Ripley's detriment; for it is Ripley herself who violates her implicit bargain with the queen, and thereby risks her own life and that of her child, in order to annihilate the queen's offspring. In other words, she prefers to break her word, deny her own drive for survival and reproduction, and enact genocide (against a race whose predation upon her own is merely natural, and against a queen who has hitherto shown a willingness at least to accept a temporary *modus vivendi* with the human species, and hence an almost human concern for morality and children) rather than live a moment longer with the knowledge that such an incarnation of biological fertility might exist. Which of these females, we might well think, is the real bitch?

We might also recall Ripley's (self-)righteous denunciation of Burke's plan to smuggle an alien back to earth, when she says that she doesn't know which species is the worst: 'at least you don't see them fucking one another over for a percentage'. One might defend her against her own criticism by saying that her deal is not for personal gain, and that it was brokered between species rather than within one; but genocide is hardly more morally appetizing than murder, and it is hardly rendered more comprehensible when attempted in a context in which it threatens immense personal loss. In reality, what offends Ripley about Burke is what offends her about the aliens: just as the queen incarnates the threat of biological fertility, so Burke's smuggling plan both literally and symbolically threatened Ripley with the consequences of being 'fucked': Burke intended to impregnate her (and Newt) with an alien foetus in order to smuggle them past quarantine checks on Earth. Here is the deepest reason for Burke's taking on the symbolic role of Ash in the first film (with its transposition of the threat of masculine sexual violence from the realm of science to that of economics); his behaviour re-enacts Ash's attempts to kill Ripley by forcing something down her throat (as his attempt to trap Ripley in the soundproof med lab, rendering mute her appeals for help against the facehuggers, reiterates Ash's double denial of her voice). Here also is the deepest appeal of her relationship with Hicks: for their union coincides with their mutual convergence upon an essentially asexual human ideal – as if each reflects the other primarily in their transcendence of any biological sexual difference, as if the erasure of the very idea of such difference is the condition of their mutual attraction.

If further confirmation were needed of Cameron's inability to distance himself from Ripley's nightmare vision – the downside of his (and our) deep identification with her fusion of the soldier and the nurturer – it is to be found in the political significance of her genocidal impulse. Like its predecessor, *Aliens* is a generic hybrid: it fuses the logic and conventions of the horror film with that of the war movie, and Cameron has more than once acknowledged that he conceived the Marine mission to LV 426 as a study of the Vietnam War – in which, on his analysis, a high-tech army confident of victory over a supposedly more primitive civilization found itself mired in a humiliating series of defeats that added up to an unwinnable war. To be sure, this analysis allows Cameron to criticize certain aspects of American culture – its adoration of the technological, its ignorance of alien cultures, its overweening arrogance. At the same time, however, the generic background of his film, together with its specific inheritance of the alien narrative universe, ensures that the structure of his criticism works only by placing the Vietnamese in the position of absolute, and absolutely monstrous, aliens; and it rewrites the conflict it claims to analyse by allowing the Marines to win the war by destroying the planet in a nuclear explosion. It thereby supports the vision of American political hubris and xenophobia that it claims to criticize, and underwrites Ripley's genocidal impulse, the deepest expression of her repression of her human flesh and blood – both her own and that of her offspring and her species. It appears, then, that the person most in need of healing here is the would-be therapist.

Excursus: *The Abyss*

Whether or not as a result of perceiving this, James Cameron's next excursion into the science fiction field contains some evidence of a transformation in his attitudes to the aspects of human life so resolutely detested by Ripley. For, in *The Abyss* (1991), the lives and the marriage of its two central characters are saved by their capacity to let themselves die in the hope of rebirth. The woman goes first, as if educating her husband. When both are trapped too many metres from their underwater mothership with only one oxygen mask between them, she chooses to allow herself to drown; her hope is that the resulting hypothermia will preserve her vital functions during the time it takes her husband to carry her back to the ship, and that hope is realized. As if empowered by her example, her husband then agrees to utilize an entirely new, SEAL-designed, breathing apparatus, intended to allow divers to operate at extreme depths; it works by filling its user's lungs with oxygen-rich fluid – hence, her husband must, in effect, allow himself to drown in order to live at the depths to which he must go in order to avert the destruction of an extraterrestrial species they have encountered. As one of the SEALs points out as a kind of reassurance, 'everyone breathes like this for nine months; your body will remember': in other words, to employ this apparatus is to return oneself to the womb. It is as powerful and beautiful an image of what is involved in human self-overcoming as one could desire; and its force in this context is redoubled by the fact that its cinematic projection required James Cameron to subordinate his best resources as a director to giving life to that SEAL's invocation of the life-giving powers of the human body and its memory of existence between conception and birth – when it survives and flourishes only in parasitic dependence on human femininity.

On self-termination

Cameron's attitude to the making of sequels, as established with *Aliens*, is re-enacted in his next exercise in the science fiction genre – *Terminator 2: Judgment Day* (1993), the sequel to his own first film. The same implausibly pervasive repetitions of basic plot structure, specific scenes and particular seams of imagery are evident – ranging from a reiteration of the first film's chase structure and its culmination in a double climax pivoting on the death-dealing terminator's capacity to overcome even the dismemberment of his body, to Cameron's magnification of a toy lorry (crushed under the wheels of the terminator's car at the beginning of the first film) into an enormous, fully functioning truck of exactly the same appearance hijacked by the new terminator to hunt down John Connor in the sequel's opening chase sequence. Equally predictably, however, these massive reiterations are blended with equally insistent patterns of displacement and transformation, the whole hanging together with almost algorithmic precision, and turning ultimately on Cameron's introduction of a second (kind of) terminator into his second *Terminator* film.

In his sequel, the machines send back a prototype T-1000 (made of mimetic polyalloy, a liquid metal that can imitate anything of similar volume that it samples by physical contact) and target it on John himself rather than his mother. This single move determines every other displacement of the key characters from the first movie within the matrix of roles that film established: it allows Arnold Schwarzenegger to appear in the Kyle Reese role, as another instance of the older model of terminator he played in the first film, but now programmed by the resistance to combat the T-1000; this allows Sarah Connor to appear as a kind of human terminator, dispensing the opposite of love to her son, intending to kill the future inventor of the SkyNet technology, and seeing herself and her world as already post-nuclear; and this in turn allows John Connor himself, displaced from the unseen future, to concern himself again with the (re)construction of his own family.

This last displacement in many ways simply reiterates the bizarre family structure at the heart of *Terminator*, despite the fact that it prevents him from authoring his own birth in any literal sense; for, once again, we find not only that John Connor is the prime mover of the plan to save his own mother, but that he in effect brings her together with a new or surrogate father – the reprogrammed terminator. As Sarah herself puts it: 'It would always be there, and it would die to protect him. Of all the would-be fathers who came and went, only this machine measured up; in an insane world, it was the sane choice'.

That testimony appears to underline the very repression of the flesh and of sexual difference that we noted in *Aliens*; it identifies true fatherhood with an absence of flesh and blood, and invokes an idea of a family forged in the absence of sexual intercourse. To be sure, Sarah has given birth in the usual way to her son, but her sense of her own motherly relation to him is one in which he is not so much her own flesh and blood as everyone's, the embodiment of humanity's hope for a future: when he acts on his sense of his own particular connection to her, ordering the terminator to help him get her out of the mental hospital despite the risk of encountering the T-1000, because she is his mother, Sarah's response is to deny that connection; she tells him to protect himself, even when her interests are threatened, because his destiny as the saviour of the race is more important.

On the other hand, the film also makes clear that the person who utters those words about the perfect family is herself in a far from perfect state; it does not endorse but rather contextualizes and diagnoses their import. Education and change are at the heart of this film in a number of ways – as we see in the terminator's education in the ways of human beings, most specifically in its learning to achieve its goals without killing, and in Dyson's coming to learn and take responsibility for what he has not yet done; but its key instance of self-overcoming is that of Sarah Connor herself.

At the end of the first film, we see her on the verge of trans-forming herself into a warrior's mother; the second film begins by displaying the results of that self-transformation. The Sarah Connor who later finds herself trying to assassinate a fellow human being for something he has not (yet) done is someone who believes (and lives out the belief) that a warrior's mother must be all warrior and no mother – a non-nurturing soldier. In the service of the goal of preparing her son for his destiny as saviour of the human race in the war against the machines, she has become a killing machine herself. And Cameron's understanding of the source of her incarnation of deathliness is striking: it is her foreknowledge of the future.

The film's study of Sarah opens with her unsuccessful attempt to convince her psychiatrist that she has changed; but the video-taped interview in which she gives expression to her true feelings focuses on her Cassandra-like foretelling of the nuclear war of which Kyle Reese spoke, and on the impact of that knowledge of impending apocalypse upon her own sense of the world. Its impact, in short, is that she perceives herself, her fellow human beings and their world as already dead: 'You think you're safe and alive; but you're already dead. Everything is gone – you're living in a dream. Because I know what happens – it happens.' For Sarah, her knowledge of what will happen collapses the future into the past, and thereby destroys the present; because for her the future is fixed, no longer open to determination in at least some degree by the thoughts and actions of those currently alive, those thoughts and actions lose any human significance, and the significance of the lives that they go to make up also vanishes in the face of the utter loss of human significance that future nuclear war represents. She dreams of that war as annihi-lating children because it annihilates the future, and the primary symbol of the future in the present (the primary locus of the human sense of humanity as having a future, and of the human sense of the future as open and meaningful) is the child. In short, to know that the world will end is itself the end of the world; what Sarah knows spells the death of her world, and of herself in it – she is already dead too, and she knows it. Hence, her presence in that world can only spell death for those she encounters – not only for her son, who finds that his mother does not exist for him, but for anyone who opposes her (for what can it matter if she kills someone who is already dead?).

Three things serve to rescue Sarah from the most extreme consequences of her nihilism – to turn her away from completing her execution of Miles Dyson. First, she sees herself – a would-be assassin and killer of children, a destroyer of the human family, a terminator – in her victim's eyes; second, she learns from John's attempt to stop her that her failure to be a mother to her son has not annihilated his capacity to be a son to his mother, and hence not annihilated her capacity to acknowledge herself as his mother; and, third, she learns from the terminator's acceptance of John's orders that even technology is not destiny. These three factors are not unconnected – hence their three-fold impact occurs within a single scene in the film; for it is plain that, in her eyes, the ultimate cause of the death of the future is technology, which she understands as the expression of an essentially death-dealing masculinity. She sneers at Dyson for thinking that building SkyNet is a creative act, seeing it rather as the antithesis of genuine, life-giving creativity as represented by female generativity; but Dyson's willingness to sacrifice himself to destroy the technological origins of SkyNet, the terminator's willingness to sacrifice itself in the same cause and her awareness of her failure properly to mother the product of her biological creativity together suggest that technology is no more destined to deny life than biology is destined to affirm it. What matters is what human beings make of them, whether they acknowledge their creatureliness and its creations, or deny them. 'No fate but what we make.'

Since Terminator 2 presents Sarah's knowledge of the future as the source of the deathliness in her and in her world, it must present her recovery of the future as a function of annihilating that knowledge. If she is to overcome herself, the future must become unknown. The film makes this release possible by determining that the indispensable basis of the research that leads to SkyNet, and thence to nuclear war, should be the remains of the first terminator, rescued by the CyberDine Corporation from the robotic metal-press. It follows from this that the future's (and hence Sarah's) emancipation from doom can be achieved if all traces of the first terminator are destroyed. As befits a Cameron sequel, this destruction takes a doubled form: first, John tosses the pieces of the first terminator (stolen from CyberDine) into the furnace; then, the second instance of that first terminator invites Sarah to lower it into the same furnace – its self-sacrifice imitating that of its unknowing creator, the nearest it can achieve to self-termination (which its programming forbids). And Sarah herself takes hope from its example, allowing herself to think of its self-sacrifice as suggesting the falsity of its earlier view that 'it's in your nature to destroy yourselves': 'for if a machine can learn the value of human life, maybe we can too'.

Rather more interesting than this concluding moral, however, is what the concluding events of this film say about the relation between it and its predecessor. For, of course, in destroying any trace of the first terminator, and thereby erasing the narrative (of nuclear war followed by human resistance to extermination by machines) that it enabled, *Terminator 2* destroys not only the future reality from which its own two terminators come; it destroys the possibility of any future *Terminator* films, and it destroys the future which enabled the events of *Terminator* itself – the film which is its own source or origin, its indispensable past. In other words, *Terminator 2* self-terminates, and, in so doing, it self-terminates both *Terminator* and the *Terminator* series.

This second sequel in Cameron's directorial career thus makes profoundly radical use of the power inherent in any sequel to rewrite the significance of the predecessor to which it is inevitably indebted, and to determine the possibilities it leaves open to any future sequel. But in this case its exercise is not inherently vengeful or self-aggrandizing – as if driven by the anxiety of influence or inheritance; it is rather liberating or empowering. For just as it frees Sarah from her death-in-life, so it frees Cameron himself from the nihilistic narrative universe that he had created, and from the need to return to it in any further sequels. In short, it freed him from any sense of confinement by his own origins as a director, reopening his own cinematic future.

But, in so doing, he certainly appears to have foreclosed one possible mode in which that future might be realized. For we saw earlier that the spatio-temporal disruptions made possible by the science fiction genre, and utilized with unusual power in Terminator's time-travel narrative, functioned as a kind of internal representation of the disruption inherent in the experience of viewing science fiction movies as such (which might be defined as projections of a future world that is simultaneously a world past). Sarah's nihilism is Terminator 2's internal representation of that viewing condition – which suggests that, for Cameron, representations of the future as knowable, as picturable in a way indistinguishable from reality, are incitements to conflate our relationship to the past (over which we can exercise no control) with our relationship to the future, whose openness is a condition of our capacity to think of our own lives as significant. Terminator 2's self-termination amounts to a refusal or transcendence of that incitement, and hence a denial of one of the determining characteristics of the genre it inhabits. It is, to say the very least, unsurprising that Cameron himself has thus far avoided any further work in that genre.

However, the displacements to which Cameron subjects the world of his first film in order to effect this self-transcendence also allow him to explore further another aspect of what one might call the ontology of film. This involves what Terminator 2 has to say about Linda Hamilton's potential for stardom, about what has and can become of her on film. At the end of Terminator, just as her character was on the verge of self-transformation, so Hamilton herself appeared to have the chance of becoming a star; and by the end of Terminator 2 she has demonstrated the depth of her capacity to make her character's physical, psychological and spiritual vicissitudes real on screen. The soft, unformed physique of the first film has become a sleek, streamlined weapon; the emotional vulnerability of her younger self has calcified, and then is recovered to re-inform her renewed maternal impulses and her sense of hope for the unwritten future. And yet, despite this capacity to absorb and represent the complex and unsympathetic trajectory of her character, and to bear up under the physical demands of a typically pyrotechnic and kinetic Cameron blockbuster, we now know that Linda Hamilton did not become a star – that her specific physiognomy proved incapable of projecting a life in the movies free from the conjunction of character and director that first made the possibility of stardom real for her. Can we even begin to answer the question: why not?

Terminator 2 offers a certain understanding of what it is to be a film star that might at least help us to formulate this question more sharply. It follows from the film's doubling or splitting of the terminator role it inherits from its predecessor. On the one hand, we have the same actor representing a differently programmed reiteration of his earlier 'character'; on the other, inhabiting the 'villain' role thereby left vacant, we have a new actor representing the next generation of terminators, whose distinctive capacity is to mimic anything it samples by physical contact. We might think of these two types of terminator as each embodying one of the two conflicting vectors of any mode of acting – the constancy of the individual actor beneath or behind his differing roles (a cause of much disorientation and humour in the film) and the bewildering variety of characters he is called upon to inhabit (as uncanny in its way as the T-1000's brief re-embodiment of every human being it impersonated in its death-throes at the foundry). If, however, following Cavell, we acknowledge that the relationship between these two vectors in screen acting is determined by the material basis of the medium, hence by the camera's automatic reproduction of the individual human physiognomy placed before it, then we would expect the actor to be prior to the character in the film – with the individual actor lending himself to the character, accepting only that within it which fits and discarding the rest (as opposed, say, to yielding himself to or working himself into the character, as might a theatre actor).[7] We should therefore expect stardom to turn more on an actor's constancy than his inconstancy, upon the effect of his physiognomic consistency across a body of films than upon any ability to change himself in accordance with the demands of an independently given part.

Against this background, it will seem rather less than accidental that, whilst Linda Hamilton's gift for inhabiting her character and its vicissitudes seems actually to have prevented her from attaining stardom, the actor whose appearance in both *Terminator* films helped to project him into the highest reaches of cinematic fame was the one who, by playing the same, physically indistinguishable character, allowed the camera to transcribe and re-transcribe his utterly distinctive physiognomy without obstacle or interruption (and the one who, in his unparalleled ability to take physical direction, to do and hence to be exactly what his director wishes, earns from Cameron the label of 'the perfect actor')[8] – Arnold Schwarzenegger.

2007 postscript: the anti-terminator Terminator

Since my reading of the two *Terminator* movies entails that the series could not possibly continue, should I view the release of *Terminator 3: The Rise of the Machines* (Jonathan Mostow, 2003) as having falsified it? On the contrary: I take the incoherence of that movie as providing the strongest possible confirmation of my earlier view. And, fittingly enough, the source of its failure lies in its inability to make its own narrative starting-point cohere with the ending of *Terminator 2*, and so with the complex relation between past, present and future as that was established within the earlier movies and between the world of those movies and the world of its viewers.

For the fundamental difficulty confronting the writers and director of *Terminator 3* was that its release would postdate the year of Judgement Day as that was established in the first two movies. Hence, the temporal location of the new film's intended audience made it impossible for the older John Connor of *Terminator 3* to deny that Judgement Day had in fact not happened – that the future apocalypse (foreknowledge of which had condemned his mother to a form of death-in-life from which only a rewriting of the future could release her) had been avoided. Moreover, in exercising his pre-Judgement Day freedom to rewrite the future of both mother and son in *Terminator 2*, Cameron chose to effect the necessary revisions by annihilating the very traces of the first two terminators without which he had established that SkyNet simply could not be built, and so could not initiate Judgement Day. According to the narrative logic established in *Terminator* and *Terminator 2*, then, it was not only Judgement Day, but SkyNet itself and so all its machine progeny, and hence the whole future history around which both films were built, that had self-terminated.

How, then, could a third movie be made about subsequent events within the *Terminator* universe?

On the evidence of *Terminator 3*, only by an utterly arbitrary directorial fiat. For when this delicate issue arises, a third of the way into the film, when the impending activation of SkyNet has already been established, the third incarnation of the terminator simply denies that Judgement Day was averted by the earlier actions of Sarah and John Connor, flatly declaring: 'Judgement Day was only postponed; it is inevitable'. Indeed, minutes later, we are told that the day of the film's events is in fact (the new) Judgement Day itself. Note that we are now owed not only a specification of the alternative route by which the technology necessary for SkyNet was developed, but also an explanation of why the apocalyptic outcome of this development is 'inevitable' (that is, not just the outcome of this potentially alterable course of events, but the unavoidable outcome of any possible course of events). And we are given neither. In other words, we are given no reason whatever for the renewed existence of the world of *Terminator 3*: it has been (re)created *ex nihilo*, with complete gratuitousness but absolutely no love.

As such, it is not a generous gift but a poisoned chalice; for now it will necessarily seem that new life has been breathed into this annihilated world only in order that its original appointment with nuclear destruction and a long drawn-out, brutal revolt against human enslavement to technology be kept. It is as if the film's makers are taking revenge on their created world for the way in which the irreversible passage of time in their own world – what Nietzsche calls 'time and its unalterable "It was"' – has constrained their room for artistic manoeuvre. For in their revulsion against the way Cameron has already determined the previous history of their cinematic universe they inflict upon their imagined future, and so upon its inhabitants, the obstinate unrevisability that precisely distinguishes past from future. In their hands, the past and the future swap places: the past is treated as entirely ignorable or dismissable and the future as utterly closed, and both are thereby eviscerated of their human significance.

The vengeful arbitrariness of this act of (re)creation infects every aspect of the world thereby created. John Connor (played by Nick

Stahl) oscillates unpredictably throughout the film between declarations of belief and disbelief in the openness of the future; and his actions follow a similarly confused path, given that they imply on the one hand that SkyNet might be stopped, but on the other that he will marry the old schoolfriend he has just re-encountered and fight the machines with her. As Kate Brewster, Claire Danes must do what she can with a character whose independent spirit apparently does not extend to questioning the sentimental vision of her marrying the first boy she ever kissed (even when his reappearance in her world leads to the death of her fiancé and father), and who spends much of the film either imprisoned or unconscious; her embarrassed delivery of her 'Just die, you bitch!' line to the new, physiognomically female terminator (the T-X) sums up her predicament. The T-X itself (played by Kristanna Loken) is given problematic new powers: we are told it has been specifically developed to terminate other terminators, quite as if the two previous generations of terminators had lacked this capacity, and that it is capable of controlling other machines (via nanotechnological transjectors) – a power so devastatingly effective that, if she could only remember on a consistent basis that she possessed it, the film would have been over within half an hour. Her female appearance is given no motivation whatever, except for the opportunity it provides for casual misogyny, of the kind manifest in Kate Brewster's 'bitch' line and in the older terminator's gleeful inclination during one of his fights with her to force his enemy's head down a toilet bowl.

The T-101, played once again by Arnold Schwarzenegger, is no less incoherently programmed. Unlike his previous incarnations, he seems to understand human popular culture effortlessly; his proclaimed immunity to John Connor's instructions wavers unpredictably; and, most damagingly of all, the director attempts to gift him with the machine equivalent of free will. For it emerges that the resistance captured him after he successfully assassinated John Connor (on 4 July 2032), and he was reprogrammed by Kate Brewster herself for his present mission (better not to ask how that mission could possibly avert John's termination, given that he must live until 2032 for it to be possible). However, when the T-X reprogrammes him again for her own purposes, he is shown to be battling internally against that reprogramming, and eventually to have overcome it. But this entirely undermines his status as a machine, a status properly respected by both previous films (in the first, his programming remains unaltered; and, in the second, his ingenuity in overcoming damage inflicted by the T-1000, as well as his decision to self-terminate, are entirely consistent with his pro-resistance programming). In the third film, by contrast, there is simply no reason why the T-101's previous programmes should lurk beneath the new one, like previously endorsed but currently rejected courses of action – except, of course, a movie's star desire to be humanized and so rendered lovable, and a director's willingness to pander to that desire regardless of the damage its satisfaction inflicts on the movie he is making.

These nonsensicalities of characterization, plot and situation are unusually evident to the gaze of the viewer for two reasons: first, because the visual texture of *Terminator 3* is too thin to distract our attention – with its even lighting, its cramped scene-setting and its narrow repertoire of camera placement and focal length, it seems more appropriate to a television movie or a film expected to go straight to DVD rather than one intended for theatrical release; second, and most importantly, because the film fails decisively in its most basic promise to its audience – to deliver convincing and thrilling action scenes of the kind that James Cameron made his own in the previous *Terminator* movies. The first such extended sequence sets the tone for the rest of the film: evidently desiring to outdo even the set-pieces of *Terminator 2*, Mostow puts the T-X at the wheel of an enormous truck equipped with a crane, whose arm is deployed sideways in such a way as to plough through lines of telegraph poles, cars and the facades of buildings, with the T-101 clinging to its hook. But the sequence goes on for far too long; and as pole after pole is decapitated and building after building is reduced to rubble, the audience loses its conviction in the material reality of what it is seeing. A real crane arm would have been decisively bent out of shape by the first such impact on a building, just as a real T-101 would at the very least have been knocked off its precarious perch (and, of course, minutes later he is so removed, when the crane arm impacts with a fire engine – because that is required by the plot); and if the brute resistance of matter to human artefacts, bodies and purposes lacks credibility, so too will the characters' struggles (graceful or clumsy) to overcome it.

After this initial demolition of our suspended disbelief, we are hardly surprised to find that, when the T-101 comes to extract Sarah Connor's coffin from its resting place by punching through its protective marble covering, that slab of rock in fact looks exactly like the sheet of polystyrene that was no doubt actually in front of the camera. With such a consistent inability to make the world of the film seem real, to give its plot the appearance of sense, or to acknowledge the nature of the past and the future (both within and outside its cinematic universe), it is hard to think of *Terminator 3* as anything other than an attempted exercise in grave-robbing – and one which discovers, as does the T-101 in the burial chapel, that the coffin's supposed contents have vanished into thin air, beyond any possibility of resurrection.

Source: 20th Century Fox courtesy the Kobal Collection

3

MOURNING SICKNESS

David Fincher's *Alien*³

If this film resembles its predecessor in any respect, it is in its rejection of the expected way of noting its own status within the series of *Alien* films. James Cameron's title avoided the number '2' altogether (whilst discovering it obsessively within the film itself); David Fincher's incorporates the necessary numeral, but only after subjecting it to a radical displacement. In one respect, to present the number '3' as a superscript simply emphasizes the fact of the film's belatedness (its appearance after not one but two highly idiosyncratic directors have imposed their very different personal visions on a very distinctive original idea), as if Fincher feels that anything he might do with 'his film will be super-scriptural, a writing over the writings of others, as if this third film in the series cannot but constitute a palimpsest. But such a constraint is also a liberation, a form of empowerment; for the creator of a palimpsest can either reiterate the work of his pre-decessors, or obliterate it without trace, or subject it to radical displacement. More specifically, the advantage of directing 'Alien III' is that it means making a contribution to a series, not a sequel. For Cameron, there was no distinction between the Alien universe and Ridley Scott's realization of it, or at least none until and through his own reworking of that original realization; but for Fincher, Cameron's response to his inheritance opens up the possibility of distinguishing in each case between the director and his material, and gives him the chance critically to evaluate the strengths and weaknesses of their specific inflections of that common subject-matter. And given that Fincher's structural belatedness links him more closely to Cameron than to Scott (with his enviable, truly creative and ineliminable priority), we might expect him to be rather more sensitive to his immediate predecessor – rather more concerned to establish a critical distance between 'Alien II' and 'Alien III'.

But, of course, to attach a number as a superscript to a preceding symbol typically denotes the result of a mathematical operation – that of multiplying the symbol by itself a given number of times. Applying this to $Alien^3$, we get: Alien × Alien × Alien. What might this indicate about the film thus named? To begin with, it acknowledges that the film is dealing with the third generation of the alien species (the alien stalking the convicts on Fiorina 161 is the offspring of the alien queen ejected from the *Sulaco*, who was herself the offspring of the alien queen who laid the eggs on LV 426), and it signals in advance that it will itself directly be concerned with three aliens (the facehugger on the *Sulaco*, the alien offspring of the convict's dog, and the new alien queen). It further suggests that the film takes itself to be a certain kind of intensification of the Alien universe with which we are by now familiar: its nature has been determined only by those elements present in the first film in the series; all other (essentially extraneous) material has been eliminated, and what results is a kind of condensation or sublimation of the essence of the Alien universe. Beyond this, we might recall that $Alien^3$ could also be rendered 'Alien cubed' – and think of the coming film's unremitting emphasis upon various attempts to confine its alien (in a toxic waste container, in a maze of corridors, in a lead mould and ultimately in a sheath of super-cooled lead). The setting of these attempts – the oppressively enclosed, maximum-security prison that is the film's world, and that is itself closed down in the film's epilogue – only intensifies the implication that Fincher's primary preoccupation as a director is with closure. His aim is not to open up the Alien series but to shut it down; this step in its unfolding will be its last.

We commit these bodies to the void

As if to underline this, Fincher opens $Alien^3$ with a title sequence that, in effect, ends the film. In a superbly edited sequence of very brief, beautifully composed shots intercut with the film's main titles, we see an alien facehugger (hatched from an egg left by the queen before her ejection) invade the *Sulaco*'s cryogenic compartment, penetrate Ripley's cryotube and attach itself to her face; some drops of the alien's acid blood start a fire in the compartment, and the ship automatically transfers all three cryo-tubes to one of the *Sulaco*'s emergency escape vehicles, which is then ejected and plummets into the atmosphere of Fiorina 161. As the vehicle crash-lands in water, we are told that the planet houses an Outer Veil mineral-ore refinery which functions as a maximum-security work correctional facility for 'Double-Y chromosome' prisoners.

Each element in this opening sequence is very short, and sometimes difficult to grasp in all its implications, but the overall significance of the sequence is undeniable even on a first viewing: the fate against which Ripley has been struggling ever since her ordeal began, the worst possible incarnation of her nightmare vision of sexual difference and female generativity, has been realized before the film has even properly begun. From the moment we see her extracted from the EEV and placed on the operating table, identified as the only survivor of its crash-landing, we know that she is (as she later puts it, as if echoing Sarah Connor) 'already dead'; she cannot physically survive the alien's inevitable emergence, and since her deepest impulse throughout the series has been to stake her spiritual identity upon her refusal to be penetrated (whether by the alien or by men), neither can her psyche be expected to survive the knowledge of its introduction.

The sheer brutality of this opening is breathtaking in its auda-city: Fincher has taken the full measure of our long-deepening identification with Ripley's capacity to handle herself, her pow-erful embodiment of the ideal of the nurturing warrior, and of the satisfaction we took in her apparent triumph at the end of *Aliens*, and utterly negated them. And everything that is to come in his narrative of Ripley's adventures on Fiorina 161 (as scripted by David Giler, Walter Hill and Larry Ferguson) has thereby been stripped of significance – her thoughts, deeds and experiences will amount at best to a kind of death-in-life. When measured against what has already happened to her, nothing of any true importance can happen to her except the gradually dawning realization of what has already happened to her – the realization that her life is already over.

Fincher thereby deprives himself of resources that one might hitherto have considered essential to the repertoire of any director working with this material – the capacity to maintain suspense or to generate narrative drive, the ability to manipulate the audience's desire to know what will happen next, to make the fate of one's protagonist appear to hang on the twists and turns of a plot. Fincher's relationship with his audience must, accordingly, differ radically from that of his predecessors – particularly James Cameron; by so forcefully refusing to satisfy the expectations we bring to his film, he forces on us (and upon himself) the question of what satisfactions we might hope for from a film from which hope has been so quickly and so decisively excised.

It is the general failure to recognize this opening sequence as Fincher's way of refusing familiar cinematic pleasures that accounts, in my view, for the relative lack of critical and commercial favour accorded this film in the series. Particular disappointment was expressed with the film's concluding half, in which Ripley and the convicts attempt in various ways to trap the alien in the maze-like corridors of the foundry: the audience acquires no overall sense of the geography of the refinery, and is barely capable of distinguishing one shaven-headed male from another before the alien catches and kills them, let alone of recognizing one strategically significant intersection of corridors or sealed door from its less fateful counterparts. But Fincher is not here trying, and failing, to generate the usual structure of suspense and fear: the terrain of this final hunting of the beast is unsurveyable, and the unfolding of its events is disorienting and uncompelling, because Fincher has always already lost (and has already done his utmost to deprive his audience of) any faith in the intrinsic significance of such narrative artefacts. The business of avoiding or trying to kill the beast comes across as meaningless because for Fincher it is meaningless; he has set up his Alien universe in such a way that such sequences of events, in which reside the essence of storytelling (our telling of stories to one another, and our attempts to think of our own lives as narratives), appear only as irrelevant distractions. He is trying to tell us that the dimension of 'plot' – the inflections and outcome of inter-linked events – is not where the heart of his, and our, interest in the Alien universe should really lie.

The first phase of the film after its title sequence continues this brutal negation of our expectations by turning its attention to its immediate predecessor. As we have seen, James Cameron con-cluded *Aliens* by rewarding Ripley for her attainment of the ideal of the nurturing warrior by allowing her to acquire a family without having to acknowledge the fertility of her flesh. Fincher begins his film by not only depriving Ripley of both husband and child – she wakes to find them already dead, as if they had always been no more than a dream – but also forcing her to instigate an autopsy on Newt. The sequence in which Clemens is shown marshalling and deploying the surgical instruments needed to open up and display Newt's torso to Ripley's horrified gaze is almost unbearable in its intensity, as if Ripley herself is going under the surgeon's knife. But the true subject of this dis-passionate dissection is in fact *Aliens*, and hence James Cameron; Fincher has, in effect, identified Cameron's pivotal contribution to the series and extirpated it from the Alien universe as if it were not only dead but potentially infectious, as if *Aliens* (despite, or rather because of, its commanding invocation of the adrenalin rush of action, suspense and narrative drive) had taken the series away from itself, condemning it (and any successor which accepted Cameron's terms for it) to inauthenticity and lifelessness. Finch-er's autopsy finds no more trace of genuinely alien life in *Aliens* than Clemens finds in Newt; in performing that surgery, he is declaring that he intends to return the series to itself – to our seemingly unquenchable interest in its protagonist and her opponent, and to the metaphysical questions that have inspired and sustained their mutual fascination and repulsion.

Fincher's determination to cut to the metaphysical bone is declared in the culmination of this first portion or act of the film, which presents the cremation of Hicks and Newt in the foundry's furnaces. The scene is once again organized and edited with great elegance and economy: Superintendent Andrews' more formal, merely dutiful pronouncement before the bodies are despatched is succeeded and overwhelmed by a heartfelt speech from Dillon, the leader of the convicts and the inspiration behind the 'apocalyptic, millenarian, Christian fundamentalism' that binds these criminals together in their self-imposed exile from the human world; and both are intercut with the alien's birth from its canine host (infected by a facehugger brought down in the EEV from the *Sulaco*).

Andrews speaks of the two bodies as having been 'taken from the shadow of our nights, released from all darkness and pain'; he articulates a mode of religious belief which conceives of itself as embodying a means of escaping or transcending suffering and death, a perspective from which their significance might be diminished or explained away. By contrast, Dillon asks:

> Why are the innocent punished? Why the sacrifice, why the pain? There aren't any promises, nothing is certain – only that some get called, some get saved. We commit these bodies to the void with a glad heart, for within each seed there is the promise of a flower; within each death, no matter how small, there is always a new life, a new beginning.

In effect, then, Dillon denies that his faith provides any answers to these questions, any solutions to these 'problems' – because human suffering is not a problem to be resolved or dissolved, as if even unmerited pain that is deemed essential to bringing about a greater good (as when Christian theology claims that the suffering of the innocent might be outweighed if it is part of a divine plan to achieve an overwhelming good for all humankind) were any less painful and undeserved for the innocent individual who is required to suffer it. Dillon knows that rain falls on the just and the unjust alike; the natural world is not so organized as to distribute rewards and punishment according to moral desert, and any adequate religious response to that world must acknowledge this.

For Dillon, then, human life is not comprehensible apart from its vulnerability to contingency, pain and death – the law of the body; hence authentic human existence is to be achieved not by denying or explaining away our embodied mortality, but by acknowledging its burdens. And these burdens include not just the world's independence of our will, but also that of the self (at the very least, the self that refuses this new vision of the world). Dillon talks of a new life, a new beginning – of a transformation of the human self; but he roots the promise of that new life in the death of the old self, and he talks of that old self as something from which we are saved, from which we are called.

The first claim implies that change and redemption can grow only from a full acknowledgement of the old – and his convict community make manifest what he takes that to involve. For in staying together within the circumstances of their imprisonment they acknowledge the justice of their punishment and hence acknowledge their own depravity, their identity as 'murderers and rapists of women'; but they also think of that specific depravity as internally related to human nature as such – as an aspect of an original human sinfulness beyond any individual exercise of the will towards evil. They thus attempt to live with, to inhabit, a radically bleak conception of themselves and their common human nature; it is only their struggle to 'tolerate the intolerable' that keeps them open to the possibility of transformation and rebirth. But his second, further claim is that this new life is not something we can call upon, invoke or initiate, from within ourselves – it is something to which we are called; to be saved is to experience grace, a gratuitous exercise of God's transforming love that we neither merit nor control, but to which we can either close ourselves off or keep ourselves open.

Why, then, does Fincher edit the cremation scene so as to conjoin Dillon's words about a new life emerging from every death, no matter how small, with the new birth of alien life from the death of a dog? The flower that this promises is not likely to give anyone a glad heart. But the dog's owner answers his own question when he asks: 'What kind of animal would do this to a dog?' – any animal whose nature requires it. By reminding us that the alien will as happily impregnate nonhuman as human species, Fincher implies that life, the realm of the biological, with its unstoppable drive to survive and reproduce, and its equally ineliminable openness to death and extinction, is simply (no more and no less than) natural; the alien just does what its nature demands, and the threat of being preyed upon and of dying is not the intrusion of an utterly alien force into the life of a given species but rather its essence and precondition – part of what it means to be a part of the natural realm. Such matters are what flesh-and-blood is ineluctably heir to, and hence are not to be denied (as Andrews' Christianity attempts to deny them) but acknowledged (as Dillon's Christianity attempts to acknowledge them).

If, however, we must acknowledge our embeddedness in nature and in life, with all its arbitrary gifts and withdrawals (of lovers and children, of talent and fortune, of health and disease, of life and death), and its bequest to every living being of an apparently ineliminable drive for its own survival and satisfaction, the question remains: can any perspective on these matters simultaneously accept them as part of the human condition without collapsing into despair at the absurdity or meaninglessness of life? Can human beings fully acknowledge what and who they are and still affirm their lives as meaningful? Can Ripley?

By the end of the cremation scene, Ripley has been made to experience to the full the contingency of human life, its vulnerability to arbitrary shifts of fortune. Having lost the two people whose entirely fortuitous advent into her life held out any hope that her capacity to love and nurture others might be fulfilled, she now finds herself in a world that is itself bereft of any products of human culture more advanced than the Industrial Revolution – a world whose medieval living conditions force her to salvage scraps of malfunctioning technology from rubbish heaps, and even to shave her head and genitals. Fincher is reducing Ripley to bare skin and bone, in search of the ineliminable essence of who she is.

We already know, however, from the previous *Alien* films, what that essence is, what singled her out from the *Nostromo*'s crew as the alien's worthy other and fuelled her duel with the queen: her nightmare vision of human sexuality and generativity. Hence Fincher's brutal stripping away of the inessential Ripley leaves us, and her, confronting a world that is the fullest possible realization of that nightmare: Fiorina 161 incarnates the world of her fears, the fantasies that make her who she is. It houses a community of men whose natures exactly embody the vision of masculinity that has driven her resolute protection of her sexual and physical integrity thus far. It incorporates an alien, whose stalking of the ducts and corridors of the prison merely incarnates the truth of the prison itself from her perspective, and with whom she has already lost her personal battle – not because of any lack of resolution on her part, but simply because of the alien's ability to exploit her vulnerability (specifically, her inability as a finite creature to maintain consciousness indefinitely). She has been drugged, raped and made pregnant; and her offspring's birth will be the death of her. Little wonder that she struggles to make her voice heard in this world, fighting against the torn lining of her throat and the convicts' horrified fixation on her femaleness rather than her individuality.

Fincher is here once again coming to terms, or settling scores, with James Cameron; for *Aliens* also begins with Ripley enduring a hypersleep nightmare in which she has been impregnated by, and is about to give birth to, an alien. Cameron presents his film as giving Ripley the therapy she needs to wake from such nightmares; Fincher presents his film as awakening Ripley from Cameron's dream, his fantasy of what constitutes a fulfilled existence for his protagonist, and his fantasy of human life as something that with the right degree of effort on our part can be made to come out right. For Fincher, nothing – not even achieving the requisite degree of emotional resilience, the ideal combination of male warrior and female nurturer – can guarantee anyone a happy ending, or render them immune to accident or ill fortune. And Ripley in particular is no more cut out for a happy domestic life than the convicts surrounding her are cut out for happy, fulfilling relations with women. What defines her is also what has condemned her to a life inhabited so deeply and for so long by the alien that she 'can't remember anything else'. In this sense, Ripley is not just one of the alien family (as she expresses it, and as Fincher implies when his camera stresses the family resemblance of their physiognomies), she is the alien; it incarnates the nightmare that makes her who she is, and that she has always been incubating. Hence the alien in *Alien*[3] appears more as a loitering carnivore, killing time by killing prey, than as a parasite: its own capacity to reproduce is utterly dependent on the successful outcome of Ripley's pregnancy – as if Ripley herself is its queen, the source of its own life. Hence, too, the film presents Ripley's own nature or identity as at once a maze through which she is condemned to run without hope of escape and as yearning to break out from its confinement within her – as something she encloses that is closing inexorably around her.

What, then, are we to make of the fact that in *Alien*³ Ripley not only experiences heterosexual intercourse for the first time, but initiates it, and appears to regard it as enjoyable and fulfilling? Is this not entirely out of character for someone with her perspective on the nature of human sexuality – particularly so soon after the funeral of her closest companions? Everything turns here on the immediate and general contexts of the relevant scene. Most obviously, it occurs immediately after Fincher has deprived Ripley of her non-biological family and forced her to confront the surgically displayed physical reality of female flesh and blood (in the form of Newt's autopsied body). Against this background, Ripley's sex with Clemens appears as an attempt to seek emotional comfort in sexual contact with a man – as if Fincher's brutal inversions of Cameron's Alien universe (his rejection of Cameron's identification with, and indulgence of, Ripley's horrified aversion to the biological reality of sexual intercourse and maternity) have brought her to overcome her previous abhorrence of human embodiedness as such.

However, this triumph of Fincher's shock therapy is very short lived: after all, Clemens is almost immediately slaughtered by the alien, who then takes over the role of Ripley's protector – quite as if its phallic violence and exclusive interest in its own offspring were a more accurate representation of the nature of sexual partnership than Clemens' gentle goodwill. Fincher's broader framing of the scene appears to confirm this; for it is preceded by Ripley's rape and impregnation by the alien, succeeded by her giving birth to its offspring, and is itself displaced by an act of murderous aggression (we see Ripley ask Clemens if he is attracted to her, and we see him thank her afterwards, but the space between is occupied not by a romantic representation of their lovemaking but by the alien's first and lethal attack on a prisoner). He thus equates the sex between Ripley and Clemens with Ripley's impregnation by an alien – as if confirming the inescapability of Ripley's own perception of heterosexual intercourse as a murderous assault, of pregnancy as a parasitic infestation and of birth as the body's lethal betrayal of itself. The fact that the alien appears immediately after Clemens' second penetration of her body (with a hypodermic syringe) only reinforces this; it is as if, by allowing the sexual penetration of her body, Ripley has violated the virginity on which she conceives that her power to repel the alien rests, and hence has invited the alien back into her world. She cannot escape from herself that easily.

However, the full significance of the film's equation of the Ripley–Clemens encounter with the earlier Ripley–alien encounter emerges only if we ask whether Ripley really is utterly unaware of what happened to her in hypersleep. After all, there is evidence even in the title sequence that the facehugger's penetration disturbs her sleep, as if leaving some trace of itself in her subconscious mind; and the process by which she comes to realize what happened can as easily be seen as one of overcoming her initial repression of that fact as of discovering something entirely new to her. We can accept that her morning sickness might appear as the symptoms of excessive hypersleep; but how could she fail to understand the significance of the alien's refusal to attack her after killing Clemens, or to draw from Bishop's confirmation of an active alien presence on board the *Sulaco* the conclusion that – since Newt and Hicks were free of infection – she must have been the victim? Certainly, her reaction to the conclusive, horrifying neuroscanner image is barely tinged with surprise.

Suppose, then, that from her first moments on Fiorina 161, Ripley is – at some level – aware that she has already been the subject of sexual penetration; then two further ways of understanding her sudden, unprecedented desire to have sex emerge.

According to the first, her sexual intercourse with Clemens is a symptomatic repetition of that original encounter – just what one would expect of someone currently unable fully to acknowledge a deeply traumatic experience. This sudden compulsion is her body's way of at once declaring and concealing what has happened to it, and to her: she is driven to enact the one deed whose nature makes it both an exact representation of the original trauma and a perfect cover story for it.

According to the second reading, by contrast, Ripley's original impregnation by the alien is what makes it possible for her to have humanly meaningful sex with Clemens. After all, the nurturing warrior of *Aliens* (and even the cat-lover of *Alien*) is hardly bereft of the ordinary human desire to give and receive love; she is simply horrified by the physicality of its natural medium or means of expression, in which it can be literally as well as metaphorically creative, and hence is incapable of consciously acting so as to achieve what she desires. But in the world of *Alien*[3], as defined by its title sequence, Ripley has, without willing it, already undergone her worst nightmare of heterosexual intercourse and survived; hence (assuming she knows this about herself), it is a world in which actual, human heterosexual intercourse has been demystified, and so become a real option for her.

The calm self-confidence with which Sigourney Weaver plays the scene with Clemens (the warm matter-of-factness with which she voices her invitation) suggests that the second of these readings is the correct one – that her sex with Clemens is a brief but intense achievement of self-overcoming (confirming that the truth about human sexuality is concealed by the incarnate nightmare of alien impregnation), rather than a symptomatic validation of her present self-understanding (confirming that alien impregnation incarnates the monstrous truth about human sexuality). In the end, however, that achievement is quickly rendered otiose; the reality she must confront is one in which Clemens is dead and she is host to an alien queen – in which the briefly glimpsed truth about human sexuality has been obliterated by the making real of her nightmare. What matters now is how she responds to that massive reiteration.

At first, her reaction is suicidal; but since, as she puts it, 'I can't do what I should', she tries to enlist the help of others – first by inviting the alien's lethal attentions, then by trying to get Dillon to re-enact one side of the mutual extermination pact she originally made with Hicks. He refuses – entirely unsurprisingly, since Christianity regards suicide as the worst of all sins, the sin against the Holy Spirit: it is the ultimate expression of despair, in which the sinner turns in upon herself in such a way as definitively to exclude God. In Dillon's terms, the suicide does not so much acknowledge her sinful self as allow it entirely to enclose and overwhelm her, and thereby close herself off from the possibility of grace. By at first pretending to accede to her request, and then striking his fire-axe against the cell bars on which she is outstretched, he intends to teach her to overcome this impulse, to see that she can survive its grip on her and turn her circumstances to good account.

And this, indeed, is what she does; her invulnerability to the alien's attentions is indispensable to the final success of the convicts' attempts to destroy it. But then she faces her final ordeal: the arrival of the Company's scientific team. She has prevented them capturing the warrior alien; but the queen is moving inside her. Bishop II, who claims to be the human designer of the android series, offers to arrange for its surgical extraction and destruction, holding out to her the chance of having a life, having children, and knowing that the alien is dead. But Ripley does not – she cannot – trust him: instead, she falls backwards, arms outstretched, into the furnace that recently swallowed the bodies of her husband and child. As she descends into the flames, the alien queen bursts out; Ripley holds it gently in her gloved hands and lays its crowned head on her breast, as if to suckle it.

The logic of the Alien universe, and of Ripley's own nature, is here finally consummated. Since the alien itself originates from within her, since it is an incarnate projection of her deepest fears, she can succeed in eliminating it only by eliminating herself. And their joint elimination amounts to the elimination of the Alien universe itself, since their joint presence has made it what it is; it is as if, after its expansive, affirmative phase in *Aliens*, this monstrous cosmos has been subjected to a contraction so radical that only its absolute annihilation can constitute an adequate conclusion. The achievement of closure here, so absolute and on so many levels at once, has an elegance that almost disguises its nihilism.

But are we, in the end, meant to see Ripley's achievement as her elimination of herself or as her elimination of that in herself which dictated the nature of the alien and its universe? Has she simply destroyed herself, or is her self-destruction also a self-overcoming? After all, literally speaking, her death destroys the source of alien life within her, and indeed is the only way in which it might be destroyed; and she plainly gives comfort and succour to the alien queen in its first and last moments of life outside the womb – quite as if she has undergone the realization of her worst nightmare of birth, and not only survived it but found herself capable of mothering her offspring. To be sure, she soothes it in silence, as if rendered mute by her fate; but her fall is succeeded by the film's concluding reproduction of her concluding mayday message from the *Narcissus*, as if her last deed might amount to the recovery of that first accession to her own voice, in despite of her alien other. And the Christian imagery of her death – Fincher's presentation of her death-dive as a crucifixion through which the human race is redeemed – further asks whether we can find anything life-affirming in this self-immolation.

Dillon certainly would. For in the eyes of his community, the alien was a dragon, a demonically powerful murderer and rapist whose very nature placed them in the position inhabited by the victims of their own crimes – in short, it was an incarnate projection of their sinfulness. Hence Ripley's refusal simply to allow the alien to reproduce itself through her, to act as a vehicle for its onward transmission through the human world, exemplifies the community's motive for remaining on Fiorina 161 – their collective resolve to acknowledge the sinfulness within them, to prevent themselves from reproducing it, and to await the grace that might allow them to overcome it. For Dillon, Ripley's actions would declare that she has received that grace – that she has been saved from herself, called to imitate Christ; she has taken the sinfulness of the community upon herself even unto death, and the purity of her self-sacrifice holds out the promise of redemption.

But can we really see the absolute closure of the Alien universe as a new beginning? What might it mean, in such a world, to believe in the resurrection of the body?

We are not what was intended

David Fincher's next (his second) film, with its focus on the hunt for a serial killer each of whose victims dies in a manner intended to exemplify one of the seven deadly sins, plainly develops further the interests which first found expression in *Alien*³ – in questions about the significance of religious belief, the possibility of making human sense of human life and of the world human beings make and inhabit, the idea of closure and its overcoming. But *Se7en* (1995) undeniably shows that Fincher is perfectly capable of utilizing narrative conventions when he wants to: it has a tightly organized and utterly gripping plot (written by Andrew Kevin Walker), in which its two detective protagonists race against time to locate and interpret the clues which will indicate not only the identity of the killer but the nature of his intentions before he can carry them out. But it also excels at manipulating the generic expectation of its audience (most famously with its climax, in which both the detectives and the killer are woven into the sequence of events they would normally be attempting either to prevent or to complete from the outside, as it were); and it is, at the most fundamental level, a critical study of the conditions which make such generic exercises possible – in particular, a study of the assumption that the killer's intentions and actions might make any sense, and hence of what it is for human actions as such to have any meaning whatever.

It is fundamental to the approach that Detective Somerset (Morgan Freeman) takes to this case that the killings they encounter are not just deeds – merely more instances of the utterly unthinking, mindlessly brutal things human beings do to one another. They have a meaning, and if Somerset can understand their meaning, understand what the killer is trying to say in and through his treatment of his victims, then he might be able to predict their course and identify their perpetrator. What, then, is John Doe trying to say? What is the meaning of his tableaux?

It is tempting to answer that, in each case, an individual who is guilty of a particular deadly sin is murdered in a manner that confirms his guilt, and that simultaneously functions as a religious admonition to the broader human community in which such sinful behaviour is pervasive, and accepted without criticism or question – even lauded. However, one difficulty with this interpretation is that the dead are not in each case guilty of the relevant sin (in the 'Lust' murder, it is surely not the prostitute but her client who is lustful); another is that those who are guilty do not always die (this is true not only of the lustful client, but also of Victor Allen, the 'Sloth' victim, and of Detective Mills, the exemplar of 'Wrath'). We might further question whether John Doe can simply be described as murdering any of his victims. What he rather does is offer them a choice: either he will kill them or they must perform an action exemplary of the sin he imputes to them (keep eating, cut off a pound of their own flesh, keep taking the drugs, have sex wearing a serrated dildo). In each case, their choice relieves him of the need to murder them: they rather kill themselves, choosing to act in the way that John Doe believes has already destroyed them spiritually, even when that action will result in their psychological and/or physical destruction. It might be more accurate to call this assisted suicide, or at least assisted self-destruction.

This description certainly fits the first four crimes ('Gluttony', 'Greed', 'Sloth', 'Lust'); it doesn't exactly fit the 'Pride' case, but here John Doe gives his victim the opportunity to phone for help, and she chooses to die of her injuries instead, so he is even less obviously her murderer; and in the 'Envy' and 'Wrath' cases, John Doe chooses his own death rather than refrain from an act expressive of his sinful envy (the beheading of Mill's wife), and Mills chooses his own psychological and moral self-destruction rather than refrain from wreaking vengeance on Doe.

We cannot, therefore, take Doe's sermons simply as enacting Old Testament wrath – as if its religious meaning is that of executing divine sentences of death (after all, wrath is not the sin with which he identifies himself). The moral of his address to the community seems rather to be: our sinfulness is pervasive, and deeply rooted in (original to) our natures, and it is killing us; even when it is not literally lethal, it kills the soul, the human spirit within us. My sermons are meant to make that self-destructiveness unmissably concrete, and thereby to give us a last chance of understanding what we are doing to ourselves, what we have become, and thus give us a last chance to do otherwise. As he puts it in the excerpt Somerset reads from his notebooks, 'we are nothing; we are not what was intended'.

Note the 'we': Doe is not exempting himself from his diagnosis, as he could not in all consistency, given his sense of the absolute pervasiveness of sin. His sermons thus incorporate himself; their completion or closure depends upon his own willingness to be punished for his envy of Mills' normal life, and his inclusion further implies that the whole cycle or sequence is an expression of envy. In what sense? In part, it is an envy of God – since Doe arrogates to himself the privilege of judging and punishing the souls of others that Christianity reserves to God alone; but, more generally, it indicates Doe's belief that although he does what he does out of love, that love (which finds expression in the systematic torture and murder of other human beings, the willingness to make them suffer for what he deems to be a greater good) is essentially misdirected (as misdirected as Andrews' conception of the Christian God in *Alien*[3]). This is made clear by one of the texts that Somerset is seen photocopying in the library: it displays an intellectual topography of Dante's purgatory, in which all seven of the deadly sins are seen as distorted expressions of love – gluttony, lust and greed as forms of excessive love, sloth as a (in fact, the only) form of deficient love, and pride, envy and wrath as forms of misdirected love. (Hence, in every deadly sin, each expression of our failure to be what was intended, we can see what Doe thinks we were originally intended to be – beings constituted by properly proportioned and rightly directed love).

If John Doe does not exempt himself from his own diagnosis, neither does he exempt the detectives pursuing him, and hence the forces of law and order as such. Mills is directly incorporated into the sermons, because Doe recognizes that his otherwise admirable zeal to do the right thing, to catch and punish those who do wrong, is not properly proportioned or targeted – it can all too easily be turned upon his colleagues, his wife, even a humble newspaper photographer. And although the film in many ways opposes the character of Mill to that of Somerset, Mill's maintenance of that zeal to do good is the one aspect of his character as a detective of which Somerset is himself envious (and hence, in this respect, indistinguishable from Doe); in him, that zeal is not so much better proportioned or directed as on the point of extinction. Somerset's personal oasis of calm and order in the city's chaos is an attempt to exclude the world, and hence an expression of his sense of his own exclusion from that world, his freedom from its spiritual disorder; but when Mills makes his most unguarded declaration of his commitment to law and order in a bar, and accuses his partner of giving up on that commitment, Somerset implicitly acknowledges this critique by hurling away his metronome.

But, of course, the complicity of the forces of law and order in the sinful world that Doe diagnoses is more pervasive than this. For most of Mill's and Somerset's colleagues appear to share the moral apathy of the city's population as a whole: every crime is just another job, of no human significance, eliciting no vestige of empathy with its victims and bystanders and no particular condemnation of its perpetrator; this endless cycle of violence done and suffered is just what life is like, just the way it always has been and always will be. They are therefore constitutionally incapable of understanding Doe's enterprise as anything other than an extension of this cycle: more meaningless killing, more human lunacy. Hence, he provides them with a perfect candidate for the role of criminal – Victor Allen, whose upbringing and record exactly fit the psychological profile of a serial killer, right down to the fingerprinted plea for help found at the scene of the 'Greed' crime. Allen instead turns out to be the next victim – someone whose brain has been destroyed, and who exemplifies not only his own addiction to 'Sloth' but that of the police who are led unthinkingly to him. From Doe's viewpoint, an even better word for this sloth and apathy would be 'despair', the ultimate sin.

The question then arises: how far is the film itself complicit with Doe's perception of the world? How far can Fincher be said to have orchestrated his film so as to endorse the killer's viewpoint? Certainly, the film seems no less harshly to condemn the apathy that pervades its city than does Doe, since the highly sympathetic character of Somerset embodies that condemnation, and proposes as its only alternative exactly what Doe proposes – a properly directed love, a love which 'costs, it takes effort, work'. But even the film's most moving and beautifully realized vision of a life in which love is at work – the marriage of David and Tracy Mills – is shown to be threatened by its opposite, both from without (invaded by noise, unwilling to risk investing in its own future by bringing a child into the world) and within (Tracy's secrets, David's wrathfulness).

On the other hand, the film is also deeply marked by the oppositions that it sets up between Mills and Somerset, and some of these oppositions help to distance it from Doe's self-understanding. The list of these oppositions is long (country v. city; youth v. age; black v. white; noise v. silence; children v. childlessness), but much of it involves variations on a single distinction – that between deeds and their meaning. Mills wants only to know what was done; he thinks that simply looking at the dead body should allow him to read the identity of the killer directly off it; he has no interest in small details but in the basic, self-evident general shape of a situation. Somerset responds primarily to what a deed or situation might mean; he assumes that its true meaning will be hidden, difficult to interpret, and that significance can be squeezed indefinitely out of every small detail of a situation. Hence, Mills is entirely bemused by, and excluded from, those aspects of the human form of life in which meaning is focused, preserved and refined – libraries and the books they contain, religion, literature, music – what one might call human culture as such. Somerset is a citizen of this realm, an adept of scholarship; and the structures of significance that he lives and breathes are what make it possible for him and his partner to follow the clues that lead to John Doe.

But, of course, the clue that leads them both to John Doe's door is an FBI printout of the killer's library borrowings. In other words, John Doe is as much an adept of culture, of human practices of meaning-making and meaning-transmission, as is Somerset; they not only live in the same world, they have read the same books; the resources that Somerset deploys to locate Doe are the very resources he deploys in constructing his criminal tableaux. Dantean topography and Thomist theology allow us to understand what Doe's crimes mean because they were capable of constituting a blueprint for it; Doe's murderous activity can be mistaken for the work of a performance artist because human culture as such embodies the results of the labours of the best thinkers and artists of the race to build significance into and out of the most savage, brutal and base aspects of human existence, to make the meaningless meaningful.

Suppose, then, as Mills would have us do, that instead of approaching Doe's tableaux as cultural constructs, directing our energies to the uncovering or decoding of the significance he labours to build into his deeds, we instead strip out his aesthetically and intellectually pleasing symmetries and symbolisms and look at what he has actually done (within the film, Mills does this by looking at photographs of the crime scene, transcriptions that confront us with the thing itself and not some surrogate or symbol of it − as if cinema is inherently, materially drawn to seeing the world as Mills sees it). What we then see is the butchering of human flesh and blood. What Doe means to say is inscribed upon the bodies of his victims; hence, what he says and what he shows differ radically. He talks of spiritual suicide; but his sermons show the reducibility of human life to flesh (gluttony), blood (greed), skin and bone (sloth), sexuality (lust), a skull and its contents (pride, envy, wrath). The severed head of Doe's final sermon does not merely represent or encapsulate envy and wrath; it is the material basis of the human capacity to represent the world at all, to see it as meaningful, and its detachment from the body literalizes the detachment from material reality that such constructions of culture can seem to embody.

Doe's work is indeed full of meaning, as all human works are; but it is also strictly, intrinsically senseless − not merely the work of an unhinged mind, a lunatic, but an apotheosis of the distinctively human capacity to make meaning, a capacity whose exercise disguises from us the essential meaninglessness of the reality that is both its object and its source. This is why Doe is shown to have filled 200 250-page notebooks; a team of officers working seven-day weeks around the clock would take years simply to get to the end of them. The problem is not that meaning is hard to find in Doe's deeds, but that it is far too easy − his acts are full to overflowing with meaning, unsurveyably saturated in it; their most basic significance lies in their incarnation of the self-asphyxiating excess of signification that makes the human species what it is.

This sense of our humanity as being under threat from the very capacity that civilizes or humanizes us, of being hermetically sealed within our own systems of signification, is what gives such an apocalyptic atmosphere to the film's climax. For, in Doe's final tableau, the meaning of his deeds suddenly, shockingly expands to ingest not only him but his two pursuers;[1] his sermons thereby not only swallow up good as well as evil, but also fuse the usually distinct generic functions of victim, perpetrator and pursuer – the orthodox narrative structure and drive of which this film seems to be a beautiful exemplar turns out to provide the condition for its own annihilation. On every level, no matter how closely we look, closure reigns.

Little wonder, then, that Fincher ends his title sequence with a subliminal glimpse of the following scratched phrase – 'No Key'. It tells us before we start that there will be no way out of this narrative, that there is no particular insight or super-clue that will make final sense of Doe's deeds (in part because they have no meaning, in part because they mean too much), that there can be no key to the meaning of anything in human life – and indeed to the meaning of human life as such – because it is essentially meaningless (the natural product of natural causes, just one piece of the unstoppable, blind machinery that is nature, that system in which things and creatures just do what they do).

In this sense, a religious perspective is no more significant than any other perspective – its implications no more worthy of serious contemplation. And yet . . . If it is the seamless closure of the film's final scene that conveys this message to us, then we should note that, in fact, Doe's final sermon does not and cannot guarantee its own completion; indeed, we might rather argue that its most important moral is meant to be that the closure it represents is humanly avoidable, and that this is Christianity's deepest significance. For, of course, Doe's sermons achieve closure only because Mills acts wrathfully; confronted with the knowledge of what Doe has done to his wife and unborn child, and hence done to him, he chooses to take revenge – to hurt the one who hurt him. But he could have chosen otherwise: he could have resolved to step back from that entirely natural human response, to allow the endless cycle or transmission mechanism of pain inflicted on one person being in turn inflicted on another, and so on another, to find its end in him. He could, in short, have suffered without himself inflicting suffering (as Ripley ends her life by doing). He did not; but, as Somerset realizes, Doe's sermon could not have attained closure if Mills had refrained from doing unto others as they had done unto him (and the other elements of Doe's sermon would have been equally definitively sabotaged if his victims had chosen not to do what came naturally to them, not to continue sinning).

What Doe, and hence *Se7en*, thereby delineates by negation is the distinctively Christian moral ideal we first encountered in *Alien*[3] – that of turning the other cheek, of breaking the seemingly endless sequence of human wrongdoing. But should we dwell on what is thereby delineated, or upon the fact that it is delineated by negation? If, in Fincher's cinematic world, Christianity and nihilism are each other's negation, and hence neither is representable without simultaneously representing the other, should we conclude that nihilism is the only way of achieving a truly thoroughgoing denial of Christianity, or that Christianity has always already acknowledged the worst that nihilism can tell us?

2007 postscript: play, fight, panic, replay

In the films succeeding *Se7en*, Fincher begins to combine his continuing interest in the body as both source and subverter of meaning with a quickly developing desire to interrogate the conventions and material bases of cinema as an art form.

The Game (1997) is, on one level, the story of how a depressed and alienated man (Nicholas Van Orton, played by Michael Douglas) is redeemed by means of an in-body experience – a game organized by the mysterious Consumer Recreation Services (CRS) in which he is pushed to his psychological and physical limits and ultimately deposited in a burial chamber, until he recovers the desire to live. His initial sense of meaninglessness is, in effect, countered by plunging him into a world supersaturated with significance – one in which the smallest incident links with others to form part of a single, overarching plot, and in which every provisional understanding Van Orton reaches is overturned, but only in order to reveal a deeper and more coherent purpose lying behind it. Ultimately, however, it is all a game: the ultimate meaning of the story is that it meant nothing – or, more precisely, that the mere appearance of significance suffices (and is perhaps even necessary) to make life worth living. And by presenting us with Van Orton's climactic, revelatory irruption into the CRS staff canteen, where he re-encounters pretty much everyone with any role to play in the preceding events of the film, Fincher explicitly invites us to consider the condition of the film actor as analogously suspended between an absence and an excess of meaning – the unreality of their roles declaring itself in the undismissable reality of their embodied individuality, which preceded and succeeds any possible performance, and without which no performance could seem meaningful. Perhaps also, as we watch this realization dawn on Michael Douglas' suddenly emptied face, and recall the various films in which directors have found it possible to assign to him the experience of hubris humbled, we might further understand this scene as the supporting player's revenge on the leading man – as a declaration of cinema's need for a constellation of characters if its powers are to make visible a world in which one of those characters might intersect with the trajectory of a star, and so of any star's need for some constellation or other from which he might stand out.

In *Fight Club* (1999), meaning is once again recovered by means of a practice of affirming the irreducible reality of the body and its pains, as well as its chemical constituents; and, at the same time, Fincher celebrates the extravagant powers of cinema to represent the idiosyncratic reality of the mind. The film begins its title sequence deep within the convoluted synapses of its narrator, Jack, as if declaring that the apparently external world into which it eventually emerges (via the barrel of a gun inserted into the narrator's mouth and the hand of the apparently distinct character holding it) is essentially continuous with that interior. It realizes Jack's crippling identification of himself with his modes of consumption by presenting his apartment as a three-dimensional version of an IKEA catalogue, with the price and name of each item of furniture hovering insubstantially next to it. And it ends with the revelation that Jack's friend and enemy, Tyler Durden, is in fact his alter ego, an externalized and projected aspect of himself; for whilst their climactic fight in the underground garage is clearly presented in the film, the TV monitors trained on that space register only a single man inexplicably slamming himself against walls and cars. It is thus only the film camera that can capture Tyler's reality, as it has done throughout the story we have been told; but if that reality is, ultimately, an aspect of Jack's psyche, does that mean that cinema alone is capable of capturing the real meaning of these events, or rather that it has participated in the construction of a fantasy – a fascinating and satisfying cover for their real meaning? In being so responsive to every twist and turn of Jack's inner life, can film claim an unprecedented power of disclosure (to penetrate any and every human mind) or an unprecedented capacity to conflate appearance and reality? And is Edward Norton thereby claiming Brad Pitt's mode of stardom as a possibility of his own method of acting, or is Brad Pitt rather claiming Edward Norton's method of acting as a possible root of his own mode of stardom? Perhaps David Fincher's point is that all of these claims are to be taken with equal seriousness – that cinema really does contain such a superabundance of significance.

Panic Room (2002) eschews the formal extravagance of its predecessor, and instead returns to the terrain of *Alien*[3], by literalizing its governing image of an enclosed cube in the form of an impregnable, self-sufficient hidden space embedded within an elegant New York townhouse, to which a mother and her daughter retreat when three burglars break into the premises, only to discover that the object of these criminal endeavours is hidden within the panic room itself. The story restricts itself to the interior and immediate context of the house in a manner strongly reminiscent of Hitchcock's *Rear Window* (although its opening titles more precisely recall *North by Northwest*); and its unfolding is similarly consistent with the conventions of this kind of thriller – even if this director will no doubt have taken specific pleasure in determining that what prevents the mother (Meg Altman, played by Jodie Foster) from staying safely within the panic room is her daughter's need for medical treatment: what one might call an unwitting betrayal by her flesh and blood. But in another respect, the film is not at all at home in its genre and setting, because the film camera is not: for whilst it respects the spatial unity of the narrative, never straying from the house and its garden, after repeatedly travelling right up to the limits of that physical space, it eventually declares its autonomy of it in an extended, apparently unbroken tracking shot.

The camera begins in Meg's bedroom, retreats through the banister rails, descends two floors to arrive at the front window just as the burglars draw up, then moves sideways to the front door and travels through the interior space of the lock to encounter the key futilely inserted by one of the burglars. It immediately withdraws from the lock, tracks sideways as the burglars confer at the window, then pans 180 degrees and glides through the kitchen, passing through the handle of the coffee jug before meeting the burglars at the rear basement door; then it rises directly through the ceiling to watch them fail to enter through a second back door. Finally, it retreats, rises through another ceiling and past Meg's bedroom again to the skylight, as another burglar walks past on the roof; it tracks sideways just in time to observe him breaking in through a metal service hatch and triggering the alarm.

By means of this single shot, Fincher establishes two things: first, that the space of the narrative and the space of the camera are essentially distinct or discontinuous: for in the course of the sequence the camera performs at least three physically impossible movements (through the banister rail, into and out of the lock mechanism, through the coffee jug handle, and through two solid ceilings), thereby declaring that it is unconstrained by the material limits of the townhouse that will determine every twist and turn of the characters' fates in the projected narrative; and, second, that the camera's movements nevertheless are utterly responsive to the demands of that narrative: for it moves in perfect synchrony with the improvised movements of the burglars, as if reading their minds, and thereby reading the minds of the audience of the film, who came to the cinema precisely to experience the pleasures specific to this kind of generic narrative. By putting these two points together in a single sweeping camera movement, Fincher is declaring that the cost of enjoying such voyeuristic intimacy with this potentially lethal threat to Meg and Sarah Altman is an utter inability to intervene: for what can bring us so close to the course of events is precisely what seals us out from them – the power of the camera, whose operations determine that there is no way of moving from our space to that of the characters, no route from where we are to where they are. As Fincher himself has put it, 'you're going to be telling the audience watching this: "You can't do anything about it, they can't hear you, you can't help them, as loud as you scream they're not going to hear."'[2] In depicting the Altmans' panic room, this film aims also to depict its audience as inhabiting a panic room – a space in which panic is created of a kind which cannot be communicated or acted upon, a space that confers more security than that of the Altmans, but only by imposing complete passivity. And in so declaring the specific conditions of cinematic viewing, Fincher asks the viewer to acknowledge the enigmatic perversity of the desires that these conditions elicit and satisfy, and thereby to question their own satisfactions.

By virtue of its sprawling length and its dependence on a true story from the recent Californian past, Zodiac (2007) plainly distinguishes itself sharply from Panic Room; and the nature of the story it tells makes it tempting to suggest that it is also a deliberate negation of every defining characteristic of Se7en. For it is a faithful recounting of the San Francisco police department's attempts to catch the Zodiac, one of the first of that criminal species known as 'serial killers', and hence the inspiration for innumerable literary and cinematic works, including Dirty Harry (which some of the characters in Zodiac are shown to watch when it was first released) and of course Se7en itself. But this real-life investigation stretches over many years, involves a number of different police forces as well as a variety of journalists (to whom the Zodiac sent letters), throws up a number of suspects whose plausibility fluctuates over time, and is massively hampered by the obdurate inadequacy of the clues available to the investigators – with different forensic scientists disagreeing over handwriting analyses, as well as a variety of other circumstantial evidence, and no single, coherent pattern of implication ever emerging. Some of the investigators become obsessed with the case, whilst others attempt to put it behind them as essentially unsolvable; all are in different ways damaged by their involvement, as are the other people in their lives – in some cases, beyond recovery or redemption. The most plausible suspect eventually dies just before being re-interviewed by the police on the basis of new information gathered by the application of more advanced forensic techniques; and the film ends with the acknowledgement that the case is now essentially incapable of being resolved beyond reasonable doubt.

Should we, then, conclude that David Fincher chose to return to the generic ground of his second, and perhaps most famous, film in order to underline the extent to which its unprecedented intensification and interrogation of the conventions of that genre had sealed it off from real life? Here, we need to appreciate that *Zodiac* also embodies an attempt to understand the attractions of such generic exercises; for it identifies exactly the ways in which reality frustrates the human desire to make definitive sense of it – the ways in which matter and mind resist complete absorption into our familiar patterns of understanding, explanation and judgement. We find satisfaction in the suffocating coherence of John Doe's project, and in the uncanny seamlessness with which it incorporates the detectives' (and so the audience's) desire to comprehend that project into the project itself, precisely because it assuages our pained awareness of the extent to which the meaning of real-life events lacks such coherent self-sufficiency. It is not just that the universe doesn't owe us a living (when Talleyrand refused to respond to a beggar's plea for alms, the beggar pleaded, 'Sir, I must live', to which Talleyrand replied, 'I do not see the necessity'); it doesn't show any signs of owing us a halfway satisfactory account of itself either.

But, as we have seen, this is also the deeper message of *Se7en*, which is just as alert, in its own way, to its audience's temptation to find satisfaction in a fantasy of all-encompassing, self-sufficient meaning, and just as reluctant to provide such satisfaction, precisely by revealing John Doe's actions and so his project as suffering from a simultaneous absence and excess of meaning. To this extent, then, *Zodiac* reinforces rather than subverts the conclusions of *Se7en*; and it thereby confirms the suspicion that, on Fincher's account of things, both early and late, the most fundamental human desire that our ineluctably embodied confrontation with the material world frustrates is the desire for meaning.

4

THE MONSTER'S MOTHER

Jean-Pierre Jeunet's *Alien Resurrection*

Is *Alien Resurrection* a sequel to *Alien*[3], and hence to the previous two *Alien* films? It may seem that the presence of the aliens, together with that of Sigourney Weaver as Ripley, guarantees this; but, in fact, it merely displaces the question. For can we simply take it for granted that the aliens are the same species that we encountered in the earlier films, or that the Ripley of *Alien Resurrection* is the same person whose vicissitudes we have followed from their beginning on the *Nostromo*? After all, David Fincher's furious, purifying desire for closure in *Alien*[3] resulted in the death of Ripley and of the sole surviving representative of the alien species inside her. Hence Jeunet's film, helping itself to the resources for self-renewal that science fiction makes available to its practitioners, can recover the queen and her host only by positing the capacity to clone them from genetic material recovered from the medical facilities on Fiorina 161. But, as his renegade military scientists make clear at the outset, the cloning process produces another, distinct individual from this genetic material; it does not reproduce the individual from whom the material derives. Their clone of the original Ripley is not Ripley herself – her body is not Ripley's body (however much it resembles the one consumed in Fiorina's furnace) and her mind has no inherent continuity with Ripley's (it must be stocked from her own experiences). As Call puts it, she is 'a strain, a construct; they grew you in a fucking lab'.

To be sure, as the film progresses the clone begins to recover some access to Ripley's memories and character; but that results from an aspect of her nature that reinforces her distinctness from her genetic original. For, of course, one cannot even regard Ripley's clone as human – as a member of the same species as Ripley herself. She has acid for blood, her flesh is capable of accelerated healing, her sense of smell is highly developed, and she possesses an intuitive awareness of the thoughts and deeds of the aliens surrounding her. She is, in fact, neither fully human nor fully alien, but rather a hybrid – a creature whose genetic base is constituted by a grafting of human and alien stock (consequent upon the foetal alien queen's parasitic interactions with Ripley's flesh and blood); and one manifestation of that hybridity – her participation in the alien species' hive mind and racial memory – makes it possible for her to recall Ripley's life and death.

If Ripley's clone is not Ripley, can we say that the cloned alien queen within her is identical with her genetic original, the last surviving alien entity? Questions of personal identity may seem less pressing, as well as less clear, with respect to a species for whom the collective is prior to (and indeed eclipses) the individual; but what of species identity? If the queen is the new fount and origin of alien life in Jeunet's universe, within which two hundred years have passed since the original alien species was rendered extinct, should we regard her fertility as engendering the simple repro-duction of that earlier race? In fact, we cannot – because the cloned queen is not exactly the pure origin of this new manifestation of alien life, and hence her reproductive cycle turns out to be any-thing but a simple replication of its monstrous original. For the queen's genetic hybridity incorporates a distinctively human gift from Ripley to her offspring (the gift bequeathed by original sin to all human females) – that of pregnancy, labour and birth: 'In sorrow shalt thou bring forth children'.

Jeunet's film thus finds a way of grafting two apparently opposed or contradictory modes of reproduction onto one another. Cloning suggests replication, qualitative indistinguishability, whereas hybridity suggests the cultivation of difference, a new creation. In *Alien Resurrection*, cloning engenders hybridity; even genetic replication cannot suppress nature's capacity for self-transformation and self-overcoming, its evolutionary impulse. This film does not, then, overcome *Alien*[3]'s attempted closure of the *Alien* series by resurrecting either Ripley or her alien other – as if continuing (by contesting)

David Fincher's theological understanding of the alien universe; for (as Thomas' sceptical probing of Jesus' resurrected body implies) the religious idea of resurrection incorporates precisely the bodily continuity that cloning cannot provide. The title of Jeunet's film thus refers not to a resurrection of the alien species, or of that species' most intimate enemy; it rather characterizes its hybrid of cloning and hybridity as an alien kind or species of resurrection – as something uncannily other to any familiar religious idea of death's overcoming.

And, of course, Jeunet thereby characterizes his film's relation to its predecessors as itself alien or unfamiliar: since neither of its cloned protagonists is identical with the paired protagonists of the earlier *Alien* films, *Alien Resurrection* cannot be understood simply as a sequel to them. Its alien universe is at once utterly discontinuous with and intimately dependent upon them; its underlying thematic and stylistic codes owe everything and nothing to their templates. In grafting his own distinctive cinematic sensibility onto that of the series he inherits, Jeunet thereby sees himself as creating a world whose nature is built from the same components, but in a radically new manner – a hybrid clone of its ancestor; and hence he sees himself as following out a hybrid cloning of the idea of sequelhood that has been established by the series hitherto. For to take *Alien*[3] seriously is to acknowledge that no further development of the series is possible in the terms shared by its three members; its further evolution requires their displacement. Only in such a way – only by transposing the central themes of the *Alien* series into a new key – could Jeunet acknowledge the depth and completeness of Fincher's closure of the series without accepting its finality.

Seeing with the eyes of a child

In establishing the transfigured terms of his alien universe, Jeunet naturally draws upon the cinematic sensibility manifest in his two previous films (in partnership with Marc Caro – hence already itself a hybrid sensibility): *Delicatessen* (1991) and *The City of Lost Children* (1995). Indeed, the family resemblances between the world of the latter film and that of *Alien Resurrection* go far beyond the fact that the central roles of both are taken by the same actors. Its narrative concerns the efforts of a quasi-scientific team, most of whom are clones of one of the team's co-founders, to expropriate the dream-life of orphan children, who are otherwise exploited by a variety of freakish human adults for more straightforwardly criminal purposes. These opposing but equally abusive stratagems are confounded by a small band of children, led by a strong-willed brown-haired girl, who join forces with a circus strongman named One – a simple-minded but morally pure giant, a child in an adult's body, whose basic motivation is to save his young brother from the scientists. In the world of this city, human flesh is variously deformed or mutilated, essentially unstable and subject to transformation – as if accentuating the uncanniness of the animated human body, with its internal relation to animality and its ability to incorporate the inanimate. One set of criminal forces is led by two women whose torsos are fused together, and includes a man who regards a set of killer fleas as if they were his children; another utilizes a religious sect whose members graft prosthetic devices onto their bodies to enhance vision and hearing; and the scientific team includes a brain in a vat. Technology pervades the culture, but in forms which execute their intended (and usually sinister) tasks by means of absurdly over-elaborate arrangements of highly primitive parts – as if implicitly mocking their adult creators' hubristic self-satisfaction in their own intelligence and creativity.

The correspondences between this universe and that of *Alien Resurrection* are overwhelming. The band of pirates from the *Betty*, whose purposes initially include the sale of living human bodies to a scientific team whose cloning programme requires them as hosts, but ultimately converge with the moral vision of the petite brunette robot Call, constantly manifest a childlike delight in weaponry and the unselfconscious satisfaction of physical appetite (exemplified in *The City of Lost Children* by One's brother and his insatiable desire for food). They include a disabled engineer parts of whose wheelchair reassemble into a weapon, a not-so-gentle giant, and a weapons expert whose hidden pistols are mounted on extensible metal limbs; and Ripley's clone strides at their head with the physical and moral purity, the genetic and spiritual charisma, of One amongst his new brothers and sisters. Furthermore, the highly advanced technologies of the *Auriga* — the security system based on breath-identification, the whisky-defrosting device and the pointlessly extended well through which the guards observe Ripley's clone — are tainted with absurdity and primitivism.

The world of *Alien Resurrection* is, then, undeniably an inflection of Jeunet's world; but can it properly be regarded as even a hybrid clone of the alien universe established by the earlier films? That universe has certainly hitherto conceived of science as threatening, and of technology as a necessary but feared supplement to vulnerable human flesh and blood; but it has not imagined either as absurd or risible, or elicited a kind of dark hilarity from the body's fragility (as Jeunet finds when Johnner allows his knife to bury itself in Vriess' paralysed leg, or when an alien warrior punches through General Perez' skull, or when Dr Wren's torso is penetrated by an alien bursting from the chest of the last surviving human host), or exhibited such unquestioning assurance in the robustness of humanity (and of our capacity to acknowledge it) under even the most extreme mutations of its embodiment. In these respects, Jeunet's cinematic sensibility can seem profoundly dissonant with that of the previous *Alien* films — as if his contribution to the series is a kind of parody or caricature, in which matters that his predecessors have treated as being of profound and horrifying moment appear as ridiculous or trivial.

This impression has contributed greatly to the relatively low esteem in which *Alien Resurrection* is held by many who think highly of the other members of the series.[1] But there is good reason to contest its accuracy — or at least its present critical monopoly; and we can begin to see why if we recall further relevant facets of Jeunet's previous work. To begin with, *The City of Lost Children* presents a world of absent or perverse parental figures (the children of the city are either orphaned or adopted by the malevolent Octopus, the woman whom the clones call 'Mother' is only their original's wife, and One's father dies in the film's opening scenes), in which adult sexuality appears as disgusting and dangerous (One's sole encounter with a sexually attractive woman is seen as a threat to his moral purity, the occasion only for a temptation to betray his true companions and friends, the band of children and parti-cularly his adopted sister Miette). In these respects, Jeunet's world and that of the *Alien* series are deeply attuned; as we have seen, the Ripley who dies on Fiorina 161 is one for whom motherhood is variously absent, displaced or repressed – its preconditions and condition (that is, human heterosexuality and generativity, the fecundity of the flesh) understood as a threat to her physical and spiritual integrity, as her monstrous other.

Moreover, the form and style of Jeunet's earlier film suggest a certain kind of generic justification for his preoccupation with these thematic matters, and offer a way of understanding his otherwise bewildering mode of appropriation of the alien uni-verse. For *The City of Lost Children* is plainly a fantasy or fairy-tale; it tells a story in which children are the central protagonists, and it presents the world they inhabit from their viewpoint. This is why the adults in this world appear as essentially grotesque – their purposes either obscure, ridiculous or opposed to the interests of children, their technological artefacts and religious preoccupa-tions patently absurd, their relation to their own most natural appetites hedged round with prohibition and distortion, their sexual natures utterly incomprehensible. Hence, the children in this film treat the absence of their parents with equanimity, and invest themselves in the maintenance of relationships with other children, and most importantly with siblings – children who are also family (whether real or imagined), and hence the apotheosis of asexual intimacy. Accordingly, One searches unceasingly for his lost little brother, and adopts Miette as his little sister; and Miette shows her worthiness by being prepared to sacrifice herself to rescue One's brother from the demonic dream-landscape of her world's worst adult, a sacrifice she thinks of as her way of acquiring a brother (One's brother, and One himself). We might think of this fairy-tale as a child's dream of the adult world – or, rather, a child's nightmare of it, since these children perceive the adults around them as deprived of the capacity to dream, and hence envious of their children's free and easy inhabitation of the land-scape and logic of dreams, envious enough to wish to invade it themselves, an invasion which of course transforms their dreams into nightmares from which they cannot escape.

A wider appreciation of this vital dimension of Jeunet's art might have rescued his more recent film *Amelie* (more precisely titled *Le Fabuleux Destin d'Amélie Poulin* [2001]) from its detractors by rescuing it from its far more numerous admirers. For that film once again inhabits the perspective of a damaged child in order to trace the debilitating consequences of interpreting the world as a fairy-tale, not in order to endorse the fantasy that human life is essentially comprehensible in fairy-tale terms. Jeunet makes it clear from the outset that Amelie's parents ('a neurotic and an ice-berg') systematically deprive her of any loving physical contact, of any social life with other children, even of the company of her goldfish, arming her instead with a camera as a barrier between her and her world – a present that leads to her self-anaesthetizing immersion in a world of images (from her camera, television cinema, video recorders and postcards), and so to the central strand of the film's narrative: her pursuit of the pursuer of a man who apparently criss-crosses Paris solely in order to leave torn-up photographs of himself in railway station photo booths – quite as if she falls in love with her lover-to-be's apparent fascination with another's realization of photography's (and so cinema's) invitation to narcissism. Consequently, Amelie's attempts as an adult to do good to others should not be seen as the attempts of a rightly oriented heart to correct the world's tendency to frustrate desire, but rather as the attempts of a child in an adult's body to remake her world in the image of her fantasies of it – fantasies whose pursuit leads her to manipulate others, to inflict potentially traumatic experiences of pain and pleasure upon them (at least once by forcibly returning them to scenes of their own childhood) and centrally to find indefinitely various ways of deferring any definitive revelation of herself to the man of her dreams, and so her own access to adult sexual life. It is only when she realizes that the man she and her boyfriend are pursuing is simply a photo-booth repairman, whose discarded images of himself are simply part of his procedures for testing the success of his efforts, and so an expression of the practicalities of the city's grown-up world of work, that she becomes capable of transcending that deferral, and so of overcoming her compulsive attempts to remain a child and to perceive her world as inhabited by monsters, princes and fairy godparents.

These same generic terms are certainly required if we are to understand Jeunet's hybrid clone of the alien universe, his transfiguration of its fundamentally realistic terms into others equally capable of tapping the power of the medium of cinema as such: *Alien Resurrection* exhibits the appearance and logic of dreams and fairy-tale rather than of the real world (even the world of the future, the reality of science fiction). For the world viewed in this film is one in which the central protagonists are children in all but name, human beings inhabiting a world seen as if from the perspective of a child – hence one which invites them (and us) to accept the (physical and spiritual) absurdities and monstrosities of adults as normal, and to regard their (and our) instinctive sense of what is normal (whether in ourselves or in others) as monstrously or absurdly misaligned.

Monstrous children

Even within the generally juvenile band of pirates trying to return to the *Betty*, two characters stand out as essentially childlike. Call's diminutive size implicitly suggests that this is her status, as does her fundamental spiritual innocence. She has involved herself in this potentially lethal farce purely to save the human race from itself – a race that, after creating the technology that created her (she is a robot built by robots), then chose to recall her (along with all her brothers and sisters) for immediate destruction; and her behaviour throughout the narrative is essentially compassionate. The film wavers between thinking of her virtue as a function of her programming, and as an aspect of her transcendence of it (for example, she has to be persuaded to interface with 'Father' to block Wren's progress to the *Betty*); but either way, as a new creation or offspring of the human, she incarnates the idea of childhood innocence. It is as if, from the child's perspective Jeunet invites us to inhabit, monstrosity and selfishness appear as a perversion of initial or original virtue by experience and culture, something we grow into as we grow up and hence something that might be avoided by avoiding the process of growing up; and by making his film's purest expression of that innocence a creature of synthetic circuitry rather than flesh and blood,

Jeunet further associates the perversion of innocence with our fatedness to the body and its consequences – as if sexual maturation and spiritual purity appear mutually exclusive from the perspective of childhood.

However, the true child in this group is Ripley's clone. The film's opening scenes rapidly depict her *in vitro* conception, her post-operative emergence from a translucent caul or cocoon (as if the scientists' caesarean delivery of the alien queen from Ripley's clone was simultaneously her delivery from the queen, a transfiguring reconception or recreation of the human), and her schooling in human discourse and behaviour (the flashcard-and-stun-gun methods of her teachers subverting their implicit claim to be inducting her into, giving her a voice in, a genuinely civilized human form of life); in other words, we see her birth and her primary education – as if, by the time of the *Betty*'s arrival, she is no more than a child in an adult's body. Hence, insofar as our access to the alien universe always flows through our identification with Ripley's perspective upon it, our point of view in this film is that of a newborn posthuman being – one to whom everything is new, and to whom the human perspective is no more natural than that of the aliens. In her case, then, to any child's natural oscillation between seeing the normal as absurd and the absurd as normal must be added a sense of species dislocation – the loss of any underlying sense of kinship with the alternately monstrous and risible grown-ups of her world (whether human or alien). Ripley's clone is not just seeing the world for the first time; she is seeing it as no one has ever seen it before (inhabiting it as much through smell as through vision, as much collectively as individually, as a mortal who has already died). Little wonder, then, that the alien universe as she experiences it should appear skewed or off key, an uncanny parody or caricature of the one we have come to know over the years through the adult human eyes of her original.

Jeunet declares his sense that his dream or fantasy of that universe nevertheless remains faithful to its fundamental texture by making the first spoken words of his film (which precede our first view of Ripley's clone) a recitation by Sigourney Weaver of words first spoken by Newt in *Aliens*: 'My mummy always said that there were no monsters, no real ones – but there are'. This immediately declares that Weaver will here be occupying the perspective of a child; and it implies that what she sees will be the realization of a child's nightmare vision of the world. Jeunet thereby extends an idea developed in each of the preceding films, according to which the alien species is internally related to the human world of dreams – in *Alien*, the *Nostromo*'s crew wake from hypersleep into a nightmare; in *Aliens*, the monster's return is prefigured by its eruption into Ripley's dreams, and its ejection allows mother and child both to dream peacefully once again; in *Alien³*, her enemy overcomes her resistance in her sleep. Against this background, Jeunet's presentation of the alien universe itself as having the texture of a child's nightmare appears as no more than a natural progression. But by identifying Ripley's clone as the child whose nightmare this world is, Jeunet further implies that the underlying logic of that universe can be traced to something childlike or childish in Ripley herself. More precisely, Jeunet appears to be suggesting that the vision of human fertility and sexuality which the alien species embodies is best understood as embodying the fantasies and fears of a child, and hence as expressive of a refusal or unwillingness to grow up.

But, however unwilling she may be, Ripley's clone is nevertheless required – by her accelerated biological development as much as by events on the *Auriga* – to grow up. Hence, the initial scenes of her childhood are quickly followed by her access to adolescence. Her gleeful delight in besting the *Betty*'s crew on the basketball court, her nonchalant piercing of her own flesh, the bravado of her execution of the alien who killed Elgyn – accompanied throughout by her mastery of the mallrat dialogue that scriptwriter Joss Whedon first honed on *Buffy the Vampire Slayer* – all have that air of self-certainty, that uncomplicated pleasure in one's unfolding physical and intellectual powers, so familiar from adolescence. But the clone's sense of potency is irregularly punctured in an equally familiar way, first when she is forced by Call during their first meeting to admit to an underlying uncertainty about her own identity, and then more brutally when the group's travels confront her with the reality of her own fleshly origins.

When she discovers the room marked '1–7', she cannot avoid the chance to understand the number '8' tattooed on her arm – to understand, as in all children's tales, the riddle of her own identity. Behind the door she finds the results of the scientists' previous cloning attempts – seven hideously distorted forms, whose rapid progression through various misbegotten assemblages of gills, teeth and tails to a recognizably human and conscious, but scarred and tortured, number 7 indicate the eighth clone's kinship with the aliens, and the terrifying contingency of her own physical perfection. Beyond their manifestation of the monstrousness of the scientific project which produced her, these specimens function as a representation of the development of what is at once a new species and a new individual (as if declaring that, for Ripley's clone at least, ontogeny recapitulates phylogeny): they display nature's need to engender monstrosities if new species are to evolve, and the monstrous plasticity of any individual organism in its pre-birth development in the womb (or the test tube). Ripley's clone thus confronts the multiple, inter-linked conditions of her own existence – as the meat by-product of a cloning process, as the sole member of a new species, and as a specific, individual creature.

Jeunet declares this scene's affinity with the confrontation in *Aliens* between Ripley and the alien queen in her nursery by arming Ripley's clone with a flamethrower, with which she proceeds to destroy the room and its contents. In part, of course, she is responding to the seventh clone's agonized desire for oblivion; but in widening her field of fire to embrace the whole room, Ripley's clone stirs our memory of her original's betrayal of her agreement with the alien queen when, in an access of disgust at the latter's embodiment of fecundity, she attempts to torch the whole nursery. Jeunet thereby suggests that, for his posthuman protagonist, this destruction does far more than express her outrage at the cloning project. It also declares her anguish at the fact that the project gave her life by the merest accident, as if she is driven to deny not only the wickedness of which she is the offspring, but also the sheer arbitrariness of her own existence – its non-necessity, its dependence upon brute chance. And the conflagration further expresses her revulsion against the reality of her own origination in flesh and blood, against the body's unnerving capacity to mutate, its ineliminable vulnerability to violation and distortion, its unswerving drive to reshape itself from within (to develop from egg to adult) and its essential openness to being reshaped from without (to grafting, hybridity and evolution).

Ripley's clone thus finds herself incapable of doing what her original managed to do only at the moment, and in the manner of, her death – properly acknowledging what it might mean to be a creature of flesh and blood; she cannot see that, in responding so excessively to the seventh clone's request to 'Kill me', she gives expression to a desire to annihilate the conditions of her own existence – she cannot see that, in destroying these aborted or deformed versions of herself, she is in effect destroying herself (a perception incorporated in the scene itself by the fact that Sigourney Weaver plays the role of the seventh as well as the eighth clone, so that the flesh-and-blood human being who enacts this destruction is also the one who pleads for it).

But no such phantasms of self-destruction, however cathartic, can bring about the consummation they really desire; the transition from child to adult – the programmed transfiguration of the flesh into sexual maturity – is not to be avoided. Hence Ripley's clone is not permitted to reach the safety of the *Betty* without confronting the sexual potential of her already-adult body, which means confronting the fact that the generativity of her flesh has always already been exploited – that she is, and has been from the first moment of her own independent existence, a mother: the mother of the monster.

In another of the film's more powerful sequences (a second trapdoor set into its parodic surface, through which we fall – with its protagonist – back into the deepest metaphysical dimensions of the alien universe), Ripley's clone is drawn down into the embrace of the alien species, luxuriating in her absorption into the writhing mass of its limbs and tails – as if engulfed by the very lability of organic being that she had earlier attempted to consume in fire (and that finds further expression elsewhere in the aliens' graceful adaptation to water, at once recalling their inhabitation of that medium when capturing Newt in *Aliens* and prefiguring their coming adaptation to the amniotic). But this reactivation of the alien aspect of her embodiment ends by delivering her (half-dazed, as if either still dreaming or just awakening from a dream – or perhaps in post-coital satiety, as if implying an orgasmic dimension to her experience of reincorporation into the alien community) to the alien queen's nursery, just in time to observe her offspring's delivery of another of her offspring. And, in so doing, Ripley's clone perceives the initial activation of the human aspect of the alien queen's embodiment – her subjection to a reproductive cycle involving pregnancy, labour and birth.

Jeunet here succeeds in evoking a strong sense of tenderness towards the queen – compassion for the fact of her new, utterly alien, mode of victimization by her own body, for the fact that it results from her own gestation in the body of Ripley's clone (its being a sorrow bequeathed to her simply because she is the female offspring of a female, an aspect of her fleshly origin), and for the fact that (as a monstrous incarnation of male heterosexuality) its capacity to place all humans in the position of human females should ultimately result in its own occupation of that position.

In terms of the logic of the alien universe, however, it soon appears that Ripley's clone has not so much bequeathed a human mode of reproduction to her offspring as displaced it onto her. For the child who emerges from the queen's belly instinctively sees its true mother as monstrous, and turns instead to Ripley's clone; it is so horrified by the queen that it is prepared to kill her rather than acknowledge itself as her offspring – but it is prepared to see Ripley's clone as its mother, to see itself as flesh of that flesh. In other words, the alien queen gives birth to her mother's child; Ripley's clone attains motherhood without heterosexual intercourse, pregnancy or childbirth by sacrificing her true (but involuntarily conceived and delivered) daughter to what she thinks of as death-dealing invasions of her bodily integrity.

The clone is not entirely unresponsive to her (grand)child's sense of kinship with her; she finds herself capable of treating it with a certain tenderness, is reluctant to leave it, and hence incapable of an unqualified rejection of its assumption of her maternity. But the film's culminating course of events (as the *Betty* careers through Earth's atmosphere and away from the alien-infested *Auriga*) shows that she is equally incapable of an unqualified acceptance of it.

In part, this is motivated by the clone's reluctant but real concern for the humans on board the *Betty*, in part perhaps by vengeful grief over her (grand)child's role in the monstrous end of her true daughter. But, most fundamentally, it flows from the fact that this child's sheer existence declares the generativity of her flesh and blood, and its form and nature declares its hybridity – its equal participation in human and alien nature. Hence, the clone's acknowledgement of the child as hers would entail an acknowledgement of her own generativity and hybridity, of her own posthuman mode of being and its unavoidable drive towards reproduction and mutation. And Ripley's clone does not have it within her, despite her access to memories of her original's death, to make that acknowledgement.

Hence, she finds herself compelled not only to deny the child's plea for acknowledgement, but to destroy its source, and hence the possibility of its reiteration. As she soothes the child's fears and frustrations in the *Betty*'s cargo bay, she uses her own acidic blood to incise a small hole in one of the windows, and the monstrous infant is gradually sucked through it, its pleading wails eventually silenced as the last particles of its body are squeezed out into space. This climax is an inflection of a familiar trope of the series: the first two films culminate with an alien's ejection into space through an airlock, the third with the alien queen's ejection from the universe as such. But, in *Alien Resurrection*, the alien child's end is a grotesque parody or inversion of its birth, and hence of birth as such: its recent emergence from an orifice in its unacknowledged mother's torso is recapitulated in reverse (hence negated or denied) by its being forced through a narrow opening to its death, by its undergoing a lethal expulsion from the technological carapace of its ideal mother's body. Ripley's clone watches the child's death with anguish and remorse; but this horrific destruction of her own flesh and blood is something she herself brings about, and she uses her own blood to do it – as if to deny with the very stuff of her own organic being the sole living proof of its generativity.

So when Ripley's clone stands on the threshold of a new, ter-restrial life – a stranger about to enter the strange land that her original died to save from her alien kin – her diminutive com-panion is not the monstrous infant but Call, the childlike robot whose human inheritance is spiritual rather than fleshly, a paradigm of non-fecund embodiment (the sterile offspring of machines). This closing conjunction does not exactly suggest that the film's protagonist has overcome her original's psychic anxi-eties about her own embodiment; it rather confirms that Jeunet's inflection of the alien universe has only transposed its essential thematic co-ordinates – it has not transcended them.

But, of course, the conjunction has another, more reflexive significance. For almost twenty years have passed in the life of the *Alien* series, and as its unifying focus on the intimate otherness of Ripley and the alien has deepened and clarified, so has its dependence upon Sigourney Weaver. But twenty years is a long time in the life of a female star; in Weaver's case, it takes her well into her forties – a point at which it becomes increasingly difficult for many women actors (regardless of their mastery of their craft) to obtain substantial parts, and hence to maintain an audience and a career. It is easy to see *Alien Resurrection*'s casting of Winona Ryder in the role of Call as an attempt to graft a new female star onto the *Alien* franchise, and thereby to break its dependence on Sigourney Weaver's continued attractiveness to cinema audiences; and it is also easy to see, amidst the psychic turbulence of the scene in room '1–/', something of Weaver's own anxieties about her status as a star – its dependence not only upon the fortunate interaction of her exact physiognomy with that of the movie camera, and with that of her monstrous other in this series, but also upon the continuation of that good fortune despite the inevitable physical transformations of ageing.

But the central truth of *Alien Resurrection* is surely that both kinds of anxiety are groundless. For Sigourney Weaver's performance is a marvel of economy, intelligence and physical fluidity; her subtle incarnation of genetic hybridity, her capacity to accommodate wild shifts of tone from sarcastic, adolescent one-liners to ago-nized psychic struggles, and her undeniably charismatic physical presence hold together a film that is sometimes in danger of losing its grip on its audience, and together declare that she is at the peak of her powers. It seems plain that, if the series is allowed to continue into the terrestrial context that Jeunet holds open for his successor, it will do so only if Sigourney Weaver is prepared once again to submit herself to the vicissitudes of the camera (one might say, to its cloning or replication of her physical presence) and of the character whose life (and life after death) is now inextricably linked with her own cinematic identity.

2007 postscript: rejecting a graft

Whilst I continue to think that further contributions to the *Alien* series remain a theoretical possibility, I do not regard *Alien vs Predator* (Paul W. S. Anderson, 2004) as fitting that bill, despite its reliance upon the same alien species, its reproduction of various visual design elements from the *Alien* stylistic canon, and the involvement of the same producers, as well as two writers from the original film. This is not because it is such an empty work; *Alien vs Predator* excludes itself from series membership before judgements of quality even arise.

Its contemporary setting immediately disqualifies it as a sequel to *Alien Resurrection*; and since the particular story it tells to explain how a small group of people come to be involved in the inter-species conflict it depicts doesn't even attempt to cohere with any other point on the internally consistent far-future narrative time-line of the *Alien* series as a whole (beyond invoking a distant ancestor of the Weyland-Yutani corporation), it can't even aspire to be a prequel to those earlier films, as opposed simply to recounting events that happened to occur before the ones they recount. From the outset, then, its makers effectively refuse to confront the significance of the previous four films, understood as progressively more sophisticated solutions to the progressively more complex problems of continuity and discontinuity posed by the project of continuing this series. Because of this temporal and thematic dislocation, *Alien vs Predator* has no place for Ripley's clone or for Ripley herself (its strong female protagonist and sole survivor being essentially unlike Ripley in mood, motivation or character); and it displaces Ripley's aliens into the Earth-centred cinematic universe of another alien species, whose members have from the outset effectively domesticated her essentially untameable beasts (by maintaining them in carefully secure environments to act as particularly challenging prey). And this emasculating shotgun marriage of the *Predator* and *Alien* universes lacks any rationale beyond each species' monstrously violent otherness to humanity; but even that differs in the two cases, as fundamentally as the biological drive to reproduce differs from the cultivated desire to hunt.

Understood as an attempt to graft new life onto *Alien* stock, therefore, *Alien vs Predator* must be judged a failure; but it might nevertheless count as a further member of the *Predator* series – although, given that its proximate origin is a video game, and that *Alien vs Predator 2* is due to be released in 2008, it might better be viewed as itself originating a series, and so as founding a self-sufficient (if thematically, generically and formally hybrid) cinematic universe of its own, however insubstantial. But, as things stand, the possibility of a sequel to – a genuine continuation of – the *Alien* series, and so of a further exploration of this dimension of Sigourney Weaver's stardom, remains unrealized.

Part II

Source: Ladd Company/WB courtesy the Kobal Collection

5

FILM AS PHILOSOPHY
The priority of the particular

As I hope I made sufficiently clear in the first edition of this book, the possibility that at least some films might be thought of as standing in some internal relation to philosophy is not something I regard as my own discovery. I first acquired a sense of its reality, and of its applicability to my experience of film, through the writings of Stanley Cavell. But happily, something about my way of rearticulating his ideas in the context of a well-known and much-admired set of relatively recent Hollywood movies has evidently resonated with readers; and, as a consequence, the chapters that now make up Part I of this book have been subject to the inevitably critical appraisal of my philosophical colleagues, closely followed by those in film studies and cultural theory.

I am very grateful for their willingness to spend time with my work in this way, and I have learnt much from their expressions of puzzlement and outright disagreement (as well as deriving comfort from their declarations of fellow-feeling). So I would like to take the opportunity afforded by this second edition of the book to respond to at least some of their objections, many of which have tended to focus on the highly condensed articulation of my approach in its introduction. To put the matter more bluntly: a number of readers have found these introductory remarks to be far too condensed for them to have even a tolerably clear sense of what my approach amounts to, let alone of how it might be defended. I want to argue in response that this finding betrays a misunderstanding of the relation between the book's introduction and its constituent chapters, and so a misunderstanding of the relation I envisage between film and philosophy.

The very idea of film as philosophy

First, however, I want to give a quick, but I hope a clearer, restatement of my basic idea of film as philosophy, which I originally articulated by distinguishing and so relating three ideas: film as philosophizing, the philosophy of film, and film in the condition of philosophy.[1]

The second of these is probably the most familiar form in which film is permitted access to the philosophical citadel: the activity it refers to is constructed on the model of 'philosophy of history', 'philosophy of science', philosophy of religion' and so on. This is philosophy in its essentially parasitic mode: the philosopher inserts herself into another domain of human practical activity and raises questions about its grounding assumptions or basic conceptual presuppositions of a kind that the practitioners within this domain are not capable of answering *qua* practitioners, since anything they offer in response will presuppose the very categories that are in question. This is what happens, for example, when the philosopher of science asks the scientist what justifies the principle of inductive reasoning – the assumption that observed correlations license us to conclude that those correlations hold in the domain beyond our observations. For any scientific response to that question – say, by citing the deliverances of a theory, or by arguing that the principle has worked in the past and so can be assumed to work in the future – will themselves have been legitimated by the principle in question, and hence cannot support it.

Philosophy of film follows this model by raising questions about the basic techniques, resources and presuppositions of cinema. The philosopher of film is interested in how it is possible for light projected on a screen to make present to us objects, people and events that are patently absent, in what the relation might be between actor and character in film (as opposed, say, to theatre), in what it might mean to say that a particular scene or plot development in a film expresses the intentions of its director, in the legitimacy of investing primary authorship of a film in its director, and so on. One might think of these kinds of question as bearing upon the conditions for the possibility of cinema; and I was struck by the extent to which, in the theoretical writings about film that I studied in preparing the book, films themselves are assumed to be silent with respect to such questions. They must, necessarily, realize in themselves the conditions for their own possibility; but it would appear from such writings that they do not and cannot realize that they do so – cannot reflect upon what those conditions are, or upon the fact that they are so conditioned. At best, they provide the data in relation to which possible answers to such questions must at some point be assessed for validity.

There is already something strange about this assumption, given that films – like novels, plays and paintings – are the products of intentional human practical activity, can have representational content and can take pretty much anything as their subject-matter. If so, why couldn't their ways of presenting their narrative worlds embody sustained reflection on the part of those who fashioned them upon the kinds of questions that interest philosophers, and even the kinds of questions about film that interest philosophers? I don't mean to deny that some, or even most, films show no traces of such reflection; or to claim that philosophical enquiries into the nature of film could not legitimately view any film purely as an instantiation of film as such. What I object to is the assumption that no film could conceivably adopt a more active or questioning relation to its own conditions of possibility; and what is objectionable about this is precisely that it is an assumption – that it excludes this possibility *a priori*, and treats this exclusion as somehow beyond question.

My counterproposal was, and is, correspondingly modest. It is that we look and see whether or not the real content and qualities of any particular films might put this assumption in question, by being best understood as themselves reflecting upon (let us say) aspects of the nature of film. Of course, whether or not they are best understood that way cannot be settled in general or *a priori* terms; it cannot be settled in advance of, but only by, a detailed examination of the specific films. This is why the bulk of the first edition of my book takes the form of just such detailed examinations of specific films; for it is only in the cut and thrust of argument about such concrete details of our experience of particular films that we can hope to evaluate the claim that there are such possibilities of the cinematic medium.

Even within such modest parameters, however, one might legitimately suspect that films whose conditions of possibility are sufficiently specific are more likely to exhibit a reflective relation to their own nature than others. For instance, suppose that a director of genuine ability is asked to make a sequel – perhaps a sequel to a successful, critically acclaimed science fiction film. Is it not plausible that in doing so, in taking on the inheritance of a particular set of characters in a particular narrative universe presented in a particular way, he will be forced to reflect upon the specific nature, and the particular cinematic achievement, of the film to which his own is a sequel, and thus upon the risks and opportunities this inheritance offers for the deployment of his own original talents (as manifest in his other work)? But this dialectic of inheritance and originality is just a condition for the possibility of directing a sequel, and, of course, for directing a sequel to a sequel, and so (apparently) endlessly on. So if this sequel turns out to be of any intrinsic interest and value, it seems likely that a significant part of both will derive from the way in which it reflects upon, and so embodies a critical evaluation of, this condition of its own possibility.

In this sense, a sequel by a gifted director is likely to exhibit just the reflective questioning of its basic resources that one would expect of the philosophy of film; and although those resources will certainly include matters of thematic content whose relevance to philosophical discussions is fairly self-evident (as in the *Alien* series' obsessive interest in sexuality, embodiment and procreation), it will also include more formal questions – questions concerning the ways in which that content is conveyed cinematically, and so ones relevant to investigations in the philosophy of film. But one can go further: for insofar as it sustains its achievement by reflecting upon the conditions of its own possibility, such a film would find itself in what I (still) want to call the condition of any properly self-aware philosophy.

132

One might put it this way: if philosophy has an essentially parasitic moment, in which it implicitly criticizes other academic disciplines, other dimensions of the human cultural economy, and indeed the various non-institutionalized and non-thematized dimensions of everyday life, for failing to interrogate their own most basic resources, then any philosophy that failed to interrogate its own nature in exactly the same way would stand guilty of the very crime of which it accuses those others, and so would be in a far worse condition than any of them (condemning the motes in others' eyes whilst overlooking the beam in its own). In this respect, the increasingly common generation of sequels and series in contemporary Hollywood might be seen as one way in which film attains the condition of modernism (in which its own history becomes neither a taken-for-granted resource nor an unusable irrelevance but rather an undismissable problem) and thereby the condition of philosophy. Once again, however, we cannot settle the question of whether any of these sequels actually does attain or exemplify that condition except by watching them – by attending to our concrete experience of their qualities.

This point about what is proper to the condition of philosophy will recur; in fact, the rest of this chapter will in one sense amount to retracing the circle of concepts I have just laid out in a more expansive and I hope elucidatory way. But, for now, I want to concentrate on my claim about what one might call the argumentative relevance of particular experience.

According to my conception of the matter, the ultimate touchstone for the validity of my argument that certain films, by existing in the condition of philosophy and consequently engaging reflectively on just the issues reflected upon in the philosophy of film, might be thought of as themselves philosophizing is whether or not my claims to identify such moments in these films are convincing. For example, in my reading of Scott's *Blade Runner*, I argue that Deckard's Voight-Kampff machine, designed to distinguish humans from replicants, is a figure for the movie camera's capacity to project and screen real human beings.

Of course, what shows that the Voight-Kampff machine is a figure for the camera is not the simple fact that it exists in the film and possesses some properties analogous to those of a camera; by that token the presence of a mirror or a camera in any film would determine *a priori* that that film had substantial reflexive concerns. What matters is rather how the machine figures in the structures of significance established, developed and even subverted by the film as a whole. So my claim that in presenting us with such a machine *Blade Runner* is presenting us with a particular understanding of its own nature (by critically evaluating the opportunities and limits of one of its own determining conditions) can be justified only by showing that and how the film's specific treatment of that machine betrays a genuinely thoughtful engagement with those conditions on the part of those who made it; and that can be established only by providing a convincing reading of the film as a whole in those terms.

This is why the most disappointing aspect of the critical response to my book is that even those responsive to its concerns tend not to engage in any detail with the specific readings of particular films that make up the bulk of the book itself, and that are in fact where its more general claims either stand or fall. Instead, my brief introduction to these readings has been the sole focus of attention; and the shocking discovery is made that its extravagant general claims are not there given any clear, equivalently general justification. It is as if, despite my explicit initial attempts to ward off the very idea of films as illustrating independently established philosophical theses, even sympathetic readers of my book find it all but impossible to see my readings of specific films as anything other than illustrations of a general method, and so as dependent for their interest upon my independently establishing some prior methodological theses about film and philosophy. But on my understanding of the matter, the only justification my more general introductory claims could receive is embodied in the readings that they introduce.

Reasons for resistance: philosophy

It is hard for me to see quite why this aspect of my work is so hard for others to see. But plainly, there are some very strongly contrary assumptions at work in the way philosophers (which to my mind means all of us, at some points and in certain moods) think about film – assumptions that make it seem so self-evident that films could not be engaging in genuinely philosophical reflection that there is no point in looking closely at particular films to see whether they might be doing so. (If I am convinced that a mouse couldn't possibly have come into being by spontaneous generation out of grey rags and dust, then a close investigation of the rags will seem superfluous).[2] Some of these are assumptions about film, and I shall return to that aspect of the matter in the following section of this chapter; but others are assumptions about philosophy – about what genuinely philosophical reflection is and should be. This section will focus on those preconceptions, beginning with those at work in one of the more helpful responses to my book that I know of – Julian Baggini's review for the Film-Philosophy internet Salon and Journal, under the title 'Alien Ways of Thinking'. In the process of questioning the terms of Baggini's response, I will also make my own use of some suggestions made in the same forum by Nathan Andersen, in his article 'Is Film the Alien Other to Philosophy?'[3]

Without wanting to flatten out Baggini's highly nuanced and self-questioning ways of framing his worry, I think it not unfair to see the following thought as lying at the heart of the matter for him:

> The problem I have encountered [with On Film] is that for philosophy to be anything more than an exchange of opinions, it must involve the giving of good reasons for accepting or rejecting the position under discussion. These reasons may well be other than formal arguments, but they must be reasons of some kind. Such reasons, however, appear to be lacking from the 'Alien' quartet.[4]

And a little later:

> I see it as central to the philosophical enterprise that we offer reasons as much as is possible and that reason-giving ends only when it has to, not before. In contrast, along with much film and literature, the 'Alien' films offer us symbolic representations of the world, but don't provide

us with reasons for thinking that these representations are accurate.[5]

The idea that philosophy is peculiarly, or distinctively, subject to the claims of reason is surely undeniable; at any rate, I don't want to deny it. But then, everything hangs on what one counts as a way in which reason makes its claims on us, and what one acknowledges as a way in which one might answer to these claims. Baggini is thankfully careful to distinguish the giving of reasons from the provision of formal arguments, with premises regimented in technical formulae so as perspicuously to display the conclusions they support; for the latter is self-evidently only one genus of the relevant species. But must our acknowledgement of reason's claims on us always take the specific form of giving reasons in support of our opinions or our 'symbolic representations' (which I take to mean something like our 'view' or 'vision') of the world?

There are, I think, other possibilities, and, as it happens, Andersen gestures towards two important and inter-related ones: what he calls 'reflective film criticism', and 'providing pathways for thinking'. The first involves changing one's mind about what is happening in a given film

> not because [the critics] propose that there are hidden elements in the film that cannot be understood apart from some theoretical apparatus – but because they lay out and make plain what is already on the surface, showing that close attention to the explicit dimensions of the film reveals it to hang together much better than initial audiences and critics supposed.[6]

Suppose we think of this as a mode of description that helps us to make sense of our experience of a film, and hence of the film itself. Then we will see a close link between reflective film criticism and providing pathways for thinking, which Andersen explains as the provision of

> an open space in which thinking takes place, enabling new modes of organizing and making sense of experience and

knowledge. In order for there to be a pathway for thought, there has to be a motivation for the movement of thought. Questions ... provide this motivation.[7]

I want to say a little more about my way of taking these ideas of making sense and of questioning, understood as alternative ways of meeting the claims of reason (ways that might, of course, depart from those Andersen means to chart by his words).

First, making sense. One state or condition in which reflective beings might find themselves is that of disagreement: two people holding opposing views on a given topic. Here, philosophy can usefully intervene by providing and assessing the reasons one might have for either view. But such disagreements presuppose a shared space of thought, one given by the givenness of the topic – a shared sense of its shape and significance. Sometimes, however, we want to, or need to, or simply do, reconceive that space, by finding a new way of thinking about the topic – one that reorients both participants to the dispute by altering their sense of what stances are available to them with respect to its topic. And, at other times, we find that we lack any sense of a shared space for thinking; we find ourselves utterly disoriented by our situation, unable to find our feet with others, and with ourselves, with respect to what we confront. Then we need to find our orientation by imagining how we might take a stand here, and hence by finding a way to recognize certain topics and opinions about them as defining a space of thinking that we might inhabit.

Could we justify such new ways of thinking about a topic by the giving of reasons? Well, if what we mean by the giving of reasons presupposes a given space of reasoning or thinking within which competing positions locate themselves, then obviously not. But that does not entail that such re-envisionings of the space of reasons are beyond the claim of reason; it just means that they are answerable to it in different ways. For example, when Socrates faces judicial execution, and his friends urge him to flee from his captors, he tells them that it would be wrong to do so because disobeying the Athenian polis would be like disobeying his parents. He thereby reorients their thinking about Athens by comparing the polis to a family. But the degree of conviction this imaginative connection elicits is dependent upon the extent to which it can be followed out in detail, the way in which it makes sense of various aspects of political life, the further connections it allows us to draw in a range of related cases, and our willingness to rethink our own status and our own experience of life (in the family and in the polis, but not only there) in the terms it suggests. Socrates' imagination is thus not a faculty that is essentially other to that of rationality, or essentially unconstrained by it; it is accountable in a variety of ways, but none would straightforwardly fit the model of 'giving reasons for and against an opinion'.

I would wish my readings of specific films to be understood as accountable, as answerable to the claims of reason, in just the ways described above. Those readings aim to make aesthetic sense of the films they respond to, to show how various elements within them have a significance that depends on the way they hang together with other elements to make a coherent whole, and thus allow us to make sense of our experience of them. And, of course, the way in which a given film coheres internally has definite implications for the ways in which it can be seen to hang together with other films in a given series (whether within the Alien universe, or within a given director's body of work); hence a reading of one film gains credibility insofar as it engenders a coherent reading of other films to which it is linked, and of the links between it and them.

But my reading of the *Alien* films as a series offers two other dimensions in which such accountability is at issue, and hence measurable: the relations between the various stages of Ripley's understanding of herself and her universe, and the relations between each director's understanding of Ripley's universe and that of his successors and predecessors. We might think of these as Ripley's ongoing dialogue with herself, and as an unfolding conversation between her directors; we might also think of each film in the series as embodying a dialogue between Ripley and her director. Since, in each case, the plausibility of each individual director's reading of Ripley and her universe can be measured in terms of its internal coherence, its willingness to follow through the consequences of its particular way of making sense of things, and its willingness to respond critically to opposing readings, the dialectical evolution of these interwoven conversations seems no less answerable to reason than are Socrates' discussions with the young men of Athens. As with those discussions, what is at stake in these interacting dimensions is not (or not solely) aesthetic coherence, but that unfashionable preoccupation 'the meaning of life' – the challenge of making sense of human existence.

For the accountability of Ripley's and her directors' readings of the Alien universe is to be assessed not just within that universe (as readings of the fictional world of the films), but also within our universe – our experience of the human condition. Ripley's understandings of human embodiment, sexuality and integrity are engendered by and directed towards the cinematic world of her experience; but that world is a recognizably human world. It contains alien species and extrapolations of human technological achievements, but it is not a fantasy of human reality, if by that we mean a fictional world that represses or rewrites the funda-mental elements of our finitude. If Ripley's readings of her life can seem variously empowering, self-punishing and childlike to and for her, they cannot avoid showing us how our own accom-modations with such understandings of human existence can manifest our own empowerment, masochism and immaturity.

Two points are worth emphasizing here. First, the sense I have just articulated of film as a projected moving image of human reality does not, in my view, require a particular (perhaps Bazi-nian) realistic theory about cinema, or a metaphysical ontology of any kind, if it is to count as rationally justified. My use of the ordinary word 'real' in these contexts needs as much and as little justification as my use of any other ordinary word in this text, or indeed in any text. I am certainly accountable for every word I use, as is any speaker, and at various points in my book I do try to account for this specific combination of familiar words (such as 'projection', 'image', 'human' and 'reality') in the context of film; but I am not bound to give such an accounting in any specific discourse of film theory or philosophy.

Here is one unorthodox but nonetheless recognizable sense in which philosophy can meet its obligation to the claims of reason without regimenting its discourse in the terms provided by formal logic or the predicate calculus. It can do so by meaning every word it says: that is, by developing a discourse which acknowledges (that is to say, recognizes and explores) the ways in which its words are interwoven with other words, responsive to the world and capable of being projected into new contexts (for example the contexts of film) in ways that illuminate both words and world. One might think of this as writing that acknowledges the conditions of its own possibility – amongst them, the sheer fact that words and the world are as if made for one another, yet capable of endlessly surprising one another: call it a marriage (if one is willing to understand marriage as an unending willingness for remarriage). Literature of various kinds has found its ways of acknowledging these conditions; and philosophy – in the work of such thinkers as Emerson, Wittgenstein, Austin and Cavell, not to mention Nietzsche and Heidegger – has found its own, different but internally related ones.

But I mentioned a second important point. My earlier claim about the human reality of Ripley's world quickly produced a sudden outcropping of critical ethical concepts – empowerment, masochism, immaturity and so on; and what this brings out is a formal link between making aesthetic sense of things and making moral sense of them. There is a strong philosophical tendency to think of moral disagreement on the model of opposing opinions about a particular course of action, with each opinion supported by more general ethical principles. But, as the example of Socrates and the polis implies, moral disagreement can also be a matter of differing visions of what matters in human life, different conceptions of human flourishing in the world, and so on; and discussion here may well take the form of encouraging one's interlocutor not so much to change her mind about a particular course of action but to look at everything differently – and so to find moral significance where it did not previously seem to exist, as well as to find that what previously seemed highly morally significant was in fact trivial or even essentially illusory.

So when Baggini says that 'the Alien films offer us symbolic representations of the world, but fail to provide us with good reasons for thinking that these representations are accurate', he mixes insight with error. He recognizes that what is at stake here are visions of the world rather than individual judgements about elements of it; but he also seems to assume that such overarching ways of seeing are accurate or inaccurate to the way things really are in just the way that opinions about more local events and actions might be – as if one's way of seeing human life is just one very big opinion, or an opinion about one very big subject. And this encourages us to overlook the fact that we have rather more various resources for bringing about such fundamental shifts of ethical perception than we have for contesting specific ethical judgements about a well-defined set of possible courses of action.

In particular, we make appeals to the hearts of our interlocutors – to their emotional responses and sensibilities – and to their imaginations. And although it may be tempting to do so, there is no necessity to assume that the imagination and the heart are essentially distinct from our rational faculties. They might in fact be internally related to reason, in that imaginative and emotional responses are themselves answerable to the claims of reason and also in that reason without imagination and feeling would be, morally speaking, dead. Not to put too fine a point on it: to exclude such a possibility would be to exclude in advance the relevance of literature, and the arts more generally, to moral thinking.

Think, for example, of Charles Dickens, and his attempts (in such novels as *Great Expectations* and *David Copperfield*) to convince those whose hearts are inclined against it that prevailing Victorian attitudes towards children are morally objectionable.[8] These are attempts to enlarge the moral imagination of his readers; they do not assume that his readers' hearts are already inclined in the way Dickens would like, but rather work to change their prevailing inclinations and assumptions, to lead them to a more sympathetic way of looking at children. By presenting his readers with the world as viewed from a child's perspective, even (even particularly) when this does not involve the child being treated badly or generously, he aims to get them and us to attend to a child *as* a centre of a distinctive view of the world, and so to attend to children in their own right. By this kind of imaginative exercise, Dickens can succeed not only in altering our affections, but in enhancing our understanding – or, rather, he enhances our understanding by engaging with and altering our affections and sensibility.

Of course, Dickens' way of looking at things is not the only available one; it has many (some might say, all too many) competitors. But it is not as if different ways of attending to children, or indeed to anything in the world of our experience, are themselves beyond critical evaluation – as if they are just flatly different in their orientation, and so in what they draw to the centre of our attention. In fact, it is part of Dickens' purpose in his novels to get us to recognize this, by encouraging us to see that, for example, Gradgrind's way of attending to the world is cold and even insolent; what we could possibly find out through such a coldly presumptuous approach to the world can feed no adequate moral thought, or show us what we need to respond well to the world. By contrast, Dickens' own way of attending has a characteristic emotional colouring that derives from its combination of great warmth, concentration of energy and humour. When that concentration wavers, or any of these three elements gets too far out of balance with the others, such an approach risks sentimentality – by which I mean not that sentimentality is the usual cause of Dickens' cognitive failures, but rather that it is the characteristic form that such failures take. When it is successful, however, it gives expression to a particular style of affectionate interest in and imaginative engagement with human affairs of exactly the kind that it aims to create in us, precisely by virtue of the capacity of that mode of attention to engage and reorient our own present interests and engagements.

This is perhaps the most obvious point at which resistance to any possible internal relation of film and philosophy meets up with that notorious inaugural Platonic gesture, whereby the poets – and so the arts in general – were exiled from the just city, the philosophical republic. For that endlessly reiterated exclusion is always tied up with an anxiety about art's capacity to address the imagination and the heart, as if such forms of address must bypass the head or otherwise short-circuit our capacity for reason. The question I want simply to raise here is: why the 'must'? Perhaps if we examine the phenomena in detail, this will turn out to be a prejudice rather than an *a priori* deliverance of the very faculty it aims to constrain.

Other prejudicial assumptions in this vicinity might also be thought to have a Platonic origin. For example, one critic takes it for granted that a 'narrative can yield a philosophical truth' only insofar as 'the truth that it establishes is general', one that 'does not rely on the specific details of its story'.[9] Deploying the same basic contrast, another critic asserts that 'the concreteness and particularity of art' essentially distinguish it from 'the abstract, conceptual character of philosophy'; hence, whilst willing to take popular film seriously as art, he suggests that it must be an error to take it seriously as philosophy – an error that he thinks could only be driven by 'the ancient view that the worth of art must always pale in comparison with the worth of philosophy'.[10] Suppose we accept that philosophy has a particular interest in conceptual matters (after all, I do claim that my films philosophize most clearly insofar as they evince a reflective interest in the basic conceptual conditions of their own possibility); why then does it follow that it must have an abstract and general, as opposed to a concrete and particular, character? Some philosophers – Wittgenstein and Nietzsche among them – have taken the life of our concepts to lie in their specific role in our historically and culturally specific forms of life, hence as to be interrogated philosophically only in the concrete and particular contexts of their use by individual members of given linguistic communities. Might not art's interest in the concrete and the particular therefore naturally facilitate such forms of philosophical interrogation? Might it not even prove a salutary corrective to the prevalent philosophical assumption that conceptual analysis must involve abstract, general system-building (as opposed, say, to systematically attending to the particular ways in which concepts forge and alter their relations with other concepts from context to context of their application)? If so, then the worth of art will hardly pale in comparison to that of philosophy, but it will remain possible for each to find something of worth in the other.

What, however, of Andersen's second idea – his vision of philosophy as questioning? A number of philosophical themes come together under this heading, but one of them has an explicitly Heideggerian inflection. For, as I mentioned briefly in Chapter 1, Heidegger defines the distinctively human mode of existence as that in which the essential nature of things (including ourselves) is an issue for us; in other words, we treat the essence or Being of anything and everything as a question – as something for which an answer is not given once and for all but is rather to be sought, through the systematization of our natural interest in questioning (through such modes of inquiry as physics, history and ethics) and the periodic questioning of the assumptions that such systematic practices of questioning necessarily take for granted.

For Heidegger, then, philosophy appears here not simply as parasitic on other forms of questioning but as the ultimate radicalization of the human impulse towards questioning as such. Stanley Cavell once put it this way:

> I understand [philosophy] as a willingness not to think about something other than what ordinary human beings think about, but rather to learn to think undistractedly about things that ordinary human beings cannot help thinking about, or anyway cannot help having occur to them, sometimes in fantasy, sometimes as a flash across a landscape ... Such thoughts are instances of that characteristic human willingness to allow questions for itself which it cannot answer with satisfaction. ... Philosophers after my heart will wish to convey the thought that while there may be no satisfying answers to such questions in *certain forms*, there are, so to speak, directions to answers, *ways to think*, that are worth the time of your life to discover.[11]

Three morals might be drawn from such a conception of philosophy's essence. First, there is no essential break between the natural, inherent reflectiveness of human life-forms and the inveterate reflectiveness of philosophy; what distinguishes the philosopher is the persistence and the single-mindedness with which he employs the capacity for self-questioning that informs every aspect of our ordinary existence. Hence, second, the advent of philosophizing can occur within any and every mode of human existence, insofar as those engaged in a particular form of human practical activity find themselves driven to question the nature of their own enterprise and the resources with which it is pursued, and to incorporate both the process and the product of this self-questioning into the practical activity from which it emerged. And if this is possible for the physicist and the literary critic — if Einstein's governing questions are as much philosophical as scientific, just as De Man's questions are as much philosophical as literary — why should it not be possible for the reflective film-maker?

Third, as we saw earlier, if philosophy requires a certain self-questioning or self-accounting from every other human enterprise, then it must in all consistency require it of itself. This means that any truly thoroughgoing conception of philosophy must put its own internal resources and self-understanding in question, and thus acknowledge that any such self-conception is open to question by others (even others such as Heidegger or other inhabitants of philosophical traditions so alien to familiar Anglo-American ways of thinking as to appear essentially unphilosophical), as of course theirs is open to question by it. Philosophy therefore cannot avoid the responsibility of accounting for its own understanding of itself, recognizing that it will have competitors and accepting that the critical dialogue between their proponents will never end as long as philosophy remains true to its own nature.

What I am claiming here is that the exponents of standard approaches to the philosophy of film fail to respect that third point. Rather than allowing their experience of particular films to teach them what film might be, they permit their preconceptions about the nature of film to dictate what their experience of particular films might be. Rather than allowing their experience of particular films to teach them what ethics, art, imagination, emotions and thinking might be, they permit their preconceptions about the nature of ethics, art, imagination, emotions and thinking to dictate what their experience of these phenomena as presented in or activated by particular films might be. And rather than allowing their experience of particular films to teach them what philosophizing might be, they permit their preconceptions about the nature of philosophy to determine what their experience of particular films might be.

These failures of self-questioning — one might also call them failures to be sufficiently open to one's experience, and so failures of empiricism or realism – are patently inter-related. For example, those who succumb to the first thereby repress any invitation that certain films might extend to resist the second or the third. But one could equally well say that to succumb to any of these failures is a way of succumbing to the third; and to succumb to the third amounts to an abdication of one's primary responsibilities as a philosopher. For the question of what philosophy is just *is* philosophy's defining question – the question it can never leave behind and never definitively answer (because all its other questions sooner or later lead back to it, and so either open or reopen it, by inviting us to question whether our assumptions about how to approach those more specific questions are themselves beyond question).

This, I take it, is why Stanley Cavell has said:

> To my way of thinking the creation of film was as if meant for philosophy – meant to reorient everything philosophy has said about reality and its representation, about art and imitation, about greatness and conventionality, about judgement and pleasure, about scepticism and transcendence, about language and expression.[12]

His point here is not just that the projection of these pairs of predicates to encompass the new phenomenon of film will reorient our sense of their significance in their more familiar applications to other artistic or representational phenomena such as painting or theatre or language in general, and so will be of indirect significance for the philosophy of art or the philosophy of language. For those predicates are also familiarly applied to philosophy itself, as such and in general, in its more or less well-judged and (un)conventional attempts to transcend scepticism and capture reality itself in its own distinctive discourse, whatever the specific phenomenon to which it has turned its attention. So film's reorientation of the trajectory of those predicates will inevitably reorient our sense of the significance of philosophy itself; or, rather, it will if we let it – if that possibility is truly open to and in our way of thinking, as it is in Cavell's.

Reasons for resistance: film

What, then, of those readers who found my treatment of the possible relation between film and philosophy more questionable in its apparent assumptions about film than about philosophy?

One recurrent concern is related to what one might call the specificity or narrowness of my focus. One critic was concerned by my apparently exclusive preoccupation with representational films, wondering whether this amounted to an *a priori* exclusion of films made without recourse to such conventions or conditions from any possible relevance to philosophy.[13] That was certainly not my intention: in making a case for the philosophical pertinence of some mainstream, Hollywood, representational films I took myself primarily to be making life difficult for myself. The thought was roughly: 'If films of this kind can be discovered to be philosophically significant, then which films might not?' I have no objection, whether *a priori* or *a posteriori*, to the thought that some non-representational films might also have such significance; I simply haven't in fact explored that possibility.

Other critics took my emphasis on the identity of the directors of the films I examined to be indicative of a commitment to some version of the auteur theory of film[14] – a perspective that has become increasingly unpopular in recent years in the domain of film studies, being held to run counter to the obviously communal nature of film production – rather than (as I explicitly claimed in the introduction to the first edition) of an interest in exploring the strengths and weaknesses inherent in any such perspective. Here I can do no better than to cite some words on the topic by Stanley Cavell:

> What I think is that the arts differ, that directors of film differ, and differ in the amount of control they intend to exercise; that intention and control remain seriously under-analyzed concepts in these contexts; that my allusions to a director's intentions leave its exercise wide open to investigation – he or she may have a hand in setting up each camera angle … play most of the parts, and develop each print; or he or she might extensively

delegate some or all of these matters ...; or ... dispense with one or another such task ... and subject remaining tasks to communal settlement; or there may be a committee ... that tells the director pretty much what to do in each dimension. ... As long as a reference to a director by name suggests differences between the films associated with that name and one associated with other names, the reference is, so far as I can see, intellectually grounded. It may be intellectually thin in a given instance. But that is more or less pitiable, not a matter for metaphysical alarm. And how about names associated with writers, actors, cinematographers, designers, studios? The intellectual warrant remains in each case the power in a given instance to show a difference. I wish I knew enough to invoke them all.[15]

Another reader was tempted to suggest that my book was in fact about the relation between philosophy and science fiction: that is, that it was not just not a book about philosophy and film as such, but also not even a book about philosophy and science fiction films.[16] This seems to me somewhat to downplay the various points at which my discussions of other work by each of my four directors takes me beyond the generic limits of the *Alien* series; and I hope that my choice of the *Mission: Impossible* series as the focus of discussion in Part III of this second edition of the book offers some reassurance that the phenomena that interest me can indeed be found outside the genre of science fiction. But I take it that a central part of this reader's worry had to do with what he perceived as a relative lack of attention on my part to the specifically cinematic aspects of the science fiction films I discussed; the suggestion was that I might as well have been discussing science fiction novels as science fiction films. And other readers recorded similar impressions: one talked of my focus on 'dialogue, character development, narrative and star persona' as opposed to 'more film-specific features like cinematography, editing, and mise-en-scène';[17] another encouraged me to 'become more responsive to the materiality of film, to its haptic qualities: colour, rhythm, light, sound, the plastics of the medium'.[18]

The broader worry that these objections might generate would run as follows. If my case that films can philosophize rests upon readings of films which concentrate on their deployment of features and powers that are not distinctively cinematic, then I cannot possibly succeed in showing that philosophizing is a possibility of film *qua* film. To adapt an example from another philosopher of film: my argument would then be analogous to one which attempted to demonstrate that films can philosophize by pointing out that one could make a film of a philosopher giving a lecture on scepticism about other minds. In other words, it would reduce to a triviality. It can only avoid that fate, so this line of criticism would continue, by showing how exclusively cinematic stylistic devices or modes of expression can make a contribution to philosophy. And that, of course, would be no easy achievement: one might even think that any such position would inevitably face a dilemma. For either the specific philosophical contribution made by some particular deployment of a specifically cinematic resource can be paraphrased – that is, be given coherent and accurate linguistic expression – or it cannot. If it can be paraphrased, then it cannot be a contribution that can be made only by the deployment of that cinematic resource (since the paraphrase alone would suffice); but if it cannot, then one might reasonably doubt whether this 'contribution' is really there at all, and it would anyway be hard to see how it could possibly contribute to philosophy (which is, after all, an essentially discursive enterprise).[19]

How might one respond to this constellation of anxieties? To begin with, I would again be inclined to suggest that the first edition of my book in fact contains rather more detailed analyses of the distinctively cinematic aspects of the films under discussion than these responses imply. I might, for example, point to the analysis of the opening sequence of *Alien*, as well as to certain scenes in *Blade Runner*; to the discussion of the role of the photograph of Sarah Connor in *Terminator*; to the salience given to Fincher's use of editing in his title sequence and the funeral sequence in *Alien*[3]; and to the characterization of Jeunet's camera angle, set design and staging in *Alien Resurrection* as expressive of a child's caricatural vision of the adult world. These are not, in my

149

view, minor elements in the patterning of what was of necessity (given the parameters of the Thinking in Action series) a rather short book.

I would emphasize in addition the number of instances in which I argue that, by using the resources of dialogue, character development and narrative, my films manifest a reflective engagement with what I called the conditions for the possibility of cinema – that is, a concern to think about the material basis of the medium (i.e. photography), the distinctively cinematic resources it makes available to those who work within it (the specific relation between actor and character, between the space and time of the film and the space and time of the viewer, the idea of stardom, and so on) and the specific kinds of artistic achievement those resources make possible. In other words, I repeatedly claim to find that my films reflect thoughtfully upon the nature of exclusively cinematic resources, even if they typically do not do so exclusively by the thoughtful deployment of those resources. So what my critics regard as the essence of cinema is often at the centre of my (and my films') concerns, even when the vehicles or means of its reflective investigation are not themselves embodiments of that essence.

With those qualifications in place, I would not wish to deny the relative prominence of dialogue, character development and plot in my readings of these films. But I would wish to deny the suggestion that in giving detailed attention to these aspects of my films I am not attending to them as films. For why should the fact that a given expressive resource is not unique to cinema entail that it is not one of cinema's expressive resources? Suppose we take a parallel case. Dialogue is an expressive resource of the novelist, but it is also one deployed by the playwright. Does that mean that a literary critic who attends to the use of dialogue in Dickens' novels is not thereby attending to his novels qua novels? Dialogue is also an expressive resource that some novelists either largely or entirely dispense with: one can certainly imagine a novel which was devoid of dialogue altogether. Does that mean that a literary critic who attends to the use of dialogue in Dickens' novels is not thereby attending to an essential dimension of Dickens' novelistic art?

In short, I see no reason to assume that any reading of a film which found its contribution to philosophy to reside in its deployment of resources that are not exclusive to cinema would thereby reduce itself to a triviality. To say that the dialogue of a film is essential to its philosophical interest is not equivalent to saying that a film is philosophically interesting because it records a dialogue between two professional philosophers in an academic seminar. For understanding the particular way in which a non-exclusively cinematic expressive resource is deployed in a film might nevertheless prove to be essential to understanding its nature as a film; and in certain cases what is thereby understood might be the way that film bears upon and contributes to philosophy. In such cases, the philosophical dimension of the film would be no less intrinsic to it as a film, no less determinative of its identity as a specific work of cinematic art, simply because the expressive resources deployed by its director to articulate that dimension of its significance might also be deployed in other artistic media, and might even be deployed there to make the same philosophical point. And that is why the 'dilemma of para-phraseability' mentioned above is essentially untroubling; for why should the fact that the philosophical significance of a cine-matic artwork is articulable in language be thought to cause dif-ficulty for the claim that it has that philosophical significance, and that its having that significance is essential to it? On the face of it, what is essential to a work of art's being what it is need not involve the deployment of what are deemed to be resources exclusive to its distinctive artistic medium.

That there are such distinctively cinematic resources need not be denied; and, in acknowledging that, we must acknowledge that their availability might decisively alter the expressive possi-bilities of non-exclusive cinematic resources – as the significance of dialogue in motion pictures is distinctively determinable by the various ways in which the soundtrack and the moving image of a film might be synchronized (or desynchronized). But hovering in the background of any such discussion of distinctively cine-matic expressive resources is a question about the relation between those resources and the material basis of the cinematic medium. More precisely, one might wonder whether or not the material basis of cinema determines its essential nature as a medium, and thereby determines what will count as distinctively cinematic artistic resources and achievements. Some of my critical readers have assumed that, insofar as I pay too little attention to the expressive resources that are specific to film, I neglect its material basis – its 'haptic qualities' of colour, rhythm, light and sound. Others have assumed that, on the contrary, I have oriented all of my specific readings around a set of very specific, Cavellian assumptions about the material basis of cinema (understood as photographic) and derived therefrom a rather too tightly focussed conception of what is genuinely specific to the medium of cinema, and so of what must inform any genuinely artistic achievements within it. I want to suggest that both lines of criticism are essentially misplaced.

Following Cavell, I certainly do take the concept of a medium to be indispensable in differentiating kinds of art work, and in understanding specific instances of those kinds; but our use of that concept must be understood as applying not simply to a physical material but to a material-in-certain-characteristic-applications, and hence as having a necessarily dual sense. For instance, the claim that sound is the medium of music would be empty in the absence of the art of composing and playing music. Musical works of art are not the result of applications of a medium that can be defined by its independently given possibilities; for it is only through the artist's successful production of something we are prepared to call a musical work of art that the artistic possibilities of that physical material are discovered, maintained and explored. And such possibilities of sound, without which it would not count as an artistic medium, are themselves media of music – ways in which various sources of sound have been applied to create specific artistic achievements, e.g. in plainsong, the fugue, the aria, sonata form. They are the strains of convention through which composers have been able to create, performers to practice and audiences to acknowledge specific works of art.

My Cavellian account of cinema involves a parallel dual deployment of the concept of a medium in relation to that of its material basis. In his first book on film, *The World Viewed*, Cavell begins by analysing the material basis of film (in terms of photography in its relation to reality); he then characterizes the medium of film in terms prompted by that analysis (as a succession of automatic world projections); and he goes on to identify various film media – that is, a range of character types and genres whose particular applications in good movies disclose the artistic potential of these media in this medium. But the overarching order of exposition here does not reflect the order of excavation or derivation in Cavell's work, and so is potentially misleading.

For this is not an instance of what is generally called an argument from medium-specificity – that is, it is not an attempt to read off an art form's generic and specific possibilities from the independently given properties of its medium.[20] The terms of Cavell's idiosyncratic specification of the medium of film are not read off from merely material properties of photography, but rather accrue their very particular sense from his critical interpretations of specific films and specific achievements of film. And the same is true of his characterizations of the various media of film. For example, his work has famously focussed on two genres that he was the first to identify: the comedy of remarriage and the melodrama of the unknown woman. But he does not approach the matter by first specifying the features necessary and sufficient for genre membership and then testing individual candidate films against that specification. Rather, each member is seen as mounting a critical study of the conventions hitherto seen as definitive of that genre (say, by establishing that the absence of one such convention can be compensated for in certain ways); it thereby discovers new possibilities of that generic medium, and hence of the medium of film as such.

My own work is intended to operate in a parallel way. I am committed to the thought that the medium of cinema has distinctive possibilities; but my working assumption is that these possibilities can be discovered as such only through an artistic achievement in that medium whose significance is to be understood as exploiting that possibility, and as thereby acknowledging some aspect of its material basis. Similarly, in thinking of the four *Alien* movies as engaging in a critical dialogue about the Alien universe, I take the basic conventions or conditions of that universe not as determined in advance of the conversation, but as to be determined by it – as Fincher's *Alien*[3] determines that Cameron's idea of Ripley's participation in family life is not only inessential to but actually subversive of her identity and so of any truthful engagement with the reality she inhabits, and as *Alien vs Predator* determines that the presence of members of the alien species in a film does not automatically admit it to membership of the series, but can at best establish them as inhabiting a parallel universe.

Two points are worth emphasizing in conclusion. First, the specific terminology employed here – the dual notion of a medium of cinema, as well as the particular terms in which its possibilities and its material basis are characterized – is not to be taken as theory-laden, as if authorized only by the authority of some supposed Cavellian ontology of film, any more than my frequent use of the term 'reality' presupposes a particular metaphysical stance or my use of the term 'truth' presupposes a particular theory of truth. Their use in my book (as in Cavell's books) is justified to precisely the extent to which its readers are willing to accept their projection into the specific contexts in which I find myself inclined or compelled to employ them in order to account for my experience of specific films, and so to acknowledge them as intelligible projections of utterly everyday words. Hence, second, the legitimacy of the claims I make about the medium and media of film, and about its material basis, ultimately depends upon a willingness to accept my specific readings of particular films as true to (our experience of) them, and so as successful acts of critical interpretation. In other words, everything comes down once again to the credibility of specific acts of critical judgement; as I tried to elucidate in the previous section, the justificatory burden of my whole enterprise is carried by the claims I make about the specific films under discussion.

The spontaneous generation of a mouse

Now, however, a concluding reflexive worry arises. If the extreme, insubstantial brevity of my book's introduction in comparison to its four main chapters really was internal to my conception of the project I had embarked upon, have I not now allowed certain predictable misunderstandings of it to tempt me into betraying that conception by writing a supplementary chapter such as this – in which I discuss general conceptual questions about the nature of philosophy and of film in abstraction from detailed readings of particular films? I would rather claim that this chapter is an attempt to clear away certain misconceptions that seem in retrospect to have prevented at least some of my readers from looking more closely, and in the right mood or spirit, at the book I actually wrote. My aim here has not been to articulate and defend any general views of my own about either film or philosophy that I (carelessly or carefully) left implicit in the first edition of my book, but rather to identify and put in question a range of assumptions about what film and philosophy must be whose apparent prevalence has helped to occlude the kinds of possibilities that my book always aspired to realize. Of course, those original chapters may, even on closer examination, turn out to be no more than a heap of grey rags and dust; but at least this chapter – rightly understood – should not be regarded as adding to the heap, but rather as trying to remove certain obstacles to any such examination.

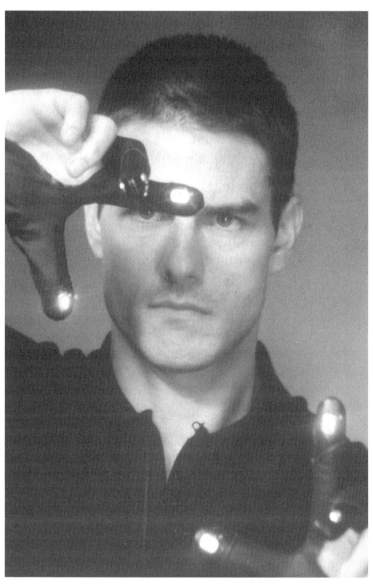

Source: 20th Century Fox/Dreamworks courtesy the Kobal Collection

6

PRECRIME, PRECOGNITION AND THE PRE-REFLECTIVE COGITO

Steven Spielberg's *Minority Report*

If Chapter 5 essentially looked backwards, aiming to remove certain obstacles to a proper appreciation of the nature of my project in the first edition of this book, then this chapter aims to look forward – to prepare the ground for Part III of this second edition in a number of useful ways.

To begin with, since Part II of this book is, in effect, transitional in its nature – being my attempt to forge a natural link between the main body of the first edition (now Part I) and the new but equally concrete material that constitutes the heart of the second edition (its Part III) – I did not want it to consist solely of a more general, and so inevitably a more abstract, discussion of film and philosophy. For even though, as I noted at the end of Chapter 5, that discussion has a purely negative purpose (one of clearing away misunderstandings rather than constructing a positive theoretical system of any kind), it nevertheless might appear to betray my central concern throughout this project – namely, to give priority to the particular: to specific films and my experience of them. So this chapter is designed to correct that imbalance within Part II taken as a whole, and thereby to ensure that this guiding methodological commitment stays at the centre of my readers' attention.

But why *this* particular film? First, viewed as a hybrid or synthesis of the genres of science fiction and crime thriller, *Minority Report* (Steven Spielberg, 2002) will help to facilitate the transition from my primary concern with varieties of science fiction films in Part I of this book to my central focus on a series of espionage thrillers in Part III (thus helping to dispel any anxiety that my intuition of an internal relationship between philosophy and film applies only to the domain of science fiction). Second, since the star of Minority Report is also the star of the Mission: Impossible series, this chapter will also initiate a change of focus in the book's investigation of the condition of cinematic stardom – from Sigourney Weaver to Tom Cruise. And finally, given the prefatory or preparatory role I wish this discussion to have, it is striking how far Minority Report makes a variety of uses of the 'pre-' prefix, but particularly the idea of a preview or prevision, central to its own reflective concerns. To see that, however, we must turn to the film itself.

Absolute metaphysics: PreCrime and moral luck

In the middle decades of the twenty-first century, the USA is about to decide whether to implement at the national level a police and judicial system known as 'PreCrime'. By utilizing information embodied in visions of the future experienced by three mutant humans called 'precogs', this special police unit has been able to identify murderers before they commit their crimes, immobilize them with a headpiece known as a 'halo' and incarcerate them in a state of suspended animation for the duration of their sentence. During its trial period of operation in the District of Columbia, PreCrime has almost entirely eliminated cases of premeditated murder. Homicidal crimes of passion continue to occur, and other crimes such as theft and assault, which are less 'destructive of the metaphysical fabric that binds us than the untimely murder of one human being by another' (as one of PreCrime's founders puts it), are, thus far, beyond or beneath the precogs' foresight; but, within its parameters, Pre-Crime has evinced no flaws, and its leaders are eager to expand its range. Minority Report begins at this moment of national decision, which has prompted the Department of Justice to send an emissary named Danny Witwer (Colin Farrell) to assess (and perhaps take over) the PreCrime system for itself, and at which the Chief of the unit (named John Anderton [Tom Cruise]) confronts a precognitive vision of himself murdering a man he doesn't even know. The scene is set for another Hollywood science fiction blockbuster based on the paranoid imagination of Philip K. Dick.[1]

Witwer's fascination with PreCrime is not just a matter of individual and departmental self-interest. He is exercised by what he calls 'the legalistic drawback to PreCrime methodology' – the fact that precriminals are incarcerated despite not actually having committed any crime; and he is also impressed by the ways in which people have begun to deify the precogs. Both issues resonate with him because of his religious background: he spent three years in a seminary before joining the police, and then the Justice Department, and he always carries a rosary. But their salience is not simply an expression of his idiosyncrasies. The PreCrime policemen are plainly familiar with, even wearied by the need to respond once again to, Witwer's legal and moral qualms; and they (perhaps shamefacedly) admit to their Chief that they think of themselves, in their entanglement with matters of destiny, as more like clergy than cops. Anderton is the most articulate advocate of the genuine criminality of their arrestees; but he is equally unyielding in his rejection of any religious interpretation of the precogs. The early debate between Witwer and Anderton over both issues – the failed priest contending with the resolute materialist – sets the agenda for the rest of the movie.

What, exactly, is the difference between a criminal and a pre-criminal? Is this understood in and by the film to be a matter of action as opposed to intention, as if criminals actually execute an illegal plan that precriminals merely formulate and resolve (perhaps with unusual purity) to implement? The relation between intention and action has been at the heart of much modern controversy in moral philosophy, in large part because of Kant's highly influential arguments to the effect that the morally relevant essence of action is in fact intention – the orientation of one's will, over which he argues that we have complete responsibility, as opposed to the bodily movements that constitute the action itself together with the consequences of that action in the wider world, over which he argues that we lack control, and hence for which he claims that we should not be regarded as answerable.

The issue has crystallized around the question of whether there can be such a thing as moral luck – whether we can make sense of the idea that matters lying outside our control (such as the apparently significant ways in which what we bring about in the world outruns or otherwise escapes the rein of our intentions in acting) might legitimately be deemed to alter our moral status. For example, is the moral status of a would-be murderer affected by the fact that his long-prepared, perfectly aimed bullet fails to kill the President because it happens to hit a bird that swoops across the line of fire? Why should a would-be murderer whose failure actually to kill is a matter of luck or contingency of this kind be regarded as any less guilty, from a moral point of view, than a would-be murderer whose plans are not so thwarted? And yet, what could be more morally significant than whether or not a given person has actually killed someone? For to be a murderer is surely to be responsible for another's death; and whatever might be said of the unsuccessful would-be murderer, he has not actually killed anyone.

Kant's sensitivity to this issue is unsurprising given his Christian upbringing and culture. He would, for example, be familiar with the following, canonical passage from the Sermon on the Mount:

> Ye have heard that it was said by them of old time, Thou shalt not commit adultery: But I say unto you, That whosoever looketh on a woman to lust after her hath committed adultery with her already in his heart.[2]

If, then, the Kantian way with moral luck appears designed drastically to restrict the realm of moral responsibility, and so to make it easier to be virtuous, its Christian inflection brings out the way in which it can drastically increase the scope of the self's moral surveillance of itself. It is a small step from the thought that intention is the essence of action to the thought that intention is action, and hence inhabits an interior domain that is subject to all the strictures that are primarily applicable to actions alone. As Nietzsche noted, such a vision hardly makes it easier for the self to live with itself.

Spielberg carefully makes the implicit religious resonance of Witwer's apparently legalistic moral qualms all but unavoidable by centring the opening sequence of the film, which follows a particularly dramatic 'redball' case (in which the PreCrime unit receives precognitive warning of a crime only minutes before its unpremeditated commission), around an attempted murder provoked by a spouse's acts of adultery. Indeed, the impending ocular trials of John Anderton, who later resorts to backstreet surgical removal and replacement of his eyes in his attempts to escape from the authorities and their retinal-recognition scanning systems, and so to avoid the PreCrime containment facilities (what he will describe as 'rotting in hell with a halo'), will seem less unpredictable – even predetermined – to those aware that the passage from Matthew I just cited continues with the following, equally notorious divine injunction: 'And if thy right eye offend thee, pluck it out, and cast it from thee; for it is profitable for thee that one of thy members should perish, and not that thy whole body should be cast into hell'.

But our present concern is this. When the PreCrime unit intervenes at the last possible moment to prevent Leo Marks from killing his adulterous wife and her lover, should this be seen as a piece of good luck for the previctims alone, or also for the precriminal? Why not regard Leo as having, whether by the grace of God or by happy accident, thereby avoided a fate to which he might otherwise have succumbed – that of actually becoming a murderer? Or does the very narrowness of the gap between intention and action in this case – the fact that the diversion of the scissors' trajectory from human flesh to window-glass occurs only at the very last second   rather reinforce John Anderton's conviction that Marks should be treated just as one would treat an actual murderer? If the PreCrime unit's interventions prevent crimes from happening, should they be seen as preventing actual criminals from having their usual deleterious impact in the world, or rather as preventing people from actually becoming criminals?

Part of the interest of this film is that it begins by highlighting the possibility that such questions are based on a misunderstanding of the nature of precriminality. For the PreCrime police deny from the outset that the difference between a precriminal and a criminal is the difference between someone who intends to commit a crime and someone who actually does so. To be sure,

precriminals have not actually committed a crime – one of the
police declares that 'the commission of the crime itself is absolute
metaphysics' – but neither have they merely intended to do so; a
precriminal is someone who not only intended to commit a
crime, but who actually would have done so in the absence of the
PreCrime unit's intervention. As Anderton puts it, 'the precogs
don't see what you intend to do, only what you will do'. So the
PreCrime unit's actions cannot be regarded as one amongst a
range of happy accidents that might prevent Leo Marks from
becoming a murderer; the unit is only ever in a position to
intervene if the successful implementation of his intention is
beyond the reach of such accidents.

In other words, to block Witwer's legal and moral qualms,
the PreCrime system has to invoke a strong notion of predetermination – something that offends Witwer's sense of human
freedom to have done otherwise, but which Anderton regards as
utterly commonplace. For him, 'predetermination happens all the
time'; and he illustrates this by rolling a wooden ball along the rim
of a semi-circular desk in the control room. Witwer instinctively
catches the ball as it rolls over the end of the desk, initiating the
following exchange with Anderton: 'Why did you do that?';
'Because it was going to fall'; 'Are you sure?'; 'Certain'; 'But it
didn't.'

The film gives Anderton the last word in this exchange, but its
conjunction of word and image goes rather less decisively in his
favour. For the ball is one of those on which the names of precriminals and previctims are incised as part of the process of
transcribing the precog's visions and validating the PreCrime
unit's actions; and the curving rim of the desk brings immediately to mind the image of a roulette wheel. So Anderton's absolute belief in the absolute metaphysics of precriminality hangs
together with a vision of individuals as akin to physical objects,
mere matter in motion. We might construct a game of chance,
involving the calculation of probabilities as well as intuition and
courage, around the entangled trajectories of ball and wheel, but
the outcome of the throw of the ball is not in reality a matter of
gambling, but one of utter certainty. All we need to attain such
certainty about the ball's destination (it might be thought) is

enough of the right kind of information about the physical properties of ball and wheel; and all we need to attain the same kind of certainty about human beings, Anderton implies, is the kind of information provided by the precogs.

The conceptual problem here is not that we ordinarily regard human beings' actions as essentially unpredictable: as Hume pointed out, if we could not reliably predict another's actions in a range of circumstances on the basis of our knowledge of her character, then our relations with other human beings would be very different, and our idea of human beings as possessed of a character would be under grave pressure. But there is a difference between predictability and predetermination. For example, predictability hangs together with the idea of room for reasonable doubt, just as being possessed of a character is compatible with, indeed partly determines, the idea of being capable of doing things out of character; whereas predetermination of the kind Anderton invokes in his comparison of people with balls on a roulette table excludes such discontinuities between character, intention and action, as causal laws are thought to exclude any insufficiency of cause to effect. But Anderton in fact lacks any body of causal laws, together with any sufficiently large body of information subject to organization by such laws, that might apply to the human beings he convicts. His future world is not one in which Laplace's vision of physical (or more generally natural scientific) predetermination, of a kind that would make human freedom an unnecessary hypothesis, has been realized; all that Anderton has is the visions of the precogs.

Of course, the film does provide us with a natural scientific story about the precogs. They are the offspring of neuroin addicts who had ingested an impure version of that drug; it affects the user's neurological systems, and these unlucky addicts gave birth to children whose brains and nervous systems were severely affected by a consequent mutation at the genetic level. A team of scientists attempting to heal them discovered that the sleep of those few children who survived beyond the age of twelve was regularly disrupted by nightmares that had them clawing at the walls of their bedrooms; as one member of the team puts it, 'they dreamt only of murder over and over, one after the other; and the real nightmare was that these so-called dreams were about to come true, the murders were actually happening'. Having noted these correlations between dream and future reality, the three children – Arthur, Dashiell and Agatha (Samantha Morton), the most gifted – were transferred to a room known as the Temple, and are permanently kept in a state midway between waking and sleeping, floating in a pool of photon milk that simultaneously supplies them with nutrients and enhances the images they receive, the three individual streams of which are analysed and synthesized by a complex array of computers to provide the evidential basis for the PreCrime unit's efforts to avert the future they envision.

This certainly seems like a resolutely materialist version of the aetiology and management of an oracle: on the one hand, bodily traces of chemical self-abuse and genetic mutation; on the other, the gleaming lines and pulsing lights of hi-tech medical care and data analysis. In this world, the medium of prophecy is electrical activity, in a way which undercuts the distinction between the organic and the inorganic. But, ultimately, the ability of these mutants to precognize the future, the uncanny fit between their dreams and tomorrow's reality, remains as mysterious to us as it was to the Ancient Greeks, who after all knew perfectly well which herbs best transported their Pythia into her visionary state, and who were no less aware of the practical uses of the knowledge they imparted. Twenty-first century science might be able to diagnose the preconditions for the exercise of their oracles' ability in unprecedented depth, and its technology might provide unprecedentedly efficient ways of recording and making use of its results; but invoking genetics and neurology gives us no answer at all to the question: how can their dreams possibly be visions of the future?

And yet, for the PreCrime system to work, its functionaries must place an unqualified degree of confidence in the essentially inexplicable correlation between the precogs' visions and what will happen. If one thought that their seeing the commission of a crime only made it likely that it would happen – if, in other words, there were room for reasonable doubt that the future would match the content of these visions – then no reasonable person would feel confident about any convictions for pre-criminality. After all, we can make plausible predictions about another's behaviour in many cases even without the benefit of precognition; but we would not countenance punishing them solely on that basis, when they had not yet committed any crime. So any conviction for precriminality requires the exclusion of doubt; it requires an absolute degree of conviction about the future (and so about the reliability of the precogs' access to that future). Hence, Anderton's absolute belief in PreCrime demands a correspondingly absolute belief in the essentially mysterious veracity of the precogs and their visions. In short, it requires faith.

The law of the Father: secular religion as a family drama

So Witwer's legal and moral qualms about PreCrime cannot be separated from his sense of the religious dimension of precognition. We can also see that the stances of the two debaters with respect to that second issue are rather more complex than they might at first appear. For if Anderton's resolute materialism (epitomized in his claim that the precogs are 'just pattern-recognition filters') turns out to depend upon a quasi-religious faith in the prophetic utterances of his science-embedded oracles, Witwer's awareness of the quasi-religious role and significance of the precogs is conjoined with a sceptical, verging on cynical, stance towards them and the system of justice erected upon them.

The film certainly invites us to share in the tendency to deify the precogs: they inhabit a temple, and the policemen waiting upon their visions are closer to clergy than cops; the precriminals they help to identify join a vast array of other haloed, comatose miscreants whose sleeping minds constantly replay the precognized images of their crimes in a penal parody of purgatory or hell; and the people of Washington, DC erect statues in their honour, venerate their powers and are encouraged to imagine them living an idyllic, even paradisal life within the PreCrime headquarters.

But Witwer is a failed priest, whose loss of faith is connected with the murder of his father; he doesn't accept that the precogs' status is genuinely divine, although he understands why so many people might be tempted to deify the merely human: 'science has stolen most of our miracles; in a way [the precogs] give us hope – hope of the existence of the divine'. In other words, there is a poetic justice in the emergence of godlike powers from 'the unintended consequences of a series of genetic mistakes and science gone haywire'; science, that thief of miracles, miraculously turns out to have a prophetic soul. But Witwer also understands the politics of religion: 'the oracle isn't where the power is; power is always with the priests, even if they have to invent the oracle'.

Whereas Anderton believes absolutely in the veracity of the precogs, and so in their status as oracles, Witwer suspects that the priests – that is, the PreCrime system based upon them – have invented it. He cannot accept that anything human is ultimately beyond doubt or error: 'there's a flaw; it's human; it always is'. And his suspicions are justified, because it turns out that every so often one of the three precogs produces a minority report – a vision of the future which fails to mesh with that of the other two, and which thereby raises the possibility of alternative futures for putative precriminals. This is what leads Anderton to invade the Temple and kidnap the most gifted of the precogs – to see whether her mind contains a minority report on his apparently murderous future; and it is the need to suppress any awareness of that possibility that leads one of the founders of PreCrime to attempt to ensure that Anderton himself will rot in hell with a halo, by implanting a vision of his future as murderous and arranging reality so that Anderton will realize that vision.

But, ironically, these confirmations of Witwer's suspicion also make manifest its quasi-religious nature. For Witwer is convinced of the fallibility of PreCrime even before any evidence is available to ground it, because he has an absolute belief in the fallibility of human beings – in what his seminary instructors would have called the originally flawed or sinful nature of humankind. Recall his instinctive reaction to the rolling wooden ball: he tries to prevent it from falling, but he is absolutely certain that it (like any and all of the fallible human beings it stands for in the PreCrime system) would fall. In this respect, Witwer and Anderton share a conception of metaphysical predetermination: the former's may face backwards and the latter's forwards, as the idea of erring origins opposes that of errors foreseen, but both men have faith in the taintedness of human nature.

If, however, human nature is fallen, then human religious institutions, as well as their quasi-scientific substitutes, will inevitably be tainted by the fallenness they proclaim. And such is the picture of PreCrime that is painted in Minority Report. For Anderton's attempts to evade his own fate reveal that this apparently incorruptible system of saving lives and dispensing dispassionate justice is founded upon destroying lives and subverting justice. The origins of PreCrime lie in a humane medical research project, jointly led by Lamar Burgess (Max Von Sydow) and Zora Hinneman (Lois Smith), into the mutant offspring of neuroin addicts. The aim was to heal them, to help them overcome the pain and suffering they inherited as a result of their parents' freely chosen destruction of their own freedom. But once the correlation between the survivors' dreams and future reality was noted, Burgess fathered PreCrime by betraying Hinneman's maternal concern for healing, and instead condemned the three precogs to a permanent state of subjection to their murderous, nightmarish dreams. It is indeed better not to think of them as human; for a human life reduced to endless night, in which they cannot even express their suffering by clawing at the walls, is barely recognizable as such.

Burgess' betrayal is, however, both more specific and more general than this: more general, in that he condemns all precriminals to a purgatory of immersion in their own most wicked imaginings, despite knowing that the precog visions lack the indubitability their judicial significance presupposes; more specific, in that he chooses to murder Agatha's natural mother (Ann Lively) rather than lose his most gifted mutant, when Ann manages to overcome her addiction, and returns to reclaim her child. He does so by hiring a drifter to attempt to murder Ann, allowing the PreCrime unit to intervene on the basis of a precognition of the crime, and then himself actually murdering her exactly as the drifter had planned and the precogs foreseen. For, when this murder was itself foreseen, it would appear to be merely an echo of the earlier prevision – an anomaly known to the PreCrime technicians as 'precog déjà-vu' – and hence eliminated as meaningless. In other words, Burgess not only founds his system for eliminating murder on a murder; he does so by exploiting a flaw in his supposedly flawless system, and by using its key oracle to murder her own mother. That this murder also eliminates a living counterexample to the idea of human predetermination, someone who proved capable of freeing herself from her freely chosen unfreedom, could only have made his plan more appealing.

But, of course, as Witwer would expect, Burgess' self-subverting creative act was not destined to remain an isolated deed. For although the second prevision of Ann Lively's murder could be eliminated from the PreCrime system, it could not be eliminated from the dreaming mind of its original recipient; so the night-mare of her own mother's murder endlessly recurs amidst the onslaught of murderous nightmares to which Agatha's managed condition subjects her, until she draws it to John Anderton's attention. And Burgess is thereby forced to repeat his original founding act, at precisely the moment of PreCrime's refounding as a national project, and so of the refounding or reconstitution of America. Preserving his system of perfect justice once again requires that its founder rededicate himself to injustice, that he bury the body of another surrogate child in its basement and rebury his original surrogate child, condemning Agatha once again to an existence that is neither death nor life.

One might think that what PreCrime lacks is a mother's influ-ence – that its internal perversions are a manifestation of the law of the Father, and that these might be corrected by the presence of a more Maternal inflection or conception of nature, justice and divinity. After all, the self-described mother of Precrime dissociates herself from Burgess' scheme, retreats into a retirement apparently devoted to cultivating her garden, and castigates her ex-partner in Anderton's presence for his treatment of the precogs. And her claim to healing purpose is apparently underwritten by the film, since she makes it whilst brewing the cup of herbal tea without which Anderton's encounter with the animated foliage of a doll's-eye plant in her garden would have been lethal.

On the other hand, it was Hinneman who placed that potentially fatal plant at the borders of her property in the first place; and her greenhouse includes other plants with similarly aggressive tendencies, quite as if her primary recreation is to cultivate the natural world in this particular direction, devoting all her thwarted scientific energies to the task of ensuring or revealing that nature's bloodthirstiness extends beyond tooth and claw to leaf and root. Indeed, she makes a point of showing Anderton how one of these disconcertingly animate plants will draw blood from her palm when she squeezes it too tightly, in order to draw the moral that 'all living organisms are alike: when the chips are down, every creature on the earth is interested in one thing only – its own survival'. If this is true, then it applies not only to Anderton but to Hinneman herself, suggesting an awareness on her part that her retirement involved sacrificing the well-being of her precog children to her own desire for security and survival. And it further implies a complete disbelief in the very idea of justice – a conception of it as essentially superficial and ultimately contrary to nature, nothing more than a constitutive delusion of those peculiar animals in whose nature it lies to engender culture and to identify themselves with its transforming powers.

We may not find Burgess' vision of absolute justice to our taste; but would we prefer a world from which justice was excluded in principle? It may be worth remembering that when, at the film's conclusion, Burgess is confronted with a choice between destroying the PreCrime system and murdering Anderton, he chooses to destroy both the system and himself; for his act of suicide falsifies the precog vision of him shooting his protégé and surrogate son, the man from whom he asks forgiveness with his final breath. Hinneman, by contrast, encourages Anderton to risk his eyesight and his existence to bring about the absolute destruction of her spiritual husband and his creation, on what turns out to be the erroneous assumption that Agatha contains a minority report concerning his own fate; and she sends him on this quest with a disturbingly sexual kiss on the lips, as if invoking the Oedipal prospect of what mother and son might permit themselves in the absence of the hated and envied father. Nevertheless, by offering us a concluding image of Anderton reunited with his wife, and looking forward to the birth of a child, the film leaves it open to us to view the equal and opposite deformations of the father and the mother of PreCrime as a function of their isolation, and hence as overcomable in some conceivable mode of marriage or mutual grafting, call it a form of genuinely human culture or cultivation.

The non-identical self: Anderton and Agatha, Descartes and Sartre

If Burgess and Hinneman are the father and mother of PreCrime, then one might think of both Agatha Lively and John Anderton as their children. At one point, Hinneman remarks that 'parents see their children as they want them to be, and not as they are'. How, then, should we, the viewers of this film, see Anderton and Agatha? What do we want them to be, and what – beyond that pressure of expectation and desire – are they shown to be?

Suppose we begin with Anderton. How did he acquire his faith in precognitive predetermination? Why does precriminality seem to him to be such a compelling category, a way in which to penetrate to the essence of human existence? Burgess supplies one answer to this question, when he characterizes Anderton's commitment to PreCrime as one 'born out of pain, not politics'; for, as the film gradually reveals (reserving its most detailed rendering of the matter for Anderton's recovery from his eye surgery, when he is at once devoid of vision and least distracted from introspection and insight), six years previously Anderton's son had disappeared when he was in his father's care, at a public swimming pool. Between one second and the next, with his submerged father distracted by the admiring gaze of a woman swimming past him, Sean Anderton vanishes, leaving behind him the wristwatch he borrowed from his father, which we follow as it floats lazily down through the rippling distortions of the water to its owner, signalling that, for him, time is about to stop.

The consequence is not exactly that Anderton becomes motionless: on the contrary, he is shown to be as hyperactive as any of Tom Cruise's other cinematic incarnations, whether in his professional life or in his more private moments (which, when not given over to jogging obsessively through the Sprawl, are devoted to restlessly reviewing the holographic records of his son's childhood). The question the film poses is rather: does this activity count as action, as Anderton's way of enacting a genuinely human form of existence? Its answer is 'No'; but what interests me here is the film's way of grounding that answer, which means Spielberg's presentation of what it is about Anderton's post-traumatic mode of life that validates it.

What is Anderton's existence shown to amount to? At work, he analyses and acts upon visions of the future which he takes to be absolutely veridical – that is, he immerses himself in representations that he treats as essentially identical with the future reality they purport to· represent. Hence, when he confronts Agatha's prophetic vision of him as a murderer, what he instinctively recoils from is what one might call the working-out of his general attitude to the future in the first-person case – for to take that attitude with respect to himself amounts to the annihilation of any distinction between what he is and what he will be. At home, he obsessively replays veridical visions of the past, representations of his lost son and his absent wife with which he is so familiar that he can and does recite his part in the dialogues they include, and into which he patently yearns to insert himself, reaching out to these shimmering images as if desiring above all to immerse himself in them, to become one with the past reality they reproduce in a way which would annihilate the present actuality of his continuing loss.

Taken together, these public and private tendencies amount to an avoidance of the present, the maintenance of a state of suspended animation (whose similarity to that of the precogs is underlined by the fact that it is partly enabled by his addiction to neuroin) by oscillating between an absolute immersion in the future and an absolute immersion in the past. In other words, it suggests that Anderton's present absence to himself is a function of his identification of himself either with what he no longer is or with what is not (and, if he is successful in his job, will never be). If so, genuine selfhood must depend upon enacting the realization that the self is not identical either with its past or its future, and (given that it nonetheless, and necessarily, *has* a past and a future) it is not identical with its present either (any more than it is essentially unrelated to it). Can one say instead that it is identical with its past, present and future taken together? But, if so, then the self is identical with an ungraspable interlacing of what no longer exists, what does not yet exist and the infinitesimal distance between them; it is, in short, identical with what (it) is not.

This formulation of Anderton's condition is by now beginning to sound like Sartre's famous articulation of the human condition in *Being and Nothingness*.[3] In that book, he defines the self (what he calls the 'for-itself') as that which is what it is not, and is not what it is – a way of being that he contrasts with that manifested by nonhuman entities (such as plants and stones, and wooden balls), the being of the in-itself, which is precisely identical with itself, entirely self-coincident. To banish the unworthy thought that this might be sheer coincidence, or at least a convergence between film and philosophy of which the film itself is ignorant, it is worth further pointing out that Sartre traces his understanding of the human way of being back to a structure that he calls 'the pre-reflective cogito'. And, of course, the founding importance of the 'pre-' prefix in Sartre's reconception of Descartes' vision of human existence precisely matches its importance in *Minority Report*.

For the world of this film is simply saturated with it. It is the world of PreCrime, precognition and predetermination, a world in which the concept of precriminality controversially attempts to situate itself somewhere between criminality and its absence, in which the PreCrime system itself has the effect of eradicating genuine premeditation in its domain whilst being secretly founded on the maintenance of the precogs in a state midway between waking and sleeping – the condition of dreaming, of being subjected to images of a reality that is not (yet and may never be) real, at once a condition that haunts Descartes himself throughout the sceptical phases of his *Meditations* (threatening to undermine its certainties and yet potentially available to stabilize them) and the condition of the viewer of this, as of any, film. One might, accordingly, say that the intelligibility of the Sartrean transformation or refounding of Cartesian subjectivity is both the condition for the intelligibility of *Minority Report* and its primary preoccupation. In other words, the film is reflecting upon a condition of its own possibility, and is thus internally related to the condition of philosophy: perhaps one should say that it is pre-philosophical. And the result of its reflections, I want to suggest, is that attaining an accurate conception of human consciousness is not settled by affixing a specific prefix to all the critical terminology, but by the use to which that exemplary prefix is then put. In other words: even the Sartrean 'pre-' can be used authentically or inauthentically. What might this mean?

In his *Meditations*, Descartes famously aims to establish the self's inability to doubt that it is thinking, and from the indubitability of this thinking he concludes not only that the self cannot doubt that it exists but also that thinking is of the essence of the self, that the human being is a thinking thing. Sartre notes that this argument, whether cogent or not, presupposes that whenever the self is in a specific cogitative state, or indeed any state of consciousness, it is necessarily aware of being in that state – for if it were not, if there were a gap or division between the self as thinking and the self as knowing that it is thinking, then neither one's thinking nor one's existence would be beyond doubt. In other words, Cartesian consciousness is essentially transparent to itself; every state of its consciousness is necessarily conscious of itself, necessarily embodying an actual act of self-reflection.

Sartre agrees that every state of consciousness is essentially marked by its capacity to reflect on itself, but he denies that it is always already doing so; and to motivate this denial he offers a vignette of wartime consciousness. He imagines a man counting his cigarettes – a matter of real moment in conditions of rationing, he is, accordingly, totally absorbed in the object of his concern, entirely immersed in the pack and its contents. Then someone asks him what he is doing; he replies that he is counting his cigarettes. Whereas, the moment before, he was in a state of absorbed contemplation of the cigarettes, he is now in a state of conscious awareness of that previous state of consciousness. The internal relation between the two successive states is evident, and our capacity always to move from one to the other is beyond doubt, but so is the difference between them. For the object of the original state of consciousness (the pack of cigarettes) is not the object of the present state of consciousness (which is the previous state, the state of absorption in the pack of cigarettes), and states of consciousness with different (Sartre calls them 'intentional') objects are necessarily different states. And if the cigarette counter further reflects upon his consciousness of his previous state of consciousness (of the pack of cigarettes), he enters a new state of consciousness, whose object differs once again from the previous two (viz. the state of reflecting upon his previous absorption in the cigarettes).

In other words, the capacity for self-consciousness is essential to human beings, but it is not something that ensures the self's absolute transparency to itself, and so its essential coincidence with itself. For when the self reflects upon a state of itself, that state of reflection is necessarily not identical with its object; it is rather a new state of the self, which can in turn be reflected upon, but only from the perspective of another, distinct reflective state. Hence, by reconceiving the self's reflective powers as pre-reflective, and so as neither always already actual nor merely possible, Sartre subverts the Cartesian assumption of the self as self-identical, and rather implies that the essence of selfhood lies in the self's necessary failure to coincide with itself – in its inability to take itself up into reflection as a whole. Self-identity thus becomes the mark of the nonhuman realm – the realm of rocks, plants and animals.

But, of course, as Descartes' meditative presuppositions suggest, the self is deeply attracted to a picture of itself as self-identical; in Sartre's terms, to think of oneself in such terms, and to attempt (impossibly) to enact that self-understanding, is a necessary possibility of human nature, and one into which most of us fall most of the time. It is, as it were, a fantasy of being what one is not, and as such a profound expression of the fact that one really is (is internally related to) what one is not. It is the condition of inauthenticity or bad faith – a condition exemplified in *Being and Nothingness* both by the waiter who attempts so completely to immerse himself in his project of being a waiter that he fails to acknowledge that he is not identical with that project (since he may choose to abandon it at any time) and by the woman who leaves her hand in her companion's grasp without acknowledging that it is hers to move if she so wishes, and hence that not moving it is a choice for which she is responsible. For Sartre, the waiter fails to acknowledge that he is not what he is; the woman fails to acknowledge that she is what she is not. Her body is not her, but neither is it utterly unrelated to her; it is her body. His job is his, but it is not him; it is not that he is not a waiter, but neither is it that he is no more than a waiter.

The Sartrean self is thus not a substance but a relation: a relation to what it is not, hence to negation, and a relation that is itself essentially negative or negating. Human existence is a matter of continuously negating what one was (relating to it as one's past, what one no longer is), what one is (relating to it as one's present, what one need not have been) and what one will be (relating to it as one's future, something one is not yet). Each temporal relation is what it is only in relation to what it is not, and the whole it makes up is therefore essentially not a totality but rather a negation of any totalizing self-conception. Precisely because human life is temporal, it exceeds its own grasp; and, if it did not, human beings would not be free, because the self-identical is essentially determined and determinate. Only those capable of relating negatingly to themselves are capable of becoming other than they were and are, of exceeding any deter-mination of themselves (even by themselves), of being essentially open to the future.

Is such a weight of philosophy too much for a mere movie to bear, let alone to weigh up in its own terms – say, by projecting a specific incarnation of its abstractions that illuminates their sense and allows their strengths and weaknesses to be evaluated in human terms? To begin with, Sartre's concepts permit us to recognize that John Anderton's present form of existence is a form of bad faith. He ceaselessly strives to live as if essentially unrelated to his currently bereaved state, by living as if he simply is his past, or as if he simply is his future. What makes it possible for him to negate this mode of self-denying self-negation is his confrontation with Agatha's vision of himself as a future mur-derer, in the context of a system which presupposes that there is no difference between who he is and who she says he will be. For when his very existence is thus put at stake, he rejects every aspect of his bad faith. He loses his faith in PreCrime, and in the future as predetermined. Unlike Sartre's waiter, he enacts the

non-identity of himself and his vocation; he is no longer consumed by being a policeman, even when those still immersed in
the requirements of that calling seem all too likely to consume
him. And, unlike Sartre's woman, he acknowledges that the non-
identity of himself and his body is nevertheless a mode of their
relation, by being prepared even to pluck out his eyes, although
not to destroy them altogether. Instead, he treats them as a possession, as his but not him, and so as a way of becoming another
whilst remaining himself – a distinction that the PreCrime
world's reduction of personhood to retinal identity, its conflation
of eyes with 'I's, represses.

The backstreet surgeon is puzzled by Anderton's desire to
retain his excised original eyes, and is informed that it is 'because
my mother gave them to me'. I take this to imply Anderton's
conception of his body as a gift from his actual mother, hence as
both his and not his; and also his conception of his symbolic
mother as having revealed to him the non-identity of his eyes
with himself by reminding him of this way of beating the retinal
scanning system, hence as having occasioned a radical break
between himself and his past. Ultimately, in order to recover
himself, and thereby recover his wife, their future child and his
future, he finds that he must run ('Everybody runs', he tells
Burgess and us, thereby announcing his acknowledgement that
genuine existence is a matter of endless process or becoming
rather than frozen repetition or anticipation of the self-identical);
and running turns out to require, even to amount to, rebirth –
first by him releasing himself and Agatha from the Temple (by
breaching the integrity of the pool, and thereby allowing them
both to be expelled from the womb of PreCrime together with its
amniotic photon milk), and later by him accepting a period of
purgatory in the confinement facility (as if needing to harrow
hell in his halo before he can merit resurrection). After all, on
a Sartrean conception of selfhood, every new moment of existence amounts to a possibility of radical self-recreation: existence
is either continuous resurrection or it is the endless purgatory of
bad faith.

The pivot for Anderton's transformation is Agatha, whose attitude to her own visions is the reverse of that embodied in the

PreCrime system founded upon her; for she systematically refuses to identify the future with her precognition of it. Despite her vision of him as a murderer, which the whole PreCrime unit takes to be absolutely veridical, she repeatedly urges Anderton – right up to his confrontation with Leo Crow in the stage-dressed apartment – to choose another path, to allow his knowledge of her vision to make it possible for his own choices to falsify it. Anderton's access to that knowledge distinguishes him from all the other precriminals in their haloed hell; but since, in principle, each of them could also have been confronted with the vision before they attempted to realize it, the PreCrime system as a whole could (on Agatha's understanding of it) have been used to show the openness of the future – its non-identity with even our most deeply premeditated intentions with respect to it. For if we really did know the future before it happened, then that knowledge would be a factor in determining it, the actual effects of which would then themselves have to be precognized, and that new precognition would in turn be capable of altering the future it envisions, which would once again have to be precognized, and so endlessly on.

This point about the paradoxicality of precognition is far more explicit in, and central to the unfolding of, the original short story than the film: but the whole of Agatha's attitude to the events she sets in train embodies it. And what she embodies is the central Sartrean perception of the human inability to take up any element of one's own existence, including one's future, immediately and as a whole, as if bringing it totally within our reflective powers. Such a perspective of total and totalizing reflection would literally be a God's-eye view on the world, and one which would annihilate our freedom – our answerability for ourselves and our existence. The hubris of the PreCrime priests is to think that they can occupy it, and the truly prophetic insight of their oracle is to see that any such position is humanly unoccupiable, and to act on that perception.

Agatha's relation to the past is similarly non-hubristic, and similarly dependent upon a perception of its essential non-identity. On one level, she brings about Anderton's ultimate liberation from his own identification with the past by recounting a vision of his son's unrealized future – a future of high school athletics, veterinary college, first love, marriage and the prospect of children of his own. This response to her perception that there is 'so much love in this house' is, one might say, a refusal to identify Sean with the totality of his actual existence, a precognition of an unrealizable future, of a world in which the dead are not dead. But she tells Anderton that, according to the mother of PreCrime, 'the dead don't die: they look on and help'. The implication seems clear. The dead are truly dead only to those who cannot accept their death, and who attempt to enact that denial by treating surviving traces of the dead as if they were alive (as if Sean's hologram were Sean himself). If, instead, they acknowledge them as dead, hence as people who had a future that they never had a chance to realize, then the dead will remain with those who survived them, remain alive to them as real individual beings – the object of their undying love.

And Agatha's relation to her own past matches that which she aims to bring about in the Andertons (John's wife, Lara, admits that she separated from her husband because 'every time I looked at him I saw my son; every time I got close to him I smelt my little boy', thereby declaring her continuing inability to distinguish past from present, husband from son – to see their non-identity). For Agatha is haunted by the loss of her mother, and more specifically by the knowledge that her true murderer has not been found. In other words, where PreCrime preoccupies itself wholly with the future, Agatha's visions involve the past as well; and where PreCrime, in her mother's case, specifically conflated one precognition of the future with another, Agatha continues to recognize their distinctness. But her pursuit of justice for her mother, and so her pursuit of Burgess, is a matter of righting a past wrong, and so does not involve conflating possible futures with the actual one, but rather involves the proper acknowledgement of a deed that was actually done.

Her actions therefore presuppose a proper sense of the difference between past and present, between the most deeply committed intention and the action itself, and between her mother and herself. Her notion of justice is not absolute, any more than her notion of evil intent; and this makes it possible for her to enact her own freedom, and to enable the freedom of others (as when she utilizes her precognitive powers in the shopping mall to place balloons and umbrellas between the fleeing couple and the PreCrime unit hunting them, leaving them free to alter the foreseen future). In short, it is in her hands that the exemplary prefix of the PreCrime world is turned from inauthentic to authentic use.

Scrubbing the image: actor, director and audience

In the original short story version of Minority Report, the precogs are introduced as follows:

> In the gloomy half-darkness the three idiots sat babbling. Every incoherent utterance, every random syllable, was analysed, compared, reassembled in the form of visual symbols, transcribed on conventional punchcards, and ejected into various coded slots. All day long the idiots babbled, imprisoned in their special high-backed chairs, held in one rigid position by metal bands, and bundles of wiring, clamps. Their physical needs were taken care of automatically. They had no spiritual needs. Vegetable-like, they muttered and dozed and existed. Their minds were dull, confused, lost in shadows.
>
> But not the shadows of today. The three gibbering, fumbling creatures, with their enlarged heads and wasted bodies, were contemplating the future. The analytical machinery was recording prophecies, and as the three precog idiots talked, the machinery carefully listened.[4]

Setting aside the datedness of this 1950s vision of the future, both in its idea of technological advances and in its dehumanizing conception of damaged human beings, the most striking aspect of Philip K. Dick's written version of what is to come is that it unhesitatingly makes words the medium of the precogs' talent. Where his analytical machinery listens attentively to what the precogs say and reassembles its content in terms of visual symbols, Spielberg's version sees what the precogs see and generates a coherent, composite, moving visual representation of the future from their more disjointed individual ones. In short, the medium of cinematic precognition and PreCrime is visual rather than symbolic or linguistic; more specifically, it is a moving image of the future, and so not just an instance of the medium of cinema, but of that genre of cinema that essentially concerns the future (whether in its representation of what may come to be or in its representation of the present as already containing what it does not contain, but intelligibly could) – science fiction.

In this respect, the PreCrime system is an inflection of its wider world. For, according to this movie, the mid-twenty-first century environment will be saturated with moving images, and so will require an essentially visual literacy from us: holographic recordings have replaced video and DVD, the telephone system is video-based, the newspapers are essentially labile (with their text and pictures not only in motion, but continually being updated), even cereal packets are crowded with animated, vocal cartoon figures. Most strikingly, public advertising is no longer a matter of static words and images which are there to be seen by all; rather, they spring into life in response to the presence of specific pairs of eyes, and are specifically designed to address those eyes – to single us out insistently from the crowd.

It is hard to avoid the implication that, for Spielberg, the moving image is the medium of the future in at least two senses. First, he plainly sees our culture as one in which moving, sound-synchronized imagery rather than words will come to pre-dominate; but he presents its predominant format as an essentially privatized and dematerialized form of the cinematic experience. For the traditional, collective viewing of a world projected for us on a larger-than-life scale is here replaced by an inherently indi-vidualized mode of transmission and reception, a narrowcast rather than a broadcast, and one its recipients seem inherently capable of ignoring, or at least from which they can learn to distance themselves – their attention a species of monitoring as opposed to viewing, its object something of which one might keep track rather than something to which one is subjected. In short, what seems to be the realization of an advertiser's dream (that of an essentially individualized importuning) is in fact a way of diminishing its effectiveness to vanishing point. For the holographic images in this film are essentially weightless or unreal: they can be walked through or brushed aside, simulacra lacking any substance of their own, not presentations of another world into which we might be drawn.

To be immersed in moving images of this kind is, paradoxically, to be set free of them; but, of course, the PreCrime system is founded on another kind of moving image – ones from a different source (which purportedly guarantees that they transcribe [a future] reality), which are typically viewable on a (transparent but solid) screen, and which are first viewed against the ceiling of a temple, projected on a supra-human scale for supra-individual reception in a space and time set aside from the ordinary flow of the city's life. Does this not sound rather like the cinemas of old, a version of the inherently public movie-going practices that may well be moving into the past even of those who are currently viewing this movie, I mean *Minority Report*? If so, then we might suspect that only under such conditions can the distinctively cinematic moving image, one which ultimately depends upon the material basis of photography rather than the digital basis of computer generated imagery (CGI), retain its mysterious, mythic power of compelling conviction.[5]

But I mentioned a second sense in which, for Spielberg, the moving image is the medium of the future: the sense in which he sees an essential intimacy between the medium of cinema and the domain of the future. It is as if cinematic science fiction is an exemplary generic instance of the cinematic medium, because the inherently photographic medium of cinema has an essential affinity with that which is not (yet) real, and yet is internally related to the real (as if something reality has it in itself to become): more precisely, as essentially non-identical with reality, as relating to it in the mode of negation.

This suggestion of an essential intimacy might seem misguided. For, as I argued in Chapter 2 of this book, the photographic basis of film, the modes of relationship it makes possible between those inhabiting the world of a film and those who view it, and specifically its inherent tendency to present its worlds as past, appears to suggest a contradiction rather than a complementarity between the genre of science fiction, with its projections of future social and technological arrangements, and the grain of the film medium. For how can we be present at the projection of a narrative of something that has happened, when that story – being set in the future – is presented as not yet having happened? The experience of viewing such a film would be like that of absorbing a memory of what is to come. In Chapter 2, I described James Cameron's way of making cinematic sense of such a puzzling form of words. Here, we confront Steven Spielberg's way of doing so.

For 'absorbing a memory of what is to come' is a description of a kind of experience undergone within Minority Report as well as one induced by it. More specifically, our condition as viewers of Minority Report resembles the condition of those within the film who view the visions of the precogs: the PreCrime cops in general, and John Anderton in particular. This identification is insisted upon in the opening seconds of the movie, in which we are first presented with the initial, inchoate elements of Agatha's vision of Sarah Marks' murder, and in effect challenged to make something coherent from it, as Anderton will immediately go on to do with professional virtuosity. And that identification in turn suggests that such conjunctions of cinematic medium and science fiction genre can be appropriated either in bad faith or in good faith. Either one regards these moving images of the future as memories of what is to come, and so regards the future as if it were essentially identical with the past; or one recognizes that no image of the future can be a precognition of it, because the future (unlike the past) is essentially open, not to be identified with any particular vision of it.

Within the film, that amounts to Anderton finding a way of reclaiming his wife and his future, and of liberating Agatha into a genuine form of existence with her fellow precogs that gives them relief from their gifts (via immersion in books, as it happens), by destroying the PreCrime system as such. But what does good faith or authenticity amount to for the film itself, and hence for its director and star?

As well as functioning as a surrogate for the viewer of this film, Tom Cruise also functions as a surrogate for his director, and of

course as a surrogate for himself. His primary role is characterized as 'scrubbing the image': having been presented with the
inchoate raw materials of an inspired vision of the future, he
analyses them, reassembles them into a single, coherent image,
and interprets its significance to a broader audience (of judges
and cops, in the first instance, but ultimately to the public at
large). It sounds like an accurate characterization of any director
of a science fiction film; more specifically, it implies a division in
any artistically ambitious director between the receiver of
inspiration as if from without (since Agatha is not Anderton and
yet is internally related to him, in particular via the hallucino-
genic drug neuroin) and the competent technician or craftsman,
who makes something more coherent and polished and inter-
pretable from that divine impulse.

   The process of scrubbing the image is, however, even more
specific. For it involves the manipulation of that image by the
movement of appropriately gloved hands, a kind of conducting
or choreography by manipular mouse that is both creative and
essentially exploratory, in that it requires Anderton to move
around within the image on the screen before him – quite as if
he first conjures up a stage-set and then proceeds to explore its
resources from every possible angle within it, as if coming fully
to appreciate what he has created. This conception of the moving
image as inhabitable by the viewer – hence of the world it presents as essentially three-dimensional and so indistinguishable
from the real world in this as in all other respects – is one that
Spielberg inherits from the director of *Blade Runner* (whose detective surrogate also explores photographic images from within). It
thereby aligns itself with other images and sequences which
deliberately acknowledge canonical science fiction movies (Kubrick's
Clockwork Orange machinery for forcing someone to keep their eyes
open reappears in the eye-surgery scene, and one fight scene
amounts to a version of a famous fantasy of Hitchcock's, who wanted
to open a film by tracking the construction of a car from its
component parts to the point at which it rolls off the production
line, and the workers open the door to find a dead body in the
vehicle). Plainly, it is part of creating an authentic cinematic vision
of the future that one properly acknowledge past achievement of

this kind, so that these past visions of what is to come are shown to be not merely past, dead and gone, but rather to continue to be present in and to the genre as viable resources for present and future exercises within it. The future of cinematic science fiction remains open only insofar as one acknowledges its past.

Cruise the director may begin by conflating Agatha's inspirations with what will necessarily be, and so by conflating cinematic visions of the future with the future itself; but he ends by acknowledging their non-identity – by accepting that the future must remain open, that the world of PreCrime is a possible future, but one that is no more than possible, and one that not only can but must be entirely rejected and annihilated, its offices and technologies in the end as emptied and disused as a struck film set at the movie's close (as if declaring that the film's presentations of a future reality are presentations as real of what is not real, and that all moving images of the future are related to the future, but negatingly).

What, however, of the film's pivotal or exemplary moving image of the future – Agatha's vision of Anderton murdering Leo Crow? Here, patently, Cruise-as-director merges with Cruise-as-actor: he is the one who scrubs this image, but it turns out to be an image of himself in action. In one of the film's most uncanny moments, this merging is embodied in a shot from the rear of his transparent holographic screen, in which Cruise's face in the analysed image almost perfectly overlaps with his real face – that is, with the image of his face in the film that we are currently viewing. Does this scene – I mean, the scene of Anderton murdering Crow – actually transpire or not? In other words, is its director's eventual realization of this scene true to his initial inspiration?

In one sense, it is; Agatha sees Anderton murdering Crow, and Crow is ultimately killed by the gun Anderton is holding, even by the pressure of Anderton's finger on its trigger. But this literal accuracy co-exists with a multitude of divergences: not only is the trigger actually pulled by Crow's pressure on Anderton's finger, but the scene turns out to contain one real person not initially discovered by Anderton's scrubbing of the image (Agatha) and one person who initially appeared to be real but turns out to be a fake or simulacrum (a huge cutout advertising image of a person).

In effect, the prophetic image of Anderton both is and is not identical with Anderton himself, since his all-consuming desire for vengeance in the name of his son turns out not to be entirely determining of his actions; and our initial perception of genuine human presence in the scene is doubly misplaced (it misses the human perspective of the oracle and attributes genuine humanity to a mere image of it, one that lacks the three-dimensionality of the image in which it appears). In other words, both we and Anderton stand under indictment, although enabled to transcend its terms. And in establishing this genuinely educative relation to his character and his audience, the film's director also presents us with a certain understanding of the relation between his inspiration and its expression – namely, as guiding but not determining his actions, so that what the camera ultimately captures includes unforeseen specificities of detail and motivation (moments of subsequent inspiration that both disrupt and further the initial inspiration) that nevertheless cohere into an artistically satisfying, finite whole. Finite rather than total, because the realization of this scene does not amount to the culmination of Anderton's life, the moment of definitive judgement upon it that he initially expects; it rather makes it possible for him to begin that life anew, to resurrect his own existence.

What, then, of Tom Cruise the actor, or more accurately the star? Does the real Tom Cruise coincide with his projected image, any more than the real John Anderton coincides with Agatha's vision of him? To begin with, what is the relation between Tom Cruise and John Anderton? As I also argued in Chapter 2, if we assume that the camera's capacity automatically to reproduce the individual physiognomy placed before it is the material basis of film, then we would expect the actor to be prior to the character in cinema. But we should also recall that the camera's capacity to transform actor into star is essentially unpredictable. Even if one might be able to say that stardom will turn more on an actor's constancy than his inconstancy, upon the effect of his physiognomic consistency across a body of films rather than his ability to adapt to the demands of essentially different roles, no one can judge, in advance of what actually results from the conjunction of actor and camera, whether that individual physiognomy (however interesting or beautiful) will demand or receive the kind of response that raises some individuals to those giddy heights. Does *Minority Report* give any indication of acknowledging these aspects of its own medium and so its own nature?

Here we might recall that the uncanny moment of Cruise's face merging with itself not only manifests his horror at the implication that what he sees of himself on screen is really him; for since that merging is an artefact of our perspective upon him – a function of our being placed by Spielberg's camera on the other side of the transparent holographic screen from Cruise – the shot also attributes responsibility for that threat of merging or identification to us, the viewers of this film (inhabitants of the real world, a world from which Cruise is metaphysically excluded, but in which he is identified with his projected image).

But the threat is more specific than that of being identified with whatever becomes of him on film; it also has to do with what specifically becomes of him on film. For I take this film to declare its knowledge of Tom Cruise's knowledge that – despite his continuing ability to open a picture, and for reasons unrelated to his personal life and beliefs – many cinema-goers positively dislike him. More specifically, they dislike his physical perfection, and something cocky and self-satisfied about his character that somehow relates to that perfection, something essentially narcissistic that they find to be undeniably conveyed through the body of his work.

As a result, in more recent elements of that work Cruise has taken on roles which have required extremities of physical suffering, damage and deformation. The most obvious example of this prior to *Minority Report* is *Vanilla Sky* (Cameron Crowe, 2001), in which Cruise plays someone who is facially disfigured, and whose desire to deny or repress that aspect of his existence generates his entry into a world of destructive and ultimately self-destructive fantasy; but the *Mission: Impossible* series (as we shall see) similarly depends upon Cruise's willingness to play with his features as if they were a mask.

In *Minority Report*, this process reaches a kind of apotheosis, since the vicissitudes of the plot require Cruise to lose his eyes, to distort his facial features, to subject his body to extremes of temperature (fire and ice in swift succession), to shave off his hair, to consume revolting food and drink, and ultimately to experience a kind of life-in-death in the PreCrime containment facility. And all this punishment is, in the end, visited upon him because of the loss of his son, which the film presents as caused by a moment of pure narcissism on his part – the desire to bathe in the admiring view of a passer-by. It is hard to imagine how much more clearly Tom Cruise could declare to his audience that he understands the effect of his projected image upon those who view it, that he is prepared to make such narcissism and its physical basis the explicit study of his work, and that he is – in the end – not to be identified either with his characters or with his projected image. The real Tom Cruise both is and is not Tom Cruise the star: he can maintain a genuinely human existence only by relating negatingly to his stardom. It is a real question whether his audience will allow him to do so.

Part III

Source: Paramount courtesy the Kobal Collection

7

THE IMPERSONATION OF
PERSONALITY

Brian De Palma's Mission: Impossible

In Part III of this book, I propose to test the coherence and
plausibility of the way of understanding film's relation to philosophy that I originally developed by reference to the *Alien*
series, by examining the only other sequence of movies I know
of that holds out some prospect of matching the unusual combination of features that made the *Alien* quartet so suitable for
my purposes – the three *Mission: Impossible* films. The first (released
in 1996) was directed by Brian De Palma, the second (released
2000) by John Woo and the third (released in 2006) by J.J.
Abrams.

Each film in the sequence centres on the same protagonist,
Ethan Hunt (played by Tom Cruise), an experienced member of
the IM force, a covert offshoot of the CIA; two of the three are
scripted by Robert Towne; and each has a different director, who
brings to bear an established and highly influential body of work
(even if, as in Abrams' case, that work is not cinematic). The
structural analogies of continuity and discontinuity at the level of
character, author and director are thus evident; but so, it might
be thought, are the differences. For first, concerning content,
there is no obvious correlate in the *Mission: Impossible* series to the
thematic preoccupations of the *Alien* quartet – nothing apparently
concerning human identity, embodiment and individuality of the
kind so familiar to modern philosophy. Second, unlike the *Alien*
quartet, the *Mission: Impossible* series owes its existence to a prior
television series. And, third, one director involved in this series of
films has no cinematic track record at all (let alone one of dis-

tinction), and the other two have a reputation for, let us say, valuing surface sheen over human and artistic depth.

David Thomson, for example, in his *New Biographical Dictionary of Film*,[1] suggests that John Woo's early work supplies 'evidence of how a culture like that of Hong Kong had become degraded, long ago, by the attempt to live up to American models', characterizes his later work in America as not so much 'streamlined poetry' but rather the kind of film 'that make[s] hay with the idea of a nuclear explosion' and goes on more specifically to say that *Mission: Impossible II* 'is – and isn't – the new version of "Chinatown"'.[2] Beyond its reminder of Robert Towne's illustrious past, the precise point of that comparison remains unclear, although clearly to the detriment of the new version. However that may be, Thomson reserves his real, unambiguous venom for De Palma:

> There is a self-conscious cunning in de Palma's work, ready to control everything except his own cruelty and indifference. He is the epitome of mindless style and excitement swamping taste or character. ... I daresay there are no 'ugly' shots in de Palma's films – if you feel able to measure 'beauty' merely in terms of graceful or hypnotic movement, vivid angles, lyrical colour and hysterical situation. But that is the set of criteria that makes Leni Riefenstahl a 'great' director. ... De Palma's eye is cut off from conscience and compassion. He has contempt for his characters and his audience alike, and I suspect that he despises even his own immaculate skill. Our cultural weakness admires and rewards technique and impact bereft of moral sense. If a thing works, it has validity – the means justify the lack of an end.[3]

It is not, then, surprising to find Thomson characterizing the first two *Mission: Impossible* films as 'those two horrible wastes of time, expertise and writing talent'.[4] I haven't yet seen any pronouncements of his on the third in the series, but my hopes are not high.

Since Thomson is not only a critic of justified renown, but one properly attuned to the basic merits of the *Alien* quartet, his particular way of speaking for the critical majority in this context deserves to be taken seriously. So, too, however, does the edge of hysteria that undeniably (to my ear at least) invades his graceful and hypnotic, vivid and lyrical denunciation. Something about the way these two directors are so quickly taken as symptomatic of a larger (originally American) cultural weakness and degradation suggests to me that their work is being made to bear the brunt of much more general anxieties about Western modernity in general, and about the possibilities of the medium of cinema itself. Is it always a manifestation of moral weakness to acknowledge the motion-picture camera's capacity to detect beauty in the flowering of an explosion or the trajectory of a human body caught up in its blast? And are the ways in which artists in film have previously taken up the challenge to make something humanly meaningful of such possibilities of the medium the only ways in which that challenge can be met? What if, for some directors in contemporary circumstances, film is experienced as being in the condition of modernism – a condition in which the conventional ways of ensuring the human significance of the projected worlds of movies have, for them, lost their power?[5]

To be sure, one way of reacting to that loss of assurance would be to cut oneself loose from those conventions altogether, and thereby from the artistic enterprise they were able to support; call this the modernizing, or postmodernist, response. For such film-makers, the history of cinema is a dismissable problem, to be transcended or simply left behind in favour of something essentially discontinuous, radically new. Another way, however, is to try to find another relation to those conventions, or another set of conventions, that can continue the basic enterprise otherwise; call this the modernist response. For such film-makers, the history of cinema is an undismissable problem; they undertake to maintain a relation to it (however critical, however troubled or kinked), and hence to continue or inherit it. Such a response will inevitably place the question of that enterprise's continued existence, and so of its present nature in the light of its past achievements and their conditions of possibility, at the heart of its own endeavour. And such questions may come even more precisely into focus when their present cinematic projects owe their existence to work done in a very different medium – one whose potency has subverted the dominance, and now threatens the continued existence, of cinema as a popular art form. Modernist film-makers operating in such circumstances are bound to take up within their work as its essential subject-matter the question of cinematic practice – its point, its conditions of possibility, its present possibility altogether.

One might say: Thomson's critique of Woo's and (especially) De Palma's work identifies it as postmodernist; it deploys cinematic techniques with great skill, but in ways that are essentially unrelated to cinema's artistic, moral and human ends, as established by the great cinematic works of the past. Hence it exemplifies an essential discontinuity in the enterprise, a body of cinematic work unworthy of the name. But it is, of course, sometimes very hard to distinguish the modernizer from the modernist; for what the modernizer merely deploys (emptily, without human meaning) is what the modernist makes his subject, thereby aligning the content of his work with its form. In Thomson's terms, the end of the modernist is that of putting the means in question, which entails that the modernist may well appear to have no independent end, or no independent interest in ends. This part of my book will explore the possibility that, at least in the Mission: Impossible movies, Woo, De Palma and Abrams should be identified as modernist rather than postmodernist film-makers.

Aliens in human guise: the televisual origins of Mission: Impossible

In Alien, Ridley Scott created a narrative world that would constitute the central inheritance of the directors who were to follow him. In Mission: Impossible, beyond the general and generic forms of indebtedness to cinema's past that he shares with Scott, the origin of De Palma's work lies outside the world of this film, and indeed outside the medium of film altogether. For, of course, before it was a film Mission: Impossible was a highly popular American television series; it ran from 1966 to 1969. How might a film director take responsibility for such a source, and for such a task of transformation and renewal? Just what kind of TV series was Mission: Impossible?

I want to take my initial bearings here from some remarks by Stanley Cavell, published in 1971:

It at first seemed that [Mission: Impossible] was merely a further item among the spies-and-gadgets cycles that spun off from early science-fiction movies or serials, mated with films of intrigue. But it went beyond that. Its episodes contained no suspense at all. Because one followed the events with interest enough, this quality did not show until, accidentally reverting to an older type, a moment of suspense was thrown in (say by way of an unplanned difficulty in placing one of the gadgets, or a change of guard not anticipated in the plan of operation). This felt wrong, out of place. The explanation is that the narrative had nothing to do with human motivation; the interest lay solely in following out how the gadgets would act. They were the protagonists of this drama. Interest in them depended not merely on their eventual success, this being a foregone conclusion, but on the knowledge that the plot would arrive at that success through foregone means, absolutely beyond a hitch, so that one was freed to focus exclusively on how, not whether. Then one noticed that there were no human exchanges between the characters in the mission team, or none beyond a word or two exchanged at the beginning, and a faint close-up smile here and there as the perfect plan was taking its totally envisioned course. The fact that the format required the continuing characters to pass as foreigners and, moreover, required one of them to use perfect disguises so that he could temporarily replace a specific foreigner, itself disguised the fact that these characters were already aliens, disguised as human. This displacement permitted us something like our old conviction in spy movies.[6]

I find the features Cavell identifies as capturing the peculiarly evanescent essence of Mission: Impossible to be true to my experience of it. And it is striking how far his talk of the mission team as aliens in human guise might seem to reinforce the Thomson case against De Palma. For to a film-maker supposedly capable only of realizing simulacra of human beings, essentially emptied of moral and motivational intelligibility, the prospect of directing characters whose sole business is (what Cavell, elsewhere in his footnote, calls) the impersonation of personality would seem like the perfect project, an exact match for his specific (anti-)talents. Moreover, De Palma's film undeniably invites its audience to take an interest in the independent life of gadgets. I think here of the articulated electric screwdriver that can remove and collect screws from the farther side of an air-conditioning grille, and the spectacles with inbuilt video positioned on a pile of books to catch the 'traitor' Golitsyn in the act; but the computer – utterly ubiquitous in the film's various plots, and essentially immune to malfunction (other than those caused by others' manipulation or the limits of its material medium) – is perhaps the contemporary gadget that best absorbs this fantasy of technological success as an absolutely foregone conclusion. About such gadgets, and the operations of which they form a central part, our interest is certainly in the how, not the whether; and this might seem to support the Thomson claim that De Palma is all means and no end.

Why, however, should such a series have been so widely and enduringly popular? Is there some particularly powerful way in which its format discovers a potential of the televisual medium? Here, I think, we need to see the connection between Cavell's impression of the mission team as in human guise and the nature of their business in the world. For, of course, their prime function in relating to their gadgets is not merely to dissimulate (to hide their true motives and identity) but to simulate (to become other people – both real and fictional); and a form of life which consists of endlessly discarding one role in favour of the next, in which one's calling is precisely to disguise one's identity with another, will not only attract impersonators of personality but threaten to transform real people into mere wearers of human guise.

One might say: this TV format consists of the unending, varied repetition of acts of theatre; Jim Phelps' taped briefings assign him the role of director in a sequence of theatrical productions. And, as I argued earlier (following Cavell), one defining characteristic of theatre is that, in it, the actor is subordinate to the character.

Various people can play a given role; one does so well by working oneself into that role, accepting and training one's skill and instincts so that they match most intimately with its possibilities and necessities. And those best suited to inhabit a world of theatre such as that of Mission: Impossible are those whose own personality interferes as little as possible with their ability to occupy an unending series of different roles.

This point, of course, applies at the level of character and actor alike. The characters in Mission: Impossible are human ciphers because that is what their job demands; and the actors who play those characters correspondingly lack any distinctive personality, any powerful expression of individual character through the physiognomy captured by the television camera's recording of their presence – that is what their job demands in this case. The apparent actorly exceptions to this claim in fact simply prove its validity. The member of the cast with the most striking individual presence was Martin Landau, but his was the role which involved the donning of a face-mask; and when Leonard Nimoy joined the series at a relatively late stage, he did not last for long, precisely because he brought with him not only a distinctive identity as an actor, but also an identification with a role in another TV series of apparently undying fame – the Vulcan Spock in Star Trek (Gene Roddenberry, 1966–69). This alien presence was not one that our series could accommodate.

A comparison with Star Trek is in fact more generally instructive here; for it too has been subject to a displacement into the medium of film, but that displacement was unimaginable without the retention of the original actors from the TV series. Indeed, what is, to my eye, the most successful of the Star Trek films (the second, entitled The Wrath of Khan [Nicholas Meyer, 1982]) is so in large part because it makes its reliance upon those actors – hence its need to acknowledge their age, and hence their ageing, their mortality – the thematic centre of the narrative world they inhabit, in ways ranging from its villain (a character escaping from an exile created in an episode of the TV series), through its McGuffin (the Genesis device, which can create animate from inanimate matter, or the reverse), to its preoccupation with the avoidance of death (Kirk's solution to the Kobyashi Maru test being to reprogramme the test conditions) and its acceptance (Spock's concluding self-sacrifice).

A similar kind of resistance would attend any attempt to recast characters in any successful TV series or sitcom; just as the loss of Farrah Fawcett in *Charlie's Angels* (Ivan Goff and Ben Roberts, 1976–81) demanded the introduction of a new character for the new actor to inhabit, so the death of the actor who played the grandfather (Lennard Pearce) in *Only Fools and Horses* (John Sullivan, 1981–2003) necessitated the arrival of another elderly relative in the Trotter brothers' world. This suggests that, in television, as in cinema but in contrast to theatre, the character is subordinate to the actor. The screen actor takes a role onto herself, lending her physical and temperamental endowment to it and accepting only what fits – the rest is non-existent; the specific, flesh-and-blood human being is the primary object of the camera's study, since the reality of whatever is placed before it is what the camera places before us. And yet, in the film of *Mission: Impossible* we accept a wholesale recasting of the team, even when it involves certain actors who bring with them not only a substantial body of work but also the aura of fully fledged cinematic stardom.

Shall we say, then, that the TV series in fact works precisely counter to the possibilities of its medium – perhaps even that its enduring (if limited) power and interest for us shows the emptiness of this idea of a medium and its conditioning possibilities? I am rather inclined to suggest that if we can understand why this series needs human impersonators as both characters and actors, we will thereby come to understand how it discloses certain possibilities of the televisual medium. I claimed earlier that any such explanation must acknowledge the theatrical mode of their inhabitation of their world; but the TV camera's relation to their theatricality has not yet been specified. Once again helping myself to ideas of Stanley Cavell's, I would like to say that the camera monitors these acts of theatre: each episode in the series allows us to attend in that particular way to the preparation for, the enactment and the immediate aftermath of, a theatrical event.[7]

What mode of attending is captured by the concept of monitoring? Some facets of the concept are implicit in the way a security guard might attend, via his bank of monitors, to the empty corridors leading from points of entry to a building; and Cavell emphasizes (long before its explicit exploitation in contemporary digital broadcasting) how the same mode of access to reality underpins that staple and paradigm of televisual coverage, the sports event:

> [A] network's cameras are ... placed ahead of time. That their views are transmitted to us one at a time for home consumption is merely an accident of economy; in principle, we could all watch a replica of the bank of monitors the producer sees. ... When there is a switch of the camera whose image is fed into our sole receiver, we might think of this not as a switch of comment from one camera or angle to another camera or angle, but as a switch of attention from one monitor to another monitor. ... The move from one image to another is motivated not, as on film, by requirements of meaning, but by requirements of opportunity and anticipation – as if the meaning is dictated by the event itself. As in monitoring the heart ... – say, monitoring signs of life – most of what appears is a graph of the normal, or the establishment of some reference or base line, a line, so to speak, of the uneventful, from which events stand out with perfectly anticipatable significance. If classical narrative can be pictured as the progress from the establishing of one stable situation, through an event of difference, to the reestablishing of a stable situation related to the original one, [television's] serial procedure can be thought of as the establishing of a stable condition punctuated by repeated crises or events that are not developments of the situation requiring a single resolution, but intrusions or emergencies – of humour, or adventure, or talent, or misery – each of which runs a natural course and thereupon rejoins the realm of the uneventful.[8]

The baseline of the *Mission: Impossible* serial lies in the repeated elements that make up the formula generating its instances or episodes: the taped instructions, the initial briefing, the technological preparations, the allotting of roles and so on, on the side of the IM team;

and, on the other, the everyday flow of activities in the realm of foreigners into which our team will insert itself. As with a live TV broadcast of an operatic performance, the camera then prepares us for a certain eventuality – here, a theatrical event – that differs in each case from its predecessors, but naturally completes itself and returns the team to its uneventful state of generalized readiness. More specifically, the technologically driven nature of this series' events (creating the sense that its success is foregone) is precisely responsive to the way in which monitoring invokes antici-patable – essentially predictable – opportunities for attention; the placing of each camera, and the meaning of a given switch from one image to another (unlike that of any particular camera pla-cement or edit in a film), is dictated by the event itself. Hence, the peculiar power of this televisual format or formula: its way of invoking the essentially anti-televisual medium of theatre in fact discovers a way of acknowledging a perceptual mode character-istic of its own medium.

'I am NOC'

By the time of his *Mission: Impossible* project, De Palma had already encountered the idea of adapting a television format for cine-matic purposes; for one of his biggest commercial successes, *The Untouchables* (1987), derived from an earlier television series of the same name, which focused on the battle between Al Capone and a small group of lawmen in 1930s Chicago. In that case, however, the relation between film and television show does not extend much beyond the title and the names of the central characters, so De Palma's work in that film cannot cast much light on his con-ception of the relations between these two media. But it does provide an occasion briefly to contest the general critical assumption about the emptiness of his deployment of generic and cinematic tropes – the sense that De Palma's relation to these structures and powers is intimate but pointless, pure show devoid of particular purpose. Once again, David Thomson exemplifies this attitude, arguing that 'The Untouchables is no more than the sum of good things in its actors – plus Sean Connery's death scene', and presenting it as one more De Palma film that dismays him precisely because of its famous set-piece sequences, which in his judgement are of a kind that 'exemplify the nullity of "movie genius" when it has no ideas'.[9]

Quite apart from inexplicably omitting to acknowledge the incalculable importance of David Mamet's dialogue and Ennio Morricone's score to the impact of this movie, Thomson also seems to me to miss the internal relation between the form and the content of *The Untouchables*. For what the film charts on both levels simultaneously is the progress of Eliot Ness' (Kevin Costner's) moral education. It begins within his opening interpretation of the world in terms of purest good against blackest evil (reflected in the excessively angelic appearance of his wife and daughter as opposed to Capone's Sun King court); then it moves to his gradual realization of the morally compromised character of even the best of men (when we are shown that it is the Irishman Malone's [Sean Connery's] vaunting, racist contempt for an Italian gangster who 'brings a knife to a gunfight' that leads him [and the camera, and so us] straight into the line of fire of Frank Nitti's machine-gun); and it culminates with his final discovery of his own willingness to suborn a judge and throw Nitti off the roof of the courtroom building in order to avenge Malone's death (Nitti's dead body being shown to have landed upon the last of five identical cars parked precisely parallel to one another, as if disrupting the mechanical patterns of law-abiding behaviour with the unruly impact of passionate, twisted flesh and blood). In short, just as the film charts Ness' discovery of the emptiness of his earlier moral thinking, so it invites us to discover the emptiness of those same categories as they are typically woven into television shows, movies and news media about cops and criminals (by, for example, the edit which explicitly links its own opening depiction of an innocent female child as the exemplary victim of Capone's violence with a tabloid newspaper's mode of representing the world). In such ways, the film aims to locate a deeper, more complex sense of good's relation to evil by deploying the very generic and stylistic tropes that usually conceal this complexity in such a way as to put them in question.

This film's most famous set-piece – the gun-battle on the marble steps of Union Station between Ness and those trying to spirit away Capone's accountant, as a runaway child's pram careers through the carnage – exemplifies the issues at stake. For this beautifully choreographed, photographed and edited sequence is patently indebted to the famous Odessa Steps montage sequence from Eisenstein's *Battleship Potemkin* (1925). But why is that anything more than an empty movie-brat gesture towards an early titan of cinema, a stylistic yoking of two utterly unrelated scenes and movies? First, because it declares the contradiction implicit in the earlier sequence – the disorienting way in which its condemnation of violence against humanity is wrapped up a montage whose delirious intensity invites its audience to experience the sheer, visceral thrill of the exercise of such overwhelmingly violent power. And, second, because it thereby declares the moral uncertainty that is now (after Malone's death) beginning to overwhelm Eliot Ness, and so us. For he is the one who first risks dragging the child into the field of fire, then chooses to give priority to capturing the accountant over removing that child from the scene, and then risks losing both child and accountant by attempting simultaneously to catch the pram and kill the gangsters. Only Stone's (Andy Garcia's) last-minute arrival avoids absolute disaster, and makes it possible for Ness, and us, to overlook the true extent of our morally compromised condition. In other words, this is not an empty deployment of Eisenstein's example, but rather a thoughtful reflection upon the emptiness and incoherence inherent in the example itself, in the character at the centre of this contemporary reworking of it and in the audiences desirous of identifying themselves with either. It is the work of a modernist, not a modernizer.

What, then, of the later *Mission: Impossible?* Can we understand De Palma's cinematic transfiguration of this TV format as the work of a modernist? In particular, can we read it as an attempt to acknowledge the aspects of that format in its relation to the televisual medium that I identified in the previous section? That would presumably mean finding an essentially cinematic acknowledgement of its distinctive aesthetic achievement, and hence of the intimate distances between television, theatre and cinema.

We might begin by examining the two scenes that open the film, preceding even its title sequence (with its loving reconstruction of the TV series' driving theme music and jump-cutting, lit-fuse sequence of images from the episode to come). The first shows the IM force team at work in Kiev, enacting a trademark De Palma scenario of sex and violence to acquire crucial information from a foreigner: we see Jack Harman (Emilio Estevez) monitoring events on a self-contained stage-set constructed within a warehouse (or sound-stage) through his computer screen. All three media are thus invoked, but the film camera's domain encompasses that of the video monitor and the theatrical performance to which it gives access; the hierarchy of this triple nesting states an ambition to declare cinema's difference, perhaps its superiority. And the first obvious difference it declares is its immediate, inherent, capacity to generate suspense: the IM force production involves injecting one member with a death-simulating drug, and the pace of the improvised performance is such that the time within which it can be brought to a successful curtain-call, and the necessary antidote injected, is running out. Will Claire Phelps' (Emmanuelle Beart's) life be foregone?

We, the film audience, see all and can do nothing; the cinematic medium subjects us to the world it projects, including the anxieties that inform it, but also mechanically screens us from it, rendering our passivity unavoidable, hence conferring on us awareness without the capacity to act upon it; is this absolute freedom, or indelible guilt? Harman knows and declares the nature of Claire's situation, and he could intrude upon the stage-set to save his colleague; but he remains transfixed at his computer, quite as if monitoring induces a kind of paralysis, a pure reception of the monitored events that utterly fails to carry over to action. The medium of his awareness offers no automatic absolution; to continue to monitor events without acting upon what one thereby perceives is something for which each perceiver is responsible. Ethan Hunt is aware of Claire's predicament, and is already on the stage-set with her; but the very thing that brings him so close is also what prevents him from helping her. To offer help would be to step out of character, to destroy the performance; and all that he is willing to do is to accelerate it. The show must run its course to completion before he is prepared to step outside the stage-space and bring back the antidote;

the actor's interests are subordinate to those of the character, hence at once to the character's audience and the character's author/director.

The effect of this cinematic suspense is thus to illuminate the differing modes of villainy that attach to each of the three modes of attention under study. One might say that, whereas the film audience is subjected to suspense, the monitor and the performer subject themselves to suspense, by choosing to suspend the humanly required course of action. And what is required to resolve that suspense is Ethan Hunt's transgression of the boundary between stage-set and sound-stage, between the space of theatre and the space of film: more specifically, he must introduce a cinematic resource into the world of theatre, an antidote to its potentially lethal demands. Since in so doing he pulls off his face-mask, revealing for the first time that Ethan Hunt is Tom Cruise, and since only Ethan Hunt ever uses face-masks in this film (so that each signature act of removing a mask reveals Cruise's face beneath, as if that physiognomy cannot be masked, is destined always to break through its guises), we might provisionally call this life-giving element 'stardom' – that epitome of the actor's priority over character in the medium whose material basis is the photographic presentation of reality. It stands for whatever in human individuality exceeds or transcends the individual's roles – that from which those various masks are suspended. And, even at this early stage, we can see from Claire's languorous attempt to brush Hunt's hand with her lips on returning to consciousness that each at once recognizes and disavows the other's role-transgressing significance.

The second pre-title scene shows us the play's author-director, seated godlike in business class amongst the clouds. Phelps (Jon Voight) immediately declares his status, when initially turning down his new briefing tape, presented to him as an in-flight movie, by saying that he prefers the theatre: that definite article, with its implicit snobbery, further suggests that any such preference would, to the director of this film, amount to a taint of villainy – a suggestion that the remainder of the movie massively confirms. Then he views his briefing on a monitor – an updating of the iconic audiotape of the TV programme that reiterates the nature of its original medium, and Phelps' implication in it and its villainy.

The content of the briefing appears to conform impeccably with the TV model, right down to its concluding promise of disavowal should the proposed mission be exposed; but the reality is very different. For whereas the TV series offered no room for scepticism about the truth and truthfulness of the briefing tapes, and hence of the authority originating them, this film will later reveal that its briefing tape is a tissue of lies. The proposed mission is the cover for a mole-hunt, the 'traitor' Golitsyn (Marcel Iures) is an IM force operative, and what he seeks to 'steal' (the second half of the NOC list, containing the true identities of every agent operating under non-official cover in Eastern Europe) is a fake designed to self-destruct and to bring destruction down upon its possessor. Further, whereas the TV series left no room for scepticism concerning the loyalty of the IM force team, in this film its leader and one key member are prepared to betray everything they supposedly stand for; and the idea of this betrayal is, we later learn, being conceived behind Jim Phelps' expressionless reception of his fake briefing.

The absence of such possibilities in the world of the TV series indicates its unquestioning acceptance of certain conventions of the spy genre it inhabits; and it is intimately tied to its capacity to create a sense of success as a foregone conclusion in every one of its operations. For no matter how fantastically reliable one's gadgets, success against an unsuspecting foreign enemy can be guaranteed only if one can exclude the possibility of an enemy within. By contrast, De Palma puts these conventions in question: the film's IM force team is multinational, thus internalizing foreigners; and its IM force as a whole is riven with internal duplicity, with every member of it capable of being other than he seems. As a result, the film's three theatrical performances are each the site of three simultaneously staged, mutually conflicting dramas.

In Prague, Ethan Hunt and his colleagues try to perform one set of roles as they track a supposed traitor's activities; but they are unsuspecting participants in Jim Phelps' genuinely traitorous counter-drama, whilst he and they are all unsuspecting participants in their boss Kitteridge's (Henry Czerny's) mole-hunt. In the film's conclusion on the Eurostar train between London and Paris, three competing dramas are again created and directed by Hunt, Phelps and Kitteridge, with only Hunt aware of every role he plays, and Max (Vanessa Redgrave) unknowingly manipulated by all three. The second, central piece of theatre – the theft of the global NOC list from the IM force mainframe in CIA headquarters – appears closer to the TV model, in that it involves an IM team united in their desire for the list confronting an unknowing enemy. In reality, however, two of the four team members have a different agenda to Hunt's, which he has anyway not fully revealed to his team; and that team is working against the IM force as such, that is, against itself. Hence, the third contending drama here is just the TV series' single, overarching script: the consistent rationale of the IM force, represented once again by Kitteridge, as he plots his own anti-Hunt drama in the very building Hunt is infiltrating.

In this sense, the narrative thrust of Mission: Impossible attacks the basic integrity of the TV series, by simultaneously attacking the integrity of the IM force, its crack team and the key members of that team. The film all but declares that this is its concern – that its subject-matter is the very existence and nature of the IM force – by taking as its McGuffin the NOC list: for this entails that the 'threat' that the IM force team aims to neutralize is (as in the TV series) a threat not to the country it serves or any of its other interests, but rather to all those in its own condition, that of operating under non-official cover, and hence a threat to itself; and what Hunt risks in using the global NOC list in his hunt for the real traitor is the destruction of IM force operations altogether. In the film, the IM force turns upon itself and very nearly tears itself to pieces; Mission: Impossible the movie questions the key condition of the TV series to which it owes its own existence, and thus puts in question its own conditions of possibility.

What induces this threat of fission? The primary act of betrayal is Jim Phelps'; and it occurs because, after the end of the Cold War, he woke up to discover that he was 'an obsolete piece of hardware not worth upgrading, with a lousy marriage and $62,000 dollars a year'. In short, he recognizes that to be a member of an IM force team is to be essentially subordinate to, hence to be nothing essentially more than, a piece of hardware, a human version of a gadget; and he responds to this sudden self-revelation by throwing a spanner in the machinery. The second act of disruption is Ethan Hunt's; and his is effected by the realization of his own already-divided loyalties, and consequent lack of integrity. In Prague, he first disobeys his team leader's command to abort in order to maintain contact with Golitsyn and the NOC list, then he abandons his mission to go to his mentor's aid on the bridge, and then he watches as this enacted conflict between his professional role and his human ties results in the violent deaths of his team. This abortion of a stage-play leaves real blood on the floor, the destruction of colleagues who have become family. It forces him to recognize that he is more than his professional role, that his identity is not exhausted by the conditions of his existence – conditions that the film insistently identifies with doubleness or internal splitting, hence fragmentation.

The IM force world as the film represents it is one in which identity in general is impersonatable precisely because it is validated by mechanical recognition of (parts of) the body. One's visual appearance, one's fingerprints, one's voice and retinas, even the heat and weight of one's body: these are what declare the reality of one's existence, and the IM force can operate precisely because all such features can be made to appear present when they are not, or to appear absent when they are really present (and one might ask: which form of words best captures cinema's screened projection of reality?). Human existence is hollowed out, reduced to the occupation of space by matter of the appropriate form and surface appearance.

Accordingly, the NOC list comes in two parts. First, there is the list of cover names, to which the contending parties all have access; what they are all in search of is the second part, the list of true names, the real identities lying behind that of the roles they play – and that proves singularly elusive. First we encounter a fake list of true names, the bait for the mole-hunt, which ultimately goes up in smoke; then, once the true list is duplicated from Langley, Hunt leaves Krieger (Jean Reno) and is uncertain which of his two disks contains it; then various attempts are made on the Eurostar to duplicate the disk with the true list – attempts which are variously jammed and disrupted by circumstance and enemy action. The implication is two-fold: that once they have been dislocated by the nature of one's work in the world, it is inhumanly difficult to bring the two halves of oneself back together again, to locate the truth of oneself behind or beyond the roles one is asked to perform; and that if one ever succeeded in doing so, the effect would be like fusing the two halves of the chewing gum Harman gives Hunt – highly explosive.

When he first uses it, the fish in the Akvarium restaurant's vast, storied tanks (their serried ranks shining with the blue-grey radiance of a bank of monitors) are set free from their confinement for consumption; but as Hunt outpaces the tidal wave of unleashed water, its loss of energy leaves them gasping on the pavement, deprived of the essential medium of their existence. He uses it again in the railway tunnel under the channel – once again in a no-man's land, this time between one country and another, perhaps even between one (Anglo-American) cultural alignment and another (Europe). He saves himself, and kills the remaining traitors in his IM force team, by destroying the helicopter by means of which they had hoped to escape. Should we, then, say that – unlike the fish – this film has allowed Hunt to escape from the self-emptying theatrical conditions of existence specified for IM force operatives in the TV series, and hence that the medium of cinema is inherently more able to acknowledge the humanity of its subjects than that of television?

This climactic scene is certainly one of liberation, and its acceptance depends upon cinema's capacity to make the fantastic real; for, of course, in accepting it we accept the literal impossibility of a helicopter attached to a train being able not only to survive being drawn into a tunnel, but also to manoeuvre with delicate malevolence within it. But then we have to say that De Palma here identifies the medium of cinema as such with the business of the IM force team – that of making the impossible a reality. And, in so doing, he locates a taint in the powers of his medium – a risk that its magic conjures up a mere simulacrum of the real world, hollowing out its constraints and conditions, and thereby tainting the heroism that depends upon our graceful and courageous bearing of reality's burdens for goodness' sake with the moral weightlessness of such fantasies. I take De Palma's decision, at the end of this scene, to place his camera so that it looks along a rotor blade of the destroyed helicopter whose tip almost slices through Hunt's exposed neck, to declare this risk; for it identifies the camera with lethal decapitation, with the reduction of a human being to a head severed from its body, and thereby identifies Tom Cruise's fatedness to stardom with his reduction to a handsome, smiling face.

A similar ambiguity emerges in the conversation between Jim Phelps and Ethan Hunt in Liverpool Street station, as Ethan lives out the realization of his self-flagellating dream in Prague – the resurrection of the father he failed. Jim attempts to persuade Ethan that Kitteridge is the real traitor; but Ethan – having just noticed the incriminating Drake Hotel stamp in Job's Bible – is in the process of realizing that Jim himself has betrayed them all. Hence, as his words appear to take up Jim's suggestion, De Palma shows us a series of flashbacks covering the events in Prague – or rather he shows us Hunt's interior discovery of the truth of those events, with every uttered word in Ethan's discourse that Jim takes to refer to Kitteridge being shown to refer in reality to Jim himself.

Once again, two conflicting plots contend with one another, this time at the level of conflicting assignments of reference to a set of pronouns; once again, the apparent meaning of a set of utterances is subverted by its covert sense, although this discrepancy is between what is said and what is seen, or imagined, by a single individual. We see Hunt once more playing a role, this time to his role-playing mentor – another mode of his interior split or doubleness; here, however, that splitting is seen to make possible his eventual liberation from the deceptions of others, for it declares the moment at which he understands what has really been going on throughout the film, and hence at which he can create a drama that incorporates the dramas in which others wish to cast him, and thereby control him. And in conveying this so economically and exhilaratingly to us, De Palma employs a key condition of talking motion pictures – their capacity to synchronize sound and vision, and hence their capacity to desynchronize them. Is he thereby declaring that this aspect of his medium is inherently liberating?

Not exactly. For we must recall that Jim's and Ethan's talk is of the past; and De Palma is here using film's marrying of sound and vision in order simultaneously to present us with that talk and with its subject-matter – that is, with the past reality to which it refers and with the stream of consciousness to which it gives (misleading) expression. The camera thereby claims the power to penetrate the interiority of its human subject – to declare the existence and nature of the inner life lying beyond that character's inherently deceptive words, deeds and appearance, and hence to confirm his humanity. But, in so doing, it simultaneously declares its own unreliability: for the past reality its images now show is not what it declared when we first viewed it – rather, every shot of that original sequence was framed so as to deceive us, as the events depicted were designed to deceive Hunt.

The camera did not present fantasy as reality: it rather framed or cropped its presentation of what really happened in such a way as to allow us to misinterpret it – just as Jim Phelps manipulated the video images relayed to Ethan from his wrist-camera to imply that he had been shot by another person on the bridge. (The same moral informs the bravura, apparently seamless 12-minute 50-second shot that opens De Palma's subsequent *Snake Eyes* [1998], inhabiting the point of view of the film's protagonist as he rushes through a bewildering sequence of glimpses of the various subplots surrounding the movie's primary drama – the assassination of a politician: the camera gives us nothing but the truth, and yet anything but the full truth.) And no particular acts of framing are necessary for such duplicity: for if the camera can declare the inner life of its subjects, even when that fails to match its expression in word and deed, it can also fail to do so. As in the second pre-title sequence of Phelps' initial briefing by Kitteridge, it can simply record everything there is to record of what they say and do, and invite, or at least allow, us to take that at face value.

Such ambiguities suggest that it is De Palma's concern to suggest that the powers of cinema are neither inherently villainous nor inherently truthful; rather, they can be turned to good or to villainy. They can either consort with those forces in our culture which reduce reality to appearance and disavow substance and meaning in favour of an endless play of interlocking images and traces, or they can disavow such reductiveness. It is my concluding contention that De Palma decisively declares his particular hand, the turn to which he wishes to subject his audience, in the second of his three theatrical set-pieces, the central sequence that everyone who has seen this film will remember.

Here the context is an epitome of the IM force world's reduction of identity to fragmentary traces of a human body: the sterile space containing the IM force mainframe's console verifies human presence by digital code and double electronic key-card, voice-print and retinal scan, and guards against human intrusion by evaluating the evidence of sound, temperature and pressure. In this space, to be is to be matter in motion. Hence, the condition for Hunt's recovery of the NOC list, and so of himself (insofar as he claims to Max 'I am NOC – was; now I'm disavowed'), is that he achieve cool, soundless weightlessness – an immaterial presence. Since the space in its alarmed state is composed of white panels outlined in black, which the triggering of the alarm turns red, Cruise must also ensure that his world remains colourless. In sum, he must attain silence and (as it were) a merely two-dimensional salience, the sheer black-and-white outline – the bare cinematic minimum, as well as the original form of cinema's projection – of personhood.

De Palma presents Hunt's presence in this purely cinematic world as dependent upon a literalization of suspense; he achieves his goal by utilizing a flexible trapeze-like harness that displaces his weight upon Krieger in the overhead airshaft. And he shows that this presentation achieves the immediate translation of literal suspense into psychological suspense – the mechanical into the human. We hang on Hunt's fate because we see even this pared-down visual schema as a human presence; even this black-and-white short with its uncanny canonical combination of slapstick and grace can subject us to exhilarating anxiety about another's well-being. No matter how systematically De Palma deprives Hunt of any complex interior and exterior life, no matter how intensively he strips away anything other than the logic of the cinematic type of the undercover spy, and then makes that logic the defining subject-matter of the character and the film, thus luring the viewer into the closed circuit of a movie's obsession with itself, it remains possible to call upon our capacities for identifying with this screened projection of his embodied mind, and hence for identifying his presence as (some transfiguration of) the human presence as that is inflected for and by the camera in the physiognomy of Tom Cruise.

There is, then, nothing mechanical or assured about cinematic reductions or hollowings-out of human meaning from its projected worlds; when we encounter such wildernesses of sense, the responsibility always lies not with the medium but with the work of specific human beings within it. And any movie that can be understood to convince us of this surely earns the right to be taken seriously as reflecting upon, not merely reflecting, such reductiveness, within and without the world of cinema.

Source: Paramount courtesy the Kobal Collection

8

THE BURDEN OF SEX

John Woo's *Mission: Impossible* II

Signifiers and signatures: Face/Off

If the mask is *Mission: Impossible*'s distinguishing mark, in both its televisual and cinematic variants, then John Woo's *Face/Off* (1997) amounts to a feature-length application for the job of directing the second movie in this series. For *Face/Off* pivots around the impossible possibility of two men literally wearing one another's faces, and so around the anxiety that the very idea of a mask might become indistinguishable from the idea of the face it masks. And because the two men concerned are tied to one another in a variety of ways – on opposing sides professionally (one a nihilistic criminal named Castor Troy and the other, Sean Archer, a federal agent committed to his capture), but indistinguishable in their compulsive-obsessive temperaments and their sense of the irreducible obligations of family bonds – the idea of faces as masks is thereby tied to two others: the idea of enemies as brothers under the skin; and the idea that ultimately no matter of principle separates the obdurate enforcer of the law from one whose existence repudiates it. It is this conjunction that will find new life in Woo's contribution to the *Mission: Impossible* series.

Although David Thomson is here prepared to make an exception with respect to his general criticism of Woo's Hollywood work, talking of *Face/Off* as his 'most interesting English-language picture, with a clever script and flamboyant performances from John Travolta and Nicolas Cage',[1] even so some might wish to ask whether Woo in effect shares the nihilism he depicts in Castor

Troy. Woo's stylistic flourishes are all here in place: the elabo-
rately choreographed fight scenes, motor-cycles versus cars and
helicopters, children as iconic victims and means of redemption,
and lashings of religious imagery; and none of this is exactly
anchored in a realistically depicted world of transplant surgery,
federal law enforcement or terrorism. So when Troy walks into a
chapel, through a flock of white doves, and declares to Archer,
'This is so religious! The eternal battle between good and evil,
saint and sinner; and you're still not having any fun … ', before
initiating the final, longest and most pyrotechnic of their con-
frontations, we are invited to wonder whether such structures of
value are no more than free-floating signifiers for Woo as well,
their significance reduced to set-dressing for his way of having
empty, meaningless fun with boys and their toys.

Suppose, however, we reflect further on the film's key idea of
faces as transposable masks. This idea at once literalizes and epi-
tomizes the postmodernist or modernizing idea of identity as a
surface phenomenon, no more anchored in its material referent
than any other concept in contemporary culture. But what the
film tracks is the extent to which that supposed freedom, that
capacity for endless displacement, is resisted by those whose faces
are turned into masks; and this resistance operates simultaneously
on the level of narrative content and cinematic form.

In the narrative, both men discover that there is nothing
superficial or simple about acquiring another person's identity by
acquiring their face, particularly when that other is an enemy. For
to see that other's face in the mirror is to see it as somehow
authentically expressive of the person who continues to exist
behind it; it declares something about their uncannily intimate
closeness to one another, as if each gives expression to something
unrealized but fundamental in the other, even if something they
each wish to extirpate from within (with Castor seeing in Sean
the possibility of devotedness to family that his own relationship
with his brother contains in embryo, and Sean seeing in Castor
the possibility of doing things simply because you can, unrest-
rained by any conception of justice or fellow-feeling, that his
own wounded isolation after the death of his son tempts him
towards in his work). But that wish is frustrated, because assuming

each man's facial identity turns out to mean involving oneself in relations of blood and comradeship with a variety of other people; and, once inhabited, these relationships have the power to make demands upon, and to reshape the commitments of, the person hiding behind his mask.

At the same time, donning the other's face is quickly shown to be insufficient to deceive those close to that other. First, the voice must be altered to match the mask; but, even more fundamentally, a match is required with what one might think of as the signature of that voice (its intonations and stress patterns, its expressive rhythm) if self-betrayal is to be avoided. And both mask-wearers find it at once exhilaratingly transgressive and extremely difficult to acquire that signature, as more generally they find it pleasurably and perplexingly difficult to acquire its bodily equivalent – the characteristic patterns of facial expression, hand gesture and gait through which the person they aspire to imitate makes manifest his distinctive bodily inhabitation of the world.

Here we see the crucial connection between narrative content and reflexive concern in this film. For, of course, the postmodern idea of identity (and of representation more generally) as floating free of its material referent finds its cinematic echo in the massively expanding use of CGI technology, which can in principle produce a screened image without any reliance upon a real object's placement before a camera, and which has often been thought to hold out the prospect of overcoming the film industry's continued reliance upon overpaid and overly demanding real people – the stars by the employment of digital actors. Against this background – one which will seem particularly hard to avoid for a director of contemporary action movies – the demands of the face-transposition plot acquire a particular resonance; for they require that, after the opening sequences, Nicolas Cage (as Castor Troy) and John Travolta (as Sean Archer) must each inhabit their characters as they imagine they would have been inhabited by the other; so that, in acting out Sean Archer's attempt to be Castor Troy, Cage must attempt to imitate John Travolta, and in acting out Castor Troy's impersonation of Archer, Travolta must imitate Cage.

As a consequence, Face/Off becomes a study of the distinctive character of cinematic acting and stardom. For suppose we accept that, in cinema as we have so far understood its possibilities, the actor is prior to the character, and that the actor's capacity for stardom depends upon the unpredictable effects of projecting his physiognomy as captured by the camera onto the screen. Then *Face/Off* tells us that a star's physiognomical signature is as much a matter of voice and body as it is a matter of his face; and it asks us whether or not we are willing or able to regard that signature as imitable, say iterable. In the first instance, the question is whether this can be done by another person, even perhaps another star, equipped as he presumably is with his own distinctive embodied signature. But lying in the background is the question of whether it might be done by an appropriately programmed computer, one capable of generating a digital image of that person, and hence perhaps of generating such images without the need for any original (at which point the distinction between representation and presentation threatens to break down, leaving us in a world of iterations that operate upon nothing real – no prior value or origin).

In my judgement, the film's answer to its own question is 'No'. To be sure, we take a peculiar pleasure in seeing the degree of success that Cage and Travolta both have in impersonating one another's expressive bodily idiosyncracies, and we are certainly capable of being startled and informed by what it is that each actor takes to be impersonatable in the other – their mutual study deepens our understanding of who each is, as an actor and as a star. It is also true that the success of these impersonations indicates a threat inherent in any actor's translation to stardom: the threat of turning oneself into an agglomeration of essentially iterable tics and gestures, and so an impersonator of oneself. But seeing Cage as Travolta and Travolta as Cage simultaneously confirms that, beyond or before their imitable expressive repertoires, there is the fundamental fact of material, bodily difference and distinctness, and the essentially ungraspable range and depth of difference it engenders.

For Cage's iteration of Travolta's bodily signature is patently and necessarily not identical with Travolta's conscious or unconscious iterations of it; it is itself signed by Cage, the man actually before the camera, just as Travolta's iteration of Cage's signature is distinctively informed by Travolta's way of signing anything and everything he does in the camera's gaze – by his own embodied way of being in the world, and so of being projected on screen (even as another actor). To put it another way, that bodily signature can at best be parodied or caricatured; to be genuinely iterated in all its richness and depth, it must be made manifest in and through the singular body that first produced it.

CGI acknowledges a more general indebtedness to the body in its dependence upon motion-capture technology (tracking the motion of sensors attached to various parts of a moving human being) in order to acquire the digital data needed to generate moving images of individual people that are plausibly human, even if they are not representations of any real individual (not even the one who wore the sensors). Woo's point in this context would be that only the technology of the camera can capture the indefinitely receding richness and depth of a real object's revelation of itself to the human eye.

CGI aside, however, it seems clear that *Face/Off* aims to demonstrate the inimitability of individuality by demonstrating the extent to which physiognomy is still destiny in cinema.

Chimerical identity: Mission: Impossible II

John Woo's sequel to De Palma's work systematically denies any indebtedness to the TV series with which *Mission: Impossible* is in such intense dialogue; no specific detail of that televisual world is reproduced in *Mission: Impossible II* that is not given its own independent (and often altered) significance in De Palma's cinematic version of that world. It is as if, for Woo, the televisual origins of the IM universe are of precisely no interest to him; that debt is one that De Palma has entirely or at least decisively discharged.

On the other hand, Woo's film does systematically declare its indebtedness to De Palma's film, as if insisting that the IM force universe is for him a purely cinematic phenomenon; and in ways that go beyond its continued focus on Hunt, his IM force and the sole remaining member of the disavowed team that survived the vicissitudes of that film. These declarations include reiterations of detail (such as the reappearance of a carpet of shattered glass across which Hunt's beloved colleague walks to confront him) and efficient transfigurations of technology (such as the use of digital cameras and viewers, and the opening conflation of video briefing with remote-viewing spectacles). They also include declarations of an intimate understanding – such as his pivotal variation on the De Palma signature theme of conflating literal with dramatic suspense in Hunt's infiltration of the BioCyte HQ, and his division of his McGuffin into two parts, distinguished by the same pair of colours that distinguished the components of De Palma's explosive chewing-gum.

Nevertheless, Woo does choose to incur another essentially cinematic debt, by aligning his basic plot with that of Alfred Hitchcock's *Notorious* (1946), starring Cary Grant and Ingrid Bergman. But it would be more accurate to say that this fact constitutes his further acknowledgement of De Palma, whose work has been understood from the outset to be the persistent expression of a sense of indebtedness to Hitchcock, and in particular to Hitchcock's ability to construct stories of crime, voyeurism, murder and psychosis that can also be understood as studies of the resources and conditions of the cinematic genres in which they participate, and of the cinematic medium itself. One might even say that Hitchcock's work (certainly by the time of *Vertigo* [1958] and *North by North West* [1959]) constitutes a key point at which the problem of telling the modernist from the modernizer – of distinguishing an interest in exploring the degree of conviction that generic and stylistic conventions can any longer elicit from a willingness to deploy them emptily, to no identifiable human interest or purpose – becomes undismissible. As I have just argued, the only way to appreciate the real richness of *Mission: Impossible* is to understand its presentation of the world of spying in exactly such terms.

One might well question the wisdom of any director who invites us so explicitly to compare his work with a masterpiece by one of cinema's acknowledged masters. But Woo, I think, means this Hitchcockian invocation to permit him to achieve a more specific, and more critical, relation to De Palma's version of the IM world, and of its protagonist, Ethan Hunt. For by drawing upon the basic plot structure of *Notorious*, in which the daughter of a Nazi (Alicia/Bergman) works with an American agent (Devlin/ Grant) to subvert a group of Nazi sympathizers by marrying their leader (Alex Sebastian/Claude Rains), Woo ensures that a relationship with a woman is central to his version of Hunt's world, and implies that the equivalent relationship in De Palma's world was at the very least insufficiently substantial or well realized – hence, that, in this respect, De Palma fails to live up to his master.

Such a criticism is hard to gainsay. As I mentioned earlier, Claire Phelps is from the outset identified as a forbidden but responsive love object for Hunt in Mission: Impossible – forbidden first as the wife of his father-figure, then as that father's possible co-conspirator, then as his victim. But Emmanuelle Beart has very little to work with in breathing life into this intermediary between male rivals; and Ethan's confirmation of her (conflicted) treachery seems decisively to negate her attractions for him: 'Of course, I'm very sorry to hear you say that, Claire' is the best he can do when – disguised as Jim – he listens to her risk bargaining with an unloving husband for his own life. Of the various indications De Palma offers of the ways in which Hunt's humanity exceeds his role, his invocation of male and female companionship growing out of the world of work carries far more plausibility than his invocation of romance.

Woo's sense of this absence, or inadequacy, leads him to embody the issue in the mythic identity he assigns his McGuffin. For the two complementary elements of Dr Nekhorvich's (Rade Sherbedgia's) experiment in molecular biology are called Bellerophon and Chimera; the disease is thus named after a monster who plagued the ancient world, which the film characterizes as possessed of 'the head of a lion and the tail of a serpent', and the cure after the prince who killed it. In fact, however, the real Chimera of legend also possessed the body of a goat; one might think of the film's silence on this matter as inviting us to see in it a certain disavowal of what links head and tail – a disavowal which matches Hunt's silence on the internal relation between himself (with his lion's mane of hair contrasting so starkly with his martial, clippered cut in the first film) and his dark other, Sean Ambrose (Dougray Scott) – the serpent in the IM bosom. For if a lion mythically signifies courage, and a serpent cunning, then a goat can only signify what Ambrose at one point calls 'the burden of sex'. And the key point of contact between *Notorious* and *Mission: Impossible* II is that Nyah Nordhof-Hall (Thandie Newton) is the key point of contact between Ambrose and Hunt.

In other words, beyond the way in which the idea of the chimerical alludes to De Palma's theme of identity in general (and Hunt's identity in particular) as an endlessly elusive fantasy or mirage of the overheated imagination, Woo means his invocation of the Chimera to inflect De Palma's related theme of the internal division between role and actor in spies, in the direction of a division within the actor as spy. Hunt is not simply Bellerophon to Ambrose's Chimera, a hero in need of a villain: he is also the Chimera's lion-head, needing to find a way of acknowledging his identity as a sexual being without simply denying its serpentine side; at which point, it is implied, the Chimera would no longer be a monstrous assortment of body parts, but rather a properly integrated, fully embodied human being – Chimera would really become chimerical (merely imaginary) by becoming Bellerophon. *Mission: Impossible* II tracks this attempted transformation.

The film underlines the intimacy of the antagonism between Hunt and Ambrose by ensuring that what we think of as our first sight of Hunt (in the doomed airliner) is in fact of Ambrose wearing a Hunt face-mask – a doubling to which he has resorted twice before, at the IM force's instigation. In fact, in a significant inversion of De Palma's practice, according to which only Ethan Hunt wore masks, and hence every mask was a cover for Cruise's stardom, almost every mask used in Woo's film is of Hunt/Cruise's face, and each time it is worn either by Ambrose or his second-in-command, Hugh Stamper (Richard Roxburgh). Tom Cruise's first task in this film is thus to play another character disguised as his own character. By thus calling on his leading man to pretend to be who he really is, and thereby suggesting that his screened reality both is and is not a pretence, Woo not only recalls the key issue of *Face/Off*; he also invites Cruise (and us) to contemplate a darker side of Cruise's stardom – a mysterious taint of violence and deceit lying behind the undeniable charm of his physiognomy and temperament. It is exactly this dual aspect of Cary Grant's screen persona that Hitchcock brings out in *Notorious*.

In *Notorious*, Grant's demonic side is externalized in the character of Alex Sebastian, the Nazi whom Alicia marries and spies upon; and part of Devlin's torment over Alicia, part of what makes him torment her over her willingness to play the role for which he recruited her despite their having fallen in love, is the anxiety that she is not only a fully sexual being with a long history of male 'playmates', but also genuinely attracted to this particular man, with whom she shares a non-sexual past through her father, and whose essentially duplicitous role in the world (combined with an obsessive sexual jealousy) so closely matches Devlin's own.

Hunt's, Nyah's and Ambrose's relationship in *Mission: Impossible II* offers a variation on this triangular theme that suggests a certain understanding of its original. After the destabilizing discovery that his professional seduction of Nyah has opened him to a more personal relationship with her (a discovery whose mood is expressed in the film's background shift from flamenco to flames – from ritualized social intercourse to the self-denying ecstasies of religion), Hunt is informed that Nyah has already made and broken a sexual relationship with Ambrose, one which his job will require that he arrange for her to renew. And even when, faced with her disgust at the thought that he could now ask her to do this, he makes it as clear to her as he can that he wants her to refuse ('Would it make you feel better if I didn't want you to do this?' 'Much.' 'Then feel better!'), she decides that she will accept it nevertheless. Here is Woo's most significant variation on the *Notorious* model; for in the analogous scene at the heart of that film, Alicia is moved to take the job precisely because Devlin refuses to affirm to her what he has forcefully declared to his boss – that he doesn't want her to do it.

Why this variation? We might imagine Ethan's response to the mystery of Nyah's choice finding expression in the following questions. Has she done this because she feels that the task is more important than our relationship? That would be bad, but understandable, given Ambrose's track record and present intentions, and no more than I, her recruiter, deserve. Or is it because, having spent the night with me, she prefers Ambrose? She as good as denied it last night; but she also began last night by asking, 'Who wants to be decent?' and ended it by remarking on

223

our having gone beyond any manual or rules ('They have a book for this?'); and my boss has just remarked that, being a woman, Nyah has 'all the training she needs to go to bed with a man and lie to him'. Her deciding for that reason would be far worse – and understandable only if what I had been able to give her during that night had lacked something, something without which she was not (sexually) satisfied.

What kind of relationship had she and Ambrose shared? Hunt has already told us that he understands Ambrose to be the kind of spy who thinks 'he hasn't done the job unless he's leaving hats on the ground', someone he later describes as needing to 'get his gun off'. The sense of violent menace around Nyah's arrival in Ambrose's Australian residence is palpable. When her presence is questioned by Stamper – whose latently homosexual relationship with Ambrose is Woo's displacement of Alex Sebastian's relationship with his mother in Notorious – Ambrose slices off the tip of one of his fingers, forcibly held erect, with a cigar-trimmer; and when Hunt makes contact with Nyah at the racecourse after her first night back with Ambrose, she responds to his criticism of her failing to follow instructions by saying, 'What are you going to do – spank me?' I take these to be grounds enough for Hunt, certainly disconcerted by falling in love, and perhaps disconcerted by, let us say, the forcefulness of the sexual response he has elicited from his lover, to suspect that Ambrose's blend of sex and violence might be a more attractive version of whatever he has to offer.

In the terms of Woo's mythology, Hunt's discomfort reflects an unwillingness to acknowledge that human sexual identity – hence both his own and Nyah's – has a serpentine as well as a leonine aspect. And it finds expression in his disavowal of his promise at the racetrack to extract Nyah immediately from Ambrose's residence. Instead, he concentrates on staging a piece of theatre for the CEO of BioCyte, in order to discover the location of the remaining samples of Chimera. This is one of two points in the film in which Hunt is seen wearing a mask; here, it indicates that he is covering up or denying something of himself. For Ambrose uses the time to deceive Nyah by disguising himself as Hunt, and requiring her to stay at his residence; he incarnates the potentially fatal consequences of Hunt's refusal to sacrifice his job for his love.

The task of overcoming Hunt's anxieties falls, then, to Nyah herself. She walks into the middle of the stalemated conflict between Ambrose and Hunt, retrieves the injection gun containing the sole remaining sample of Chimera, and fires its contents into her own bloodstream. Once again, Woo varies a theme from Notorious: for the protracted suspense of that film's final half-hour turns on whether or not Devlin will be able to rescue Alicia from her husband's (and mother-in-law's) conspiracy to poison her. But Nyah is not the unknowing, passive victim of another's actions; she takes action, declares that her own violence can find expression in ways not lethal to others, and stakes her own existence in a way which at once deprives Ambrose of what he wants and transforms her own body into the unified focus of Hunt's professional and personal goals (to save her is to frustrate Ambrose and to eliminate Chimera). Her plan thus embodies courage, cunning and sexuality; it declares that she is capable of transforming Chimera into Bellerophon in her own person, and if Hunt can properly acknowledge her achievement, he might match it.

The conclusion of the film manifests his willingness and ability to do so. Its first phase – in which he dupes Ambrose into killing Stamper and steals his samples of Bellerophon and Chimera – culminates in the second point at which Hunt tears off a face-mask, thereby revealing himself to be impersonator rather than impersonated, a man rather than a series of masks, and revealing Tom Cruise as a star capable of acknowledging the obscure darkness behind his handsome smile. Its final phase – the climactic joust between Hunt and Ambrose on motorbikes, culminating in unarmed combat on the beach – recalls that of De Palma's original movie, with its reiteration of the camera's identification with a blade poised over Cruise's features, and its final conjuring of the necessary gun for Ambrose's execution from the wind-scoured sand itself, quite as if declaring nature's siding with those who would thwart a global plague, as well as the camera's ability to realize our fantasies of good triumphing over the evil that is good's necessary other. And its epilogue shows us that, in their achievement of genuine humanity, Ethan's and Nyra's joint wish is to lose themselves in the crowds thronging Sydney's parks and harbour, to rejoin the everyday rhythms of life beyond the reach of those who would track them down and force them into roles which would make them into monstrous parodies of human existence. For when Chimera is made truly chimerical, the hero Bellerophon becomes nothing more, and nothing less, than a human being.

Divining the drama of objects: *Paycheck*

At least one of the films Woo has made since *Mission: Impossible II* suggests a continued interest in the themes arising from that project; for *Paycheck* (2003), based on a short story by Philip K. Dick, appears to realize a version of a possibility that Stanley Cavell identified in the *Mission: Impossible* television series – namely, that of the gadgets being the protagonists of the drama. The story of this film concerns an engineer named Michael Jennings (Ben Affleck), who emerges from a three-year period of employment by a mysterious conglomerate with his memory of everything he did for them in that time chemically erased. But a month before his return to the public world he posted himself an envelope containing twenty items – everyday objects such as a packet of cigarettes, a public transit pass, a key and a partly solved crossword puzzle. It turns out that he had been building a device for seeing the future, and that he used it to see his own future, so that he might arm himself against it by means of this envelope. For, after his employment is terminated, both the conglomerate and the FBI have reasons to threaten his life; and the ordinary objects in the envelope prove to be just what he needs to evade that threat, reunite with the woman with whom he fell in love during those three years and destroy the device, whose existence threatens the possibility of an apocalyptic global war.

The film itself is mysteriously inert from beginning to end – partly because of a total lack of chemistry between Ben Affleck and Uma Thurman as the leads, partly because the set designs (particularly in the conglomerate's research facility) are dismayingly inauthentic, and partly because a central, set-piece chase sequence with Woo's much-loved motorbikes is both overlong and utterly unsuspenseful. But one can see what might have attracted this director (with his modernist interests) into an unfamiliar, and evidently unaccommodating, genre. For the film's central device is a transparent figure for the screened projection of a science fiction movie, with its false promise of emancipation and its real threat to genuinely human openness to the future. And its central plot amounts to an individual's attempt to discover or construct that very plot, the plot of the very film he is in: it follows him in his attempts to find and follow a narrative sequence of dramatic scenes in which an ordinary object is able to take on extra-ordinary (indeed, life-saving) significance.

The Michael Jennings who inhabits the three-year period is never directly portrayed in this film, as if quite beyond the film's representative capacities, just as a director inhabits a world that is necessarily behind or beyond (anyway, other than) the world captured and projected by his camera. He sees the future and makes possible the particular narrative structure he prefers for it by providing the necessary means of getting from one scene to the next. And he provides this to the Michael Jennings who emerges from that three-year period lacking any memory of it, and needing to reconstruct from the contents of his self-addres-sed envelope the plot that his earlier self divined for him. In other words, Michael Jennings is both director and actor in the drama of his life (or perhaps two aspects of the director – the one whose initial inspiration gets the project off the ground and the one challenged to bring it to completion by struggling to con-figure its events in ways that re-establish his inevitably disrupted relation with that initial inspiration). Woo thereby posits the director as aspiring to be the actor's inspiring, higher self (someone who envisions the actor as able to achieve more than he thinks himself capable of achieving), and the actor as strug-gling to incarnate a conception of himself that is both beyond him and yet rooted within him, one that requires him to become the instrument of objects themselves designed to be instruments. And, for both, the basic condition of possibility for the film they jointly conspire to bring into existence is the presence and reality of material objects whose humble identities can accommodate the most dramatic of human eventualities – matters of life and death which unfold or explode from their quotidian properties in something like the way the title sequence of an original *Mission:*

Impossible episode strung its most dramatic events along a sputtering fuse lit by the striking of a humble match.

If even such objects can invite and demand this kind of dramatic contextualization or realization, one may well ask (not so much: what becomes of things on film?, but rather): what might things not become on film? What transformations and revelations of significance in the most basic elements of everydayness is it beyond the power of the motion-picture camera (that inherently dramatic object) to induce?

Source: Paramount courtesy the Kobal Collection

9

AN ACCELERATED MUTATOR

J.J. Abrams' Mission: Impossible III

Where John Woo made it his business to inherit the Mission: Impossible universe as a wholly cinematic phenomenon, Mission: Impossible III (2006) was always fated to return the series to its televisual point of origin. For its director – J.J. Abrams – had never previously worked in the medium of movies, and was invited to contribute to this franchise solely as a result of his highly influential, award-winning work on the television series Alias (2002–06) – a series that Abrams not only devised and executive produced, but to which he regularly contributed as writer and director throughout its five seasons. And, from the outset, Alias all but declared itself to be a contemporary reincarnation of Mission: Impossible – quite as if it were the same programme under another name. Accordingly, just as one would expect of any recuperation of a thirty-five-year-old original (particularly one effected in light of that original's intervening cinematic appropriations), its continuation of the format necessarily embodied a critical rethinking of its deter-mining conditions, and so an answer to the question of how a new instance of the spy genre must revise its understanding of itself if it is to compel conviction from its audience.

Alias: Mission: Impossible

SD-6, the agency for which Sydney Bristow (Jennifer Garner) has worked for seven years at the opening of Alias, describes itself to its employees as a black ops offshoot of the CIA, whose cover is that of an investment bank (Credit Dauphine). Each mission Sydney undertakes is as part of a small team drawn from a group of familiar colleagues, almost always in a foreign location (which might be anywhere on the planet); it usually involves her adopting a disguise, more specifically pretending to be someone she is not (whether real or fictional); and its success critically depends upon an exotic array of 'op tech' – sophisticated gadgetry provided by a technical services team whose abilities approximate to the magical.

So far, so uncannily similar to the status and modus operandi of the IM force. But even within the parameters of the show's pilot episode, Abrams effects a series of radical alterations to that original template. To begin with, it turns out that SD-6 is not what it claims to be: it is in fact an agency of a global criminal conglomerate known as the Alliance. When Sydney discovers this, and reports it to a branch of the real CIA, she is asked to maintain her role within SD-6, but as a CIA double agent; so every mission she goes on henceforth is itself possessed of a double aspect – as something to which she must appear to be committed on SD-6's behalf, but which her CIA handlers expect her to sabotage in ways that nevertheless maintain her cover. As the series progresses, the branch of the CIA for which she works becomes increasingly autonomous and independent of its parent agency (to the point at which it gains its own acronymic identity – APO), and increasingly reliant upon dazzling op tech and dubious techniques of violence and torture, as well as recruits (both willing and unwilling) from the agency it is targeting. In other words, it increasingly comes to merit SD-6's original, deceptive self-description, if not its true nature.

This theme of doubling already makes concrete a set of possibilities that simply didn't exist in the televisual world of *Mission: Impossible* – that the agency for which one works might be inhabited by those working against its purposes (an idea that Abrams could have acquired from the first *Mission: Impossible* movie, as he seems to acknowledge in the last series of *Alias*, when the APO team – like De Palma's IM force – have to penetrate CIA headquarters at Langley in pursuit of a mole), and even that it might itself be essentially other than it appears to be or presents itself as being. But the point about the kind of scepticism unleashed by such doubling is that it is, in principle, indefinitely reiterable. If SD-6 might be hiding its criminal nature under the alias of the CIA, then who is to say that another organization might not be hiding its nature beneath the alias of SD-6 (the Alliance), an organization that might in turn be suborned from within by those with covert purposes, or superseded by other organizations that fulfil essentially the same function under another name (the Covenant, Prophet-5), and so endlessly on?

Individuals are as much subject to this duplicity as institutions. For example, if the head of SD-6 (Sloane, played by Ron Rifkin) can conceal his criminal impulses behind the guise of a CIA chief, then he might also be concealing other projects beneath his criminal identity – perhaps projects that are no less criminal than his official SD-6 commitments, perhaps commitments to particular people in his life that conflict with his criminal responsibilities, both official and unofficial. And the principle applies to self-knowledge as well as to knowledge of others. For Sydney herself is subject to a sequence of unmaskings of covert aspects of her own motivation and identity: amongst other things, she comes to discover that her father subjected her to rigorous training in espionage skills from infancy (thus predetermining a career choice she had taken herself to make at college), and that two years of her life (during which she acted as an agent of a criminal organization known as the Covenant) elapsed within an apparently momentary gap in her stream of consciousness (a gap that coincided with the gap between the end of one series of *Alias* and the beginning of the next).

Hence, as the various series of *Alias* succeeded one another, this sceptical principle became the paranoid reality of the world it presented to us. Behind every uncovered covert purpose another was revealed, and then another behind that, until its viewers became habituated to the thought that the full significance of any action, person or institution not only could be other than it at present appeared to be, but almost certainly would be, and hence that no revelation of meaning could possibly be final. But if no such revelation is ever more than provisional, and so is always likely to be superseded by another, why should either characters in or viewers of this world retain a willingness or even a capacity to take any given layer of meaning seriously – to respond sincerely to the specific claims it makes on them? As Abrams' second televisual venture (the series *Lost* [2005–], which deploys the principle of unending unmasking in its plotting to the point of delirium) clearly demonstrates, if events and actions repeatedly turn out to mean something other than they seem to, or have the revelation of their real meaning endlessly deferred, they will soon come to seem entirely devoid of meaning, and so of human interest. Even though the spy genre has always drawn sustenance from the hermeneutics of suspicion, Abrams' willingness to develop that logic of unmasking in such a hyperbolic way risks creating an affectless parody of the genre rather than a genuine resuscitation of it.

How, then, does he avoid that fate? One strategy is embodied in the second key revision *Alias* introduces to the IM force template, which concerns the relation between the professional and the private lives of the spies in both agencies. In the original *Mission: Impossible*, every episode begins with the team leader's selection of an appropriate array of agents for the specific operation in hand; and the files of each candidate always, if glancingly, reveal something of the life each leads when not involved in a mission. Thus, the technical expert is shown to be employed by (perhaps to run) an electronics company, the sole female to have a career as a model, and the master of disguise (the wearer of masks) to be a theatrical performer. So it would be wrong to say that we gained no sense of these people's lives beyond their activities in espionage; but we certainly learn nothing about their family and friends, and in fact we are given no indication that they have any such relationships, beyond the evident but minimal cameraderie of the IM force team. At most, we learn that they have another profession – a life they lead in public, which appears essentially weightless and uninvolving, a way of passing the time between their episodic immersions in the covert profession that really defines their existence. In this sense, the aspect of their lives that is truly private – in which they express the real individuality of their character in the exercise of their talents, as opposed to occupying a role in the social world that is suited to anyone with such talents – is that which we see in the programme, not that which they pursue outside its parameters: it is their secret life as spies.

This matter is handled very differently in *Alias*. To begin with, whereas the original IM force team had only fleeting moments in Jim Phelps' apartment before their mission, Sydney's professional life is conducted as much in a sequence of HQ office complexes as in the field. And this makes it possible for her to develop far more substantial friendships with other members of her mission teams (both SD-6 and CIA); indeed, those friendships have increasingly complex ramifications in her professional life, since they engender cares and commitments that cut across, and work against, one another, and so affect her professional responsibilities. Furthermore, she has a substantial social life outside her espionage activities. She has a number of friends who think of her as working for a bank, and who are drawn more deeply into the complex machinations of the various agencies for and against which she works. She also has a fiancé; indeed, Sydney's realization of the true nature of SD-6 is initiated by their decision to execute him, because – unwilling to found a marriage and a family on dishonesty – she has told him what (she then thinks is) the true nature of her job.

But beyond friendship and romance there is family; and family ties (whether of blood or marriage) are as influential in *Alias* as any professional matters – are, indeed, increasingly indistinguishable from them. For example, the execution of Sydney's fiancé forces her father (Jack Bristow, played by Victor Garber) to reveal, first, that he is not a businessman who sells aircraft parts but an executive in SD-6, and, then, that in this covert role he too is operating as a double agent for the CIA. As the first series progresses, it is revealed that Sydney's mother (Elena Direvko, played by Lena Olin) is also a covert intelligence operative: she married Sydney's father under the orders of the KGB, and, after leaving him, began to work freelance for criminal ends, in ways that place her in conflict not only with the CIA but with SD-6 as well. Still within the first series, we also learn that Sloane is forced to choose between his sick wife and his criminal associates. In later series, Sydney's closest workmates (Dixon [Carl Lumbly], originally her SD-6 partner, and Vaughn [Michael Vartan], her CIA handler and lover-to-be) find that their spouses and parents have various roles to play in their professional lives; and Sydney herself discovers the existence of a half-sister (who works first for Argentinian intelligence and then for APO, as her partner) whose father is none other than Sloane himself, whose status as her surrogate father (established at the outset of the series, when she and her real father were estranged and Sloane appeared to be a loyal servant of his country) is thereby further complicated.

In short, *Alias* insists upon the fact that professional spies are also human beings with personal lives, in particular with familial ties. Once again, this insistence verges upon the parodic, as it becomes increasingly difficult to find a central character in this world of espionage who is not related to Sydney by blood or marriage. But it is precisely the extravagance of this dimension of *Alias* that works to counter or neutralize the threat posed by the extravagance of its procedure of endless unmasking. For their personal entanglements give depth and complexity to the characters in a way that preserves our interest as viewers in their fate, in the wilderness of unending reinterpretation that they inhabit; we care about Sydney's missions and relationships because she is not simply a spy, or a daughter, or a woman in love, but all of these things, and all at once – not a cipher, or an alien in human guise.

This difference between the two series hangs together with another: the fact that, in *Alias*, the miraculous gadgets (whilst present and highly influential) never amount to the true protagonists of the narratives, as they do with the IM force, whose members so thoroughly inhabit the status of servants of the technology, mere instruments for the instruments. Since pretty much every one of Sydney's missions promises or threatens to have personal significance for her, the magical gadgets she employs increasingly become simply one taken-for-granted means to further the human drama of the series. And what primarily ensures the success of Sydney's missions is anyway not her op tech, but rather her cleverness, her prowess as a fighter and her capacity for improvisation – what one might call the human element of the world of intelligence-gathering.

So, beyond the endless multiplicity of Sydney's disguises, her status as a double agent working within and between agencies that are one another's doubles, and her repeated confrontation with technologies of physical and genetic doubling which first permit her closest friends to be replaced by identical counterparts and ultimately are deployed to create a double of Sydney herself from her oldest enemy, *Alias'* emphasis on the humanity of its protagonists adds yet another dimension of doubling. For that emphasis ensures that every one of her small group of fellow-spies has one particularly influential alternative identity for her (as she has for them) – as father, mother, sister or potential spouse. In the world of *Alias*, then, the profession of spying is neither simply a job which has little significance for one's life as a whole nor an arena in which one's true nature can find expression independently of one's identity as relative or friend; these worlds are not independent but inter-related. Critically, however, that inter-relation is more destabilizing than it is supportive. For the fact that Sydney's key professional colleagues are also part of her family (or at least her family of friends) does not provide an external grounding or anchor for someone condemned to navigate the shifting sands and distorting mirrors of existence in SD-6 and the CIA; it rather intensifies the uncertainties of her working life, and introduces uncertainty into her private life.

Take the primary case of her parents. First, they both concealed their roles as spies, and so lied to her. But, in addition, there is the simultaneous dual relevance of both identities in her present dealings with them. For if her boss is also her father, and her enemy her mother, how will they treat her in a professional context, and how in a personal one (and how will she treat them)? Can that distinction between professional and personal contexts any longer be drawn with confidence? If not, then the central figures in her life are always something other than the role they currently occupy (whether professional or personal), and so is she; and the degree and significance of this otherness in any given context is beyond computation. She can no more rely on her father or mother acknowledging her as their daughter in professional contexts than she can be sure that their relationship with her outside the field of espionage is not an acknowledgement of the demands of that field.

On this understanding of the life of a spy, the professional requirement of impersonation – the talent, and the habit, of enacting an identity that is not yours – inevitably bleeds into the personal world (implying that even your own flesh and blood might be dissemblers to whom you cannot know that you are not dissembling in turn); and the personal requirement of honesty – the expectation of being who you are and meaning what you say – bleeds, with equal inevitability, into the professional world (intensifying the discomfort and dissociation engendered by the need, as a spy, to be who you are not – even to your nearest and dearest). In such a world, it is not so much that it is hard to grasp who others are, and who you are; it is that one loses confidence in the very idea that there is something to grasp here, about others and about oneself. And, as a consequence, the challenge it poses to its inhabitants is not so much to be, or to become, who they are, but to retain their grasp on the idea that they are each someone in particular, an individual possessed of an identity as opposed to a series of aliases behind which no true self is concealed. Or perhaps the real challenge is to acknowledge that selfhood is not essentially opposed to the inhabitation of aliases – that it might rather be a matter of how one inhabits them, of what one brings to the business of their inhabitation.

Two other substantial features of the world of *Alias* are worth noting in the light of Abrams' recruitment for *Mission: Impossible III*. The first provides a further constraint upon its logic of unmasking: the role of the figure of Rimbaldi. For, early in the first series, it becomes clear that Sloane and the Alliance (as well as its various descendants) are centrally concerned not only with the acquisition of intelligence, exotic weaponry and other familiar goals of the criminal trade, but also – and in fact fundamentally – with the writings of a fifteenth-century polymath named Rimbaldi. In one respect, this interest is continuous with those other criminal goals, since those writings embody equations and blueprints for potentially lethal technology; but Rimbaldi's work has an enigmatic quality of the kind that transforms Sloane's instrumental interest in him into a cultic obsession which also comes to pervade the activities of all the agencies involved (including the CIA and the National Security Agency). For, first, the technology his writings adumbrate is far in advance of early twenty-first-century science, let alone the emergent science of the Enlightenment, and so those adumbrations have a visionary or prophetic aspect; and, second, Rimbaldi's writing explicitly includes one genuinely apocalyptic prophecy. For it contains descriptions and drawings of a woman to whom Rimbaldi attributes world-historical significance in a cosmic battle between the forces of good and evil; and these depictions amount to a perfect premonition or presentiment of Sydney Bristow.

Once again, Abrams here differentiates his world of spying from that of *Mission: Impossible*. For the IM force do not confront any single opposition agency orchestrating the specific enemies against which their missions are serially mounted, let alone one whose interests focus on a prophetic vision in which technology and spirituality are fused (more exactly, not distinguished from each other in the ways characteristic of enlightenment modernity), and in which his deepest secret (the dual capacity to confer endless life and to induce global genocide, both ways of achieving 'the end of nature') confronts the force of family ties (with the sense they embody that human life is mortal, hence something we must always be willing to cede, and so to bequeath, to new generations). But in utilizing Rimbaldi as the ultimate, enigmatic horizon of the various inter-agency conflicts that drive the five series of *Alias*, Abrams once again presses a familiar principle of the genre to its logical limits: in this case, the Hitchcockian notion of a McGuffin – the apparently important focus of the central characters' competing efforts whose nature need never be fully explained or rendered credible because its significance resides entirely in providing a pretext for the action. Abrams' way of inheriting the cinematic world of *Mission: Impossible* will pivot upon the role he assigns to this generic staple within that world.

The second feature of *Alias* that is relevant to Abrams' work in his new medium is perhaps its most obvious one. In *Mission: Impossible*, the sole female character takes on a succession of essentially passive acting roles within the team's theatrical performances, and is rarely required to operate the technology or even to use her initiative; her world is a world of men. In *Alias*, by contrast, the central character is a woman more than capable of thinking and fighting for herself, and in relation to whom the men function in essentially supporting roles; and, as the series develops, she encounters a number of other, equally autonomous and capable women – as enemies and as partners – whose contribution to the narrative is no less pivotal. In other words, *Alias* was devised in an essentially post-*Alien* world – one in which the idea of a central, active, indeed combative female protagonist has become so familiar that any proper study of its significance now seems to require that it undergo a certain heightening or intensification. We saw earlier that John Woo's critical inheritance of Brian De Palma's cinematic transcription of *Mission: Impossible* concentrated its attention on De Palma's failure to question this aspect of his televisual source. Abrams' sequel to Woo's sequel is in effect a continuation of that criticism, and so in part a turning of Woo's questioning upon himself.

Before we turn to *Mission: Impossible III*, however, it is worth noting in conclusion some of the ways in which *Alias* is formally as well as thematically distinctive in the world of televisual espionage. One such mark of distinction might be more accurately described as a parodic intensification of a condition of production that it shares with its generic competitors, not excluding *Mission: Impossible*, and indeed with televisions shows more generally – the extent to which the environs of Los Angeles have to go proxy for every location in which the story is set. It is central to the seductiveness of Sydney's work that she might have to conduct a mission any-where on the planet; and one of the pleasures of watching her do so lies in the blatant duplicity with which the screen first declares that we have been transported to Berlin or Tangier or Moscow or Bhutan, then presents us with stock footage of these places, then reveals each to be nothing more than an alias for a very roughly corresponding portion of California. Even so, it is hard to avoid the suspicion that one aspect of the seductiveness implicit in an invitation to direct a blockbuster movie must have been the implicit possibility of (for example) actually filming scenes set in Rome in the real city of Rome.

Two other marks of formal distinction are also relevant to our concerns. First, a signature feature of all five series of *Alias* is Abrams' tendency to begin an episode with a scene (one of particular danger or mystery) taken from somewhere towards the end of the story to which that episode will be devoted, to develop that scene to a point of particular tension and then to go back to the chronological beginning of the story (with the declaration '72 hours earlier', or the like). One might think of it as an inflection of the title sequence of every Mission: Impossible episode, which threaded onto the image of a burning fuse a jumbled sequence of glimpsed scenes from the story to come. It is certainly an effective way of whetting our appetite for that story, and of encouraging us to overlook implausibilities in its development because of our impatience to discover how the climactic scene is resolved. But this presentational structure seems in addition to resonate with the McGuffin of the series: for, of course, the idea of Rimbaldi as prophesying not only the technology of the future but also a planetary apocalypse in which Sydney Bristow will be pivotally involved persistently engenders a sense that the fate of these characters is somehow always already sealed – that, for all their technological back-up, strength of will and capacity for improvisation, they are in the grip of an essentially predetermined course of events. Here, Rimbaldi, the paranoia of endless unmasking and what I will call the premonitory structure of many Alias episodes strongly reinforce one another.

This idea of premonition encodes a reference to the other formal feature of Alias that I wanted to underline – more precisely, it points towards one feature of the world it represents as acknowledging a feature of the televisual medium. For, as I argued earlier, the mode of viewing characteristic of television is that of monitoring; and monitoring is the condition to which the central characters of Alias (and, indeed, everyone in their world) are subjected with unprecedented intensity, from the perspective afforded by their professional activities. The individual members of each mission team monitor one another's words, deeds and locations, and these teams are in turn monitored by their controllers and by the security sections of the agencies for which they work. They are also under continuous surveillance, at home as well as at work, by enemies who might easily be working within as well as against their own agency; and they conduct their lives in a world that is itself subject to blanket satellite surveillance and Echelon-derived analysis of every conceivable mode of electronic communication.

As a consequence, Sydney and her espionage colleagues relate to the world as a field of essentially indistinguishable settings for inherently anticipatable events: the theatrical performances that are their missions, whether their own or those of their opponents. Hence, other people exist for them primarily insofar as they are involved in such events – whether as witting or unwitting fellow-actors or as members of an audience (either at the site of the performance or monitoring it from a distance); and, increasingly, that is how they appear to themselves. For as the palpable pleasure that they take in their professional impersonations, and in which we share, shades more and more clearly into parodic excess, so their professional existence becomes theatricalized; and this mode of perception of their professional world increasingly infiltrates their private lives, the domain of supposed normality or uneventfulness that should form the unquestioned, contrasting background to their event-structured professional lives. For the pervasive entanglement of personal and professional relationships in Sydney's life entails that, for example, her father's love for her cannot (because of the duplicitous demands of his job) be taken for granted or simply shown in his actions, but must rather be said or declared by him, in a set-piece speech whose rhetorical form inevitably works against the trust it aims to express or invite, despite (even perhaps because of) the apparently passionate sincerity with which it is delivered. Once again, then, Abrams' double vision of spies as family and family as spies makes it impossible simply to assume that a spy's life outside his or her work might secure his or her sense of themselves in the midst of that work, as opposed to subjecting it to further destabilization.

'I'm going to die unless you kill me'

The pre-title sequence of Mission: Impossible III (written by Alex Kutzman, Robert O. Orci and J.J. Abrams) is, before anything else, immediately and completely gripping. It thrusts the viewer into the world of the film (as Ethan Hunt is dragged from unconsciousness back into that world by an agonizing electric shock) with brutal speed and efficiency, of a kind that neither De Palma nor Woo manage, or even attempt, in their opening scenes. But its distinctive synthesis of content and form does more than declare Abrams' confident expertise, as well as his particular gifts and obsessions, as a director; it also poses questions to the directors whose work he is inheriting that are as radical and uncompromising as those posed by David Fincher to his predecessors in the pre-title sequence of *Alien*[3].

Abrams' opening deploys his signature structural device of premonition, and thereby declares its general indebtedness to (and so its specific differences from) the title sequence of every episode of the TV series, which means simultaneously declaring his refusal to follow De Palma in constructing exactly the same kind of title sequence as that of the TV show for his movie (a choice in which Woo's way of beginning his movie evinces no interest, which suggests that Abrams' opening further declares at least a relative lack of interest in Woo's choices, and so a desire – structurally akin to Fincher's – to return to the cinematic origins of his franchise). We begin, in other words, with a substantial scene that belongs chronologically to the latter stages of the story, and so with a situation that is not fully intelligible to us, either in its details or with respect to grasping what has brought its characters to this pass, but which nevertheless reveals a great deal about the central concerns of the film we are about to watch.

First, it introduces us to the main villain (Owen Davian, played by Philip Seymour Hoffman), who tells Ethan that he has placed an explosive charge in his head, and then threatens to kill a bound and gagged woman (whom Ethan calls 'Jules', played by Michelle Monaghan) unless Ethan reveals the location of something called 'the rabbit's foot' by the time he counts to ten. Ethan is manacled hand and foot to what looks like a dentist's chair, hence is entirely unable to intervene physically; and Davian's question appears to bewilder him, because he thinks he has already delivered the rabbit's foot to his interlocutor. Impotent and disoriented, he nevertheless tries first to reassure Jules and then to find a way of addressing Davian that will stop him from carrying out his threat. He first claims that the rabbit's foot is in Paris, then that he will only talk to Davian if he puts down his gun, then that he will only help him if stops threatening Jules (at which point, on the count of six, Davian shoots her in the leg), then that he will kill him if he hurts her; and then finally he begs Davian to let her go and promises to help him get whatever he wants, but only if he will do what's right, what he knows is right. At this point, as Ethan tonelessly repeats 'No – no – no', Davian reaches the end of his count of ten and shoots Jules in the head; and, as Ethan howls in despair, Abrams cuts to a close-up of a match-head igniting, then itself igniting a fuse, and the title music begins.

When telling Ethan about the bomb in his head, Davian sarcastically but mysteriously asks whether the idea sounds familiar to him. We shall learn of the events within the film's story to which he is referring later; but to those watching it who were also devotees of *Alias*, the idea would indeed already have sounded familiar – because it is central to an episode of the final series of *Alias*, one which was broadcast a few months before the release of his film. To build this dual-aspect structure of significance (referring us simultaneously to something within the film and something outside it) into the first words spoken in his film thus amounts to a declaration on Abrams' part that his directorial goal is to implant the preoccupations and sensibility of *Alias* into the body of work done, and so into the cinematic world established, by De Palma and Woo. More specifically, it suggests that this implantation will radically affect the intellectual structure of that work, threatening in fact to blow it apart, and that it will do so by subjecting Ethan Hunt's character to potentially explosive internal forces introduced from outside.

One might even say that the most radical effect of *Mission: Impossible* III's agonizing internalizing of *Alias* lies not so much in its suggestion that the interior of Ethan Hunt's body might be violated or turn against him, but rather in the very idea that Ethan Hunt's body might *have* an interior as well as a highly recognizable (and so disguisable) exterior. For in confronting the possibility that his material reality might amount to something more than an agglomeration of appropriate surface appearances, that the reality of the body is more than superficial, he and we will also be brought to confront the possibility that he might have or acquire an inner as well as an outer life, and so be psychically real, recognizably human, in a way that Abrams considers that neither De Palma nor Woo ever properly managed to realize in cinematic terms.

Ethan's dual-aspect vulnerability is embodied in the two other points of the dramatic triangle in this opening scene – Davian and Jules. We don't at this point know who Jules is, and so what exactly she means to Ethan; but we know enough to know that she makes him vulnerable to Davian, whose willingness to damage Ethan's body from within is equalled by his willingness to damage his mind (his heart and soul) from within. Hoffman's performance utterly convinces us, as it convinces Ethan, that his will to do harm is absolute, and that he is entirely capable of acting on it; and the final moments of the scene confirm our worst fears.

But if Davian doesn't appear to be play-acting, Ethan has been reduced to a state in which play-acting is his only resort. Deprived of any recourse to physical action, he can only rescue the situation if he can talk Davian out of his threatened course; so what we see in this scene is Ethan trying out a variety of roles or masks, discarding each as it becomes clear that it is not achieving his goal, then reaching for another – for the performance that will finally elicit conviction in his one-man audience. In short, he is forced back upon the irreducible essence of his professional identity – that of acting or impersonation, the inhabitation of an alias; and he fails. So what he confronts, in the final split-second after Davian shoots Jules in the head, is not just the death of someone he loves, but also the death of his conception of himself as capable of succeeding professionally no matter what the difficulties that stand in his way. This mission, it seems, really was impossible; so what this scene appears to present us with is the first genuine, literal embodiment of that with which the televisual and cinematic worlds of *Mission: Impossible* had always, but hitherto falsely, claimed to be concerned. And the question to which the rest of the film is devoted is: what exactly has brought Ethan, and so *Mission: Impossible*, to this point of self-subverting fulfilment?

The fuse lit by Davian's shot leads us directly to the answer to this question; for the explosion it prepares is, it appears, an engagement party for Ethan and Jules (full name Julia Mead), who turns out to be a nurse with a taste for adventurous activity holidays of the kind on which she met Ethan. In addition, we are quickly told that Ethan's parents are dead and he has no siblings, whereas Julia has a mother, a pregnant sister and a brother. So, in promising to marry her, he is at once acquiring a family, and so a range of family obligations (in their first exchange Ethan promises to keep an eye on Julia's brother's drinking at the party, which Julia describes as 'a huge responsibility'), and also committing himself to the creation of a new family of his own (as Julia's sister declares in her party speech, they are all expecting there to be offspring from the union). The *Alias* inheritance here is impossible to overlook; for whereas Clare Phelps was a member of Ethan's IM force team, and Nyah Nordhoff-Hall was at least a fellow-inhabitant of the clandestine world, Julia is a civilian – wholly an inhabitant of the ordinary world within which spies like Ethan must inhabit an alias, appearing other than they really are. So he faces the task of making and maintaining a connection with the very world from which his profession demands that he alienate himself. His initial solution is to continue to claim that he is an employee of the Virginia Department of Transportation, but to retire from field work in order to train new IM force recruits for missions of the kind he used to take on himself. The assumption is clear: field work and family don't mix, unless both elements of the mixture are modified or adulterated.

Ironically, however, it is a relationship established through Ethan's supposedly safer work as a trainer that now draws him back into the field; for his immediate boss (John Musgrave, played by Billy Crudup) informs him that his best trainee – Lindsey Farris (played by Keri Russell) – has been captured by Owen Davian and invites him to participate in her rescue. The first of the film's set-piece action sequences concerns that rescue mission, which Ethan runs with a small team (including Luther Stickel [Ving Rhames], Declan Gormley [Jonathan Rhys Myers] and Zhen Lei [Maggie Q]), and which ends in failure despite their having extracted Lindsey from the criminals' Berlin base, because Davian detonates an explosive charge that he had previously placed in Lindsey's skull as they escape in a helicopter.

Once again, then, Ethan confronts the limitations of his own power as a spy: he fails to do what he set out to do, and a woman close to him dies as a result, even if her capture and death are not a direct result of his own actions (except insofar as he declared her ready for field work and the result of her first foray is her own death). For even when the team learn that the explosive charge in Lindsey's head has been activated, there is still a chance of saving her. Ethan realizes that using an onboard defibrillator on her will short-circuit the charge; it will also stop her heart, but the same defibrillator can then be used to restart it. However, the defibrillator needs time to reach full power; and when Ethan is prevented from switching it on (by the need to save Zhen from falling out of the helicopter during its escape from enemy pursuit), the delay means that the bomb goes off before the defibrillator is ready. So Lindsey dies because Ethan decides to save Zhen's life, and because charging up the defibrillator takes thirty seconds rather than twenty; the limitations of time and space (he can't be in two places at once, doing two things at once), the determinants of material and so of human reality, defeat him.

Moreover, in trying to save Lindsey, Ethan puts his private life with Julia in jeopardy. For he is now back in the field, risking his life; and by remaining there in order to destroy the man who brought about Lindsey's destruction, he will ultimately put her life at risk. More immediately, however, Ethan's desire for vengeance embroils the team in the second set-piece operation of the film: an attempt to kidnap Davian when he attends a charity event at the Vatican. But, throughout that mission, he is embroiled in a conversation with Luther that began during the Berlin operation, and that addresses the conflict he now inhabits between his professional and his personal life. Luther argues that spies cannot have lasting relationships, because the job always comes between them and the woman; any such relationship with a civilian will be founded on 'dishonesty: a dishonesty that poisons everything'. Ethan repeatedly denies this, although without offering any reasons; and, indeed, his recent behaviour with Julia seems if anything to support Luther's position.

He did, after all, lie to her about his Berlin trip; and he does so again about the trip to Rome, even though – as he reveals to Luther in the Vatican – he and Julia get married in the intervening days. For they marry without him revealing the true nature of his job; instead – in the face of her anguished declaration that his secretiveness has ensured that 'nothing in my mind makes sense' and that she needs to know that their relationship is real – he simply asks her to trust him, whilst implicitly refusing fully to trust her. The fact that Ethan can only tell Luther about the marriage after having donned the Davian face-mask that he needs to complete the Vatican mission – at once declaring his inability to be honest even to his closest friend unless disguised and acknowledging that his new status as a husband is thus far no more than another mask, not merely a new alias for the ordinary world but a particularly dangerous form of criminality within it – suggests that he fears his friend is right.

Luther's primary anxiety is for the well-being of Ethan's wife, rather than for Ethan himself; but there is no reason to think that he isn't anxious about both, and the film itself makes it clear just how dangerous the *Mission: Impossible* principle of masking is for those who practice it, and just how far a willingness on the part of its practitioners to establish a substantial personal life behind or beyond it might (as in *Alias*) as easily destabilize as emancipate them. For the moment at which Ethan disguises himself as Davian is also the moment at which he starts becoming not only vulnerable to, but indistinguishable from, someone he thinks of as his polar opposite, whose destruction is the ultimate justification for his continued existence as a spy, with all the sacrifices that involves.

The process begins with his first interrogation of Davian after the successful kidnap, in the aeroplane that is returning them to the US. Davian not only effortlessly overrides Ethan's demand that he reveal the nature, location and destination of what is codenamed 'the rabbit's foot' – Davian's next piece of lethal merchandise on sale to the highest bidder, and the hi-tech McGuffin that powers the film's plot; he also immediately threatens to harm Ethan's loved ones. Upon being reminded of Lindsey's fate, and his failure to save her, Ethan snaps: he suspends Davian over an open cargo door, threatens to drop him if he doesn't talk, and then – as he continues to refuse – begins to slice through Davian's retaining straps one by one. Only Luther's intervention, reminding him that 'this is not you', prevents him from executing his captive, thereby indulging in exactly the kind of behaviour Davian himself tends to exhibit. As Davian himself later points out, 'you can always tell someone's character by the way they treat those they don't need to treat well'.

The transformation continues once Davian's private army engineers the impossible mission of his escape from IM force custody, by means of an attack by drone and helicopter gunship on the Chesapeake Bay Bridge (an immediate riposte to the IM force's illusions of omnipotence of a kind familiar in *Alias*, but largely unexplored in the previous *Mission: Impossible* movies). For now Davian is free to carry out his threat against Julia; and, once he has kidnapped her, Ethan becomes a tool at Davian's disposal (a cat's paw to locate the rabbit's foot), and so finds himself having to escape IM force custody and control in order to steal his merchandise from a high-security facility in Shanghai. In other words, Ethan is compelled to devote the full repertoire of his professional talents to an end that is the absolute obverse of their purported justification.

This, I think, explains why his escape from IM force headquarters begins with him wearing a leather face-mask of a kind that is irresistibly reminiscent of Hannibal Lecter, that exemplary monster in human guise, whose methods of escape from incarceration (which include biting his captor and unlocking manacles with the ink refill of a ballpoint pen) Ethan blatantly plagiarizes at a later stage in the film. It also provides one reason why the final step in this blackest of black ops – Ethan's actual theft of the rabbit's foot from the laboratory – is never shown to us: although we see him successfully reach the roof of the building, and then later exit from it with the rabbit's foot, we see nothing of the intervening process. This is not just a witty point about the logic of representation (if the mission really is impossible, it is also unrepresentable – beyond the reach of envisioning, and so of visual transcription; in this sense, the very idea of a film of *Mission: Impossible* is chimerical). It also suggests an exercise of taste, or rather a recognition of its limits – a reluctance to project for all to see the precise point at which Ethan's personal commitments have allowed his Davian mask to eat into his real face, so that there is no longer a detectable gap between the impersonator and the impersonated, and at which the technique and principle of masking thereby declare themselves as threatening complete moral unmooring.

This brings us to the film's repetition of its pre-title scene – when Ethan is awoken to find that Davian is denying that he has delivered the real rabbit's foot and is threatening to kill Julia as a consequence. It is only now that we realize that the first presentation of this scene presented the truth of it, but not the whole truth (in true De Palma fashion). For although Davian does indeed shoot the bound and gagged woman, she turns out not to be Julia (but rather Davian's disgraced head of security wearing a mask of the real Julia, as she suffers the consequences of her failure at the Vatican). In other words, what we at first took to be real is a theatrical performance designed to check that Ethan had brought the real rabbit's foot; Davian is its director as well as a knowing participant in it, and Ethan discovers that he is no more than an unknowing performer in another's charade (not so different from the many people he has fooled in his own IM force performances).

We quickly realize thereafter that most of the set-piece sequences in the film have been pieces of theatre laid on by Davian for his own purposes. The rescue in Berlin (designed to plant false information about a mole in the IM force), the Chesapeake Bay rescue (which immediately and effectively nullifies Ethan's one successful piece of counter-theatre in the Vatican), Ethan's escape from IM force custody (engineered by the real mole, Musgrave), the Shanghai theft of the rabbit's foot; all of these, but particularly Davian's use of the signature IM force masking technique against its exemplary practitioner, reveal Davian to be IM force's dark double – what it might become if its moral co-ordinates were simply inverted but its tools, techniques and resources left intact. Indeed, given that Musgrave presents his duplicity to Ethan as a matter of his making use of Davian in the best interests of the IM force and the US (providing a trail of evidence to legitimate another foray into Middle Eastern politics and reconstruction), one might say that there is no 'might' about it: Davian's operation always was an IM force operation under another name.

Davian's status as the anti-IM force echoes the distinctive nature of the film's McGuffin, the rabbit's foot that Davian is planning to deliver to customers in the Middle East for a fee of $850 million. When Ethan asks what exactly the rabbit's foot might be, his answer takes the form of one of the film's best extended speeches, delivered by Benji Dunn (the IM force technical support chief, played by Simon Pegg), a new character in the cinematic world of *Mission:*

Impossible who is patently based on an *Alias* character named Marshall (played by Kevin Weisman), and who embodies one of Abrams' most distinctive contributions to that world – a sense of humour that doesn't undercut the seriousness of our interest in its characters' fates:

> Maybe it isn't a code word; maybe it's just a really expensive bunny appendage. But I used to have this professor at Oxford – Dr. Wykeham: he was this massive fat guy, you know, this huge big guy. . . . He taught bio-molecular kinetics and cellular dynamics. He used to scare the underclassmen with this story about how the world would eventually be eviscerated by technology; how it was inevitable that a compound would be created which he referred to as the 'anti-God': an accelerated mutator, an unstoppable force of destructive power that would just lay waste to everything – buildings and pubs and streets and children and ice cream parlours. . . . So whenever I see a rogue organization willing to spend this amount of money on a mystery tech, I always assume it's the anti-God – end of the world kind of stuff. But no, I don't have any idea what it is, I was just speculating.

If the rabbit's foot is the anti-God, then it is a kind of technology that (like Rimbaldi's greatest invention) spells the end of nature; it is a force of pure destruction that would lay waste to everything, including everything that technology had previously given us. Wykeham's vision (which strongly resembles that embedded in Heidegger's later writing on technology and the divine, to which I referred in my reading of *Blade Runner* earlier in Chapter 1) is thus of technology as an expression of human creativity that contains within it the seed of its own negation – a supplement to divine creation that will ultimately subvert itself as well as that to which it is a supplement. It is hard to think of anything more alien to the vision of technology as effortlessly and flawlessly enabling that lies at the heart of the original *Mission: Impossible* television series, and that is never seriously questioned by either of the previous *Mission: Impossible* films.

In this respect, *Mission: Impossible III* is itself an anti-IM force device, an accelerated mutator of the familiar inherited template that effectively eviscerates it (in ways reminiscent of David Fincher's attitude to what the Alien universe had become in the hands of James Cameron, an attitude he articulates by literally eviscerating the bodies of Ripley's newly acquired family at the outset of *Alien³*). And it is worth noting that 'acceleration' is as distinctive a feature of Abrams' contribution to the series of films as is 'mutation'. One might even say that its key formal mutation is a matter of acceleration: for, as my attempts to summarize the film's narrative have already shown, Abrams' plot structure is full of escalating event and incident.

He certainly provides analogues to De Palma's and Woo's trademark widescreen, spectacular set-pieces: his depictions of the Vatican operation, the Chesapeake Bay Bridge attack and the infiltration of the Shangai high-rise building at the very least bear comparison with De Palma's choreographing of Ethan's attack on the Langley mainframe or Woo's editing of the BioCyte infiltration. And those set-pieces are scattered with more precise acknowledgements of his predecessor's art. De Palma's Langley sequence is recalled in Ethan's harness suspension and descent during the Vatican operation, and in the black-and-white checkerboard structure of the Shanghai building's roof (which Ethan forcefully propels himself onto rather than avoiding); whereas Woo might recognize himself in Ethan's parachute jump from that same building, as well as in the scaling-up of Ethan's escape from Ambrose's island that is the Chesapeake Bay Bridge attack.

But Abrams dispenses with their familiar three-act structure, which generates longer, slower rhythms that naturally foreground a small number of set-pieces, in favour of a much more extended, gradually accelerating sequence of inter-related episodes of the kind that a season-long run of a television series such as *Alias* naturally engenders, within which such set-pieces inevitably feel far less salient. It's as if he is aiming to dissipate a certain soporific quality he detects in the previous films by introducing a dose of contemporary televisual pacing (just as Ethan injects the drugged Lindsey with adrenalin to assist their escape in Berlin), thereby creating an aesthetic hybrid – a grafting of cinematic and televisual grammars – that demonstrates that these two media need not understand themselves as inherently alien or mutually exclusive.

Returning to the accelerated mutator that this film contains, we should note that to call the rabbit's foot the 'anti-God' is explicitly to invite the question: how much of a role does religion have to play in this film? If its significance is not exactly underlined, it is certainly real. To begin with the most obvious theological reference, the one temporarily successful IM force mission in the movie is set in the Vatican. There, we see Ethan in a priestly cassock, with op tech secreted in his missal; and we might ask whether this double-aspect setting – at once a temporal and a spiritual power – is simply one more theatrical and theatricalized domain with no substance behind the ceremony (as the sophisticated security monitoring that Ethan must evade would suggest), or whether we should rather consider the IM force operation as in effect attempting to correct the blasphemous conjunction of Davian and his anti-God with God's earthly kingdom, to extirpate the dark double of a genuinely religious view of the world as God's creation and of ourselves as its stewards. This possibility might already be enough to sensitize us to the original spiritual sense of what are now typically inert turns of phrase in familiar forms of passionate speech scattered throughout the film – for example when Ethan asks, 'What the hell is Owen Davian doing at the Vatican?', or when the IM force director Brassel (played by Laurence Fishburne) describes Davian as a 'God-damned invisible man'.

One of our religious duties as stewards is to go forth and multiply, to participate in God's creation as male and female become one flesh and reproduce themselves in a new creation. And, as I noted earlier, before Ethan begins the Vatican mission, he chooses to quell his own and Julia's doubts about the reality of their relationship by getting married. That marriage ceremony is in many ways a skeletal, even a parodic, version of itself – hastily arranged in Julia's hospital, and using found objects to stand in for the bouquet and rings; but one aspect of it is unchanged, and indeed foregrounded. It occurs before a priest (presumably a hospital chaplain), and his words provide an almost ominous counterpoint to the self-conscious hilarity of bride and groom: 'These vows are not to be taken without careful thought and prayer, so as not to be diminished by difficult circumstances, and they are only to be dissolved by death'. We have already noted one scene in which Ethan has to suffer what he thinks is the death of his spouse; we shall later see how far rescuing their relationship from dissolution will turn out to depend upon Julia suffering his death and making possible his recovery from it.

It is worth recalling here, however, that in orthodox Christianity (and is it just coincidence that, in the Vatican operation, Zhen is named 'Demea', after the character who defends religious orthodoxy in David Humes' *Dialogues on Natural Religion*?) death has a symbolic as well as a literal significance. For the imitation of Christ is centrally seen as a matter of dying to the self – sacrificing one's own rights and needs for others, and in particular shedding any conception of oneself as essentially self-sufficient, capable of bringing about whatever one aims at regardless of the vicissitudes of circumstance, and without the help of grace. This is not an easy loss for a spy – particularly one whose business is the execution of impossible missions – to accept; but it is a lesson that the film already began to teach Ethan, with his inability to save Lindsey. That opening failure will not be his last.

One other sequence invites the viewer to consider the efficacy of religious belief by considering the efficacy of prayer. I mentioned earlier that the centrepiece of Ethan's climactic attempt to extract the rabbit's foot in Shanghai is not directly shown to us; what I didn't mention was what the film shows us instead, in the gap between his successful entry into the building and his rather less successful exit from it. What we see is a brief exchange between Declan and Zhen, as they wait to learn whether Ethan can once again achieve the impossible; and when Declan notices that Zhen is quietly praying for a successful outcome (using a prayer she recited as a child whenever her pet cat ran away to bring him home), he doesn't disdain her faith but rather asks her to teach the prayer to him. It is at this precise point that Ethan breaks radio silence to inform them that he has the rabbit's foot.

Is this editorial conjunction of cinematic material meant to signify a causal connection? Is Zhen's prayer efficacious, or just a superstition, an expression of an essentially magical conception of religious faith – a stance towards certain forms of words that precisely mirrors the way superstitious people regard a rabbit's foot as good luck (to which the familiar response is: it wasn't so lucky for the rabbit)? Is God just a conceptual analogue to such objects or rather their absolute opposite, as Benji suggests may be the case with respect to the anti-God? Which of these possibilities would be better supported if we viewed the rabbit's foot as indeed the anti-God, but as being not so much what Davian pursues as what he is (something suggested not just by his con-founding presence in the Vatican, but also by the fact that all that is left of him by the film's end is one empty, tumbling shoe)? The film no more declares a definitive position on this than does Benji, whose terrifyingly offhand disquisition on the possibility that the rabbit's foot is a world-eviscerating technology is balanced by the recognition that it might be something else altogether – that it might even be exactly what it seems to be: simply a (very expensive) bunny appendage.

Perhaps it is just another coincidence that when an American philosopher named Quine wished to illustrate the ways in which our evidence about the world did not and could not determine a single correct way of interpreting it, he imagined the various ways in which different human tribes might describe a rabbit – as a rabbit, of course, but also (for example) as a sequence of spatio-temporal rabbit slices or a collection of undetached rabbit parts. But if this association of mine is not merely random or paranoid or superstitious, it would suggest that the film is sug-gesting that even a detached rabbit part is not merely or solely or simply or self-evidently a bunny appendage. To restrict oneself to characterizing reality in brutely material terms is not to avoid the need to interpret it – it is simply to impose one more inter-pretation, without taking responsibility for so doing. So when another person sees that reality as, say, God's creation, what we have is a confrontation of interpretations, not a conflict between realism and a fantasy erected upon it.

We can see, then, how far Ethan's desire to construct a personal life beyond IM force drives him to risk the destruction of the world and the perversion of his talents as a spy – to risk becoming a dark double of himself. But part of what seems to push him to this self-subverting extreme is not the sheer existence of his relationship with Julia, but rather the form that he continues to allow it to take, even as it mutates into marriage – a form in which he conceals the real nature of his work, and so leaves Julia unable to comprehend, and hence defend herself against, the risks to which she is now vulnerable.

Why this reluctance on Ethan's part? One part of the difficulty here is his deep-rooted professional habit of deception; another is his desire for self-protection, as well as the desire to protect her from essentially futile anxiety about him. But an earlier exchange between Ethan and Luther suggests a further motive. For when, after her funeral, Ethan characterizes Lindsey's significance to him by describing her as like his little sister, Luther asks, 'And you never slept with your little sister, right?' Ethan doesn't dignify the question with a response; but that means that he doesn't deny the suggestion either. And that suggestion has a double aspect: one which tells us something about the woman he didn't sleep with, and one which tells us something about the woman he is sleeping with.

The film certainly gives us reason to believe that Ethan was at the very least strongly attracted to his trainee. It is a threat to her that motivates him to break his self-denying compromise with the IM force; and the smooth, elegant complementarity of their teamwork in fighting their way out of the Berlin warehouse (bringing the physical grace implicit in their training sequences into explicit life) embodies the same sexual promise of any dance. So Ethan's comparison of her to his little sister tells us two things: that he denied himself the possibility of a relationship with Lindsey because he understood it as a kind of incest; but that that possibility had to be denied because Lindsey's talents as a spy genuinely attracted him. Accordingly, Julia can be seen as repre- senting a legitimate object of sexual interest for him – as some- one he can envisage sleeping with – because she resembles his little sister in having a taste for adventure and risk of the kind that IM force activities can satisfy, but is distinct from her in not already being a member of the IM force family. But precisely because she is not, Ethan finds it hard to be himself with her – to be who he really is, and so to make their relationship real.

The solution to the dilemma is clear: Julia has to *become* a member of the family, to enter it from the outside (as Abrams enters both the family of film-makers and the smaller family of makers of *Mission: Impossible* films) and thereby prove herself to be genuinely capable of developing the talents it requires and bearing the huge responsibilities it brings with it, but without being entirely absorbed by it (thus retaining the traces of a life before or beyond the relatively impoverished form that human life tends to take within the IM force, the sweetness or newness to which Ethan later refers when further articulating his sense of what Lindsey meant to him). Only then can Ethan become a member of her family, and a genuine partner with her in the family they hope in turn to create.

This is what shapes the structure of the film's concluding sequence, when Ethan finally locates Julia and attempts to extract her from Davian's grasp. Before he can release her, Davian himself intervenes: he activates the charge in Ethan's head, and then – taking advantage of the pain it causes – physically assaults him, before beginning the process of executing him in front of his wife. Ethan – inspired by Julia's intense gaze – somehow manages to overcome Davian in a fight that ends with his enemy being mown down by a truck; but the internal bomb continues on its countdown. Since he can't find a defibrillator, he improvises one from mains electricity and water, and tells Julia to use it on him and revive him afterwards. As he puts it: 'I'm going to die unless you kill me'. But since some of Davian's henchmen remain in the building, he also has to train her in the use of a weapon to defend them both. So she electrocutes her husband, and then succeeds in killing two would-be assassins, including Musgrave, whose suitcase turns out to contain the rabbit's foot. Finally, she deploys her medical knowledge to revive Ethan by restarting his heart without any hi-tech equipment; and the scene concludes with Ethan – his wife's body held close to his own, but at exactly the angle at which he and Lindsey moved together through the Berlin warehouse – staring in wonderment at everything Julia had achieved in his absence.

In order to survive, then, Ethan has to abdicate entirely from playing any active part in – literally, be dead to – the crisis he has helped to cause: he has to allow his wife to displace him in his role as an impossibly capable spy. The most he can do is to hastily prepare her for the actions that only she can perform – to train her as he trained Lindsey and many others, thereby inducting her into the IM force world. But what Julia herself brings to her newly acquired professional role, the capacity that proves truly indispensable to Ethan's resuscitation and thereby the resuscitation or recreation of their relationship, is not her incipient talent for braving danger, but something that belongs more fundamentally and self-sufficiently to her own professional mode of existence in the ordinary world: her abilities as a nurse.

This association of Julia with nursing – what one might think of as what she has to teach Ethan, in response to his pedagogy of espionage – involves something more than the notion of medical expertise; or, rather, her medical expertise connects her with a way of interpreting the world that foregrounds the idea that human beings are inherently embodied entities, and that their bodies are not merely surfaces presented to the gaze of others, but are inherently three-dimensional and so possessed of a physical as well as a psychological interior. In this respect, Julia's vocation or calling exemplifies a persistent preoccupation of this film: the acknowledgement of the human body as in the first instance a genuinely substantial or weighty object. This theme resounds in the bomb-in-the-skull motif, in the need to drag, haul and lift Davian's unconscious body through the cellars of the Vatican, in Ethan's use of Davian's substantial body weight against him in the aeroplane interrogation scene, and most obviously in Ethan's chosen means of access to the high-security building in Shanghai containing the rabbit's foot. For he can only enter it from the roof, which he can reach only by swinging across from a higher building standing nearby. More precisely, he uses that higher building as a fulcrum to which he attaches himself by a cable; and then he turns himself into a human pendulum, using his own body weight to generate the necessary momentum for the swing by jumping off the higher roof in the opposite direction to that in which he plans to travel. And although the moment at which he conceives of this way of achieving the impossible is depicted in the film as depending upon his seeing the real relations between the buildings in terms of their two-dimensional, geometrical essence (as he outlines their mass on the window-glass through which he sees them on the Shanghai skyline), his actually attaining his goal depends upon a willingness to apply the results of those abstract calculations to the real world – to incarnate them by jumping into thin air.

In part, this emphasis upon the body as possessed of interior substance is a figure for the human being's possession (or loss) of an inner life or selfhood. In part, it stands in opposition to the dematerializing effects of technology – as evinced not only in the anti-God's potential for utter decreation, but more generally in the way technology collapses space and time (via aircraft and mobile phones), and reduces individuals to monitored images or flashing dots on maps or the delicate tracery of their blood vessels (as when Lindsey is located in the Berlin warehouse by her vascular ID). The film incarnates this opposition in the sequence that takes Ethan from the scene of Julia's faked death to her true location and the scene of his own real, if temporary, death – quite as if viewing it as the final test Ethan needs to pass in order to rescue or recreate their relationship. For although he needs Benji's satellite data and a mobile phone to orient himself, his body is the only vehicle he has for getting to his wife in time. Hence he can only save her by running flat out, at the limit of his physical capabilities, from one place to the other – and the camera smoothly, weightlessly tracks the enthralling and invigorating sight of him (Ethan, I mean Tom) actually doing just that.

Julia's (and so the film's) attentiveness to the substantial human body also symbolizes what ultimately stands in opposition to technological dematerialization, and so presents itself in this world as constitutive of a genuine inner life: our flesh and blood – more specifically, our material reality, but understood as a figure for our family ties. What locates us in the human world is, before all, being someone's father or mother, brother or sister, son or daughter – a set of literally bodily continuities that project themselves into the future only insofar as they are also always open to additions or grafts from without, to individuals representing other families whose flesh nevertheless becomes spiritually one with ours as it literally inter-fuses with ours to produce offspring: the ordinary miracle of intercourse, pregnancy and birth. By aligning himself in this way with David Fincher's rather than James

Cameron's vision of Ripley's aspirations, but thereby with the incarnational emphases of orthodox Christianity, Abrams declares that any genuine family relations must be founded and given expression in the work of real flesh and real blood. His way of becoming part of the cinematic *Mission: Impossible* family is to create a work whose focus is the flesh-and-blood reality of its characters.

Accordingly, when, in the film's final scene, Ethan brings Julia into IM force headquarters to meet his colleagues and friends, we see not so much the induction of a new team member as a radical renegotiation of what membership might involve or allow for. For Julia is not simply a transient or uncomprehending visitor, someone who has nothing to say for herself to her hosts; she is bringing something to Ethan and to his fellow-inhabitants of that mode of life that would not otherwise be accessible to them, and without which they would be diminished: the extraordinariness of the ordinary, the familiar understood as the familial. But neither is she intending to join them – literally to become part of the team, and so to conflate familial and professional identities in the IM force in the manner unique to *Alias*; for, as we saw earlier, that conflation is more likely to damage the substance of both modes of human relationship than to enhance either. Julia's identity is grounded in something lying essentially beyond the limits of the world of professional espionage within which she can undeniably function, an aspect of her vocation (as nurse) and of herself (as female) that is rooted in the everyday world to which she and her husband can now return, as they stride hand in hand away from the IM force team and beyond the gaze of the camera towards us, the viewers, who must also re-enter that world as this film brings itself and its world to an end.

NOTES

INTRODUCTION

1 I explain why I do not regard the recent *Alien vs Predator* as a fifth member of the series in the postscript to Chapter 4.
2 As will be evident, my main source of inspiration is the work of Stanley Cavell, whose books on film include *The World Viewed* (Harvard University Press: Cambridge, Mass., 1971), *Pursuits of Happiness* (Harvard University Press: Cambridge, Mass., 1981), *Contesting Tears* (University of Chicago Press: Chicago, 1996) and *Cavell on Film*, edited by William Rothman (SUNY Press: New York, 2005), but whose philosophical reach extends much further. More occasional sources include Nietzsche, Heidegger, Sartre and Wittgenstein.

1 KANE'S SON, CAIN'S DAUGHTER

1 Barbara Creed, in '*Alien* and the Monstrous-feminine' (A. Kuhn [ed.], *Alien Zone* (Verso: London, 1990), notes this aspect of the prologue; but her argument works through certain ideas of Julia Kristeva's that are not, on my reading of the film, essential to grasping its logic; hence our accounts rapidly diverge.
2 cf Cavell, *The Claim of Reason* (Oxford University Press: Oxford, 1979), pp. 418–19.
3 In an out-take from the finished version of the film (included in the *Alien Trilogy* box set), Ripley is shown questioning Lambert about the sexuality of other crew members – suggesting that Lambert's more conventionally feminine appearance is associated with a degree of promiscuity.
4 We never see J.F. Sebastian's execution or his corpse; Tyrell is murdered in a context in which, as we shall see, his human status is in doubt; and the violence directed at Deckard – whose human status has also been doubted – will be shown to have an educative function.
5 Stanley Cavell gives a detailed treatment of the logic of acknowledgement in the fourth part of *The Claim of Reason*.
6 This is a version of Stanley Cavell's characterization, in *The World Viewed*.

2 MAKING BABIES

1 See chapters 2 and 3 of Cavell, *The World Viewed*.
2 Cavell, *The World Viewed*, pp. 23, 25–26.
3 See his interview, released with the *Alien Trilogy* box set.
4 Scott in fact filmed a scene for *Alien* in which Ripley encountered a cocooned Dallas, but discarded it for reasons of pacing – cf. his interview released with the *Alien Trilogy* box set.
5 A conjunction exemplified in a scene restored in the Director's Cut, where – in its opening sweep of the *Sulaco* – the camera pans across an open locker door decorated with pornographic photographs to an equally pornographic array of pulse rifles.
6 The Director's Cut includes an early scene in which the fifty-seven years of Ripley's hypersleep are shown to have included the death of her only daughter, to whom she promised to return in time for her birthday. The initial exclusion of this scene preserved *Aliens'* careful consistency with Ripley's nightmare vision of self and world, as declared in *Alien*; its subsequent incorporation sacrifices that consistency without modifying the counter-fleshly purity of the new family Cameron conceives of as Ripley's proper reward. It is a textbook example of the ways in which supposedly non-aesthetic considerations (the need to trim a movie to maximize potential daily box-office) can engender aesthetic achievements, and of a director's ability to lose touch with his own best insights.
7 See chapter four of Cavell, *The World Viewed*.
8 A claim recorded in 'The Making of *Terminator 2*'.

3 MOURNING SICKNESS

1 As Richard Dyer notes in his useful discussion of this film, *Seven* (BFI Publishing: London, 1999).
2 Quoted in James Swallow, *Dark Eye: the Films of David Fincher* (Reynolds and Hearn: Richmond, 2003), p. 149.

4 THE MONSTER'S MOTHER

1 It drives David Thomson to rewrite the script of *Alien Resurrection* altogether, rather than take it seriously as it stands – cf. Thomson, *The Alien Quartet* (Bloomsbury: London, 1998).

5 FILM AS PHILOSOPHY

1 This and the following section of this chapter together amount to a revised and expanded version of my paper 'Film as Philosophy: The Very Idea', *Proceedings of the Aristotelian Society*, Volume CVII, part 3, 2007.
2 Wittgenstein, *Philosophical Investigations* (Blackwell: Oxford, 1953), section 52.
3 Both articles were reprinted in *Film and Philosophy*, vol. 9 (2005), in which I first responded to both critics in ways which the following remarks are intended to elaborate, extend and supplement.
4 Julian Baggini, 'Alien Ways of Thinking', in *Film and Philosophy*, vol. 9 (2005), p. 18.

5 Baggini, 'Alien Ways of Thinking', p. 21.
6 Nathan Andersen, 'Is Film the Alien Other to Philosophy?', in Film and Philosophy, vol. 9 (2005), p. 2.
7 Andersen, 'Is Film the Alien Other to Philosophy?', p. 10.
8 Here I draw upon Cora Diamond's paper 'Anything but Argument?', in The Realistic Spirit (MIT: Cambridge, Mass., 1991).
9 Thomas Wartenberg, 'Beyond Mere Illustration', in Smith and Wartenberg (eds), Thinking through Cinema (Blackwell: Oxford, 2006) – hereafter TTC – p. 22.
10 Murray Smith, 'Film Art, Argument and Ambiguity', in TTC, pp 40–41.
11 Stanley Cavell, Themes Out of School (North Point Press: San Francisco, 1984), p. 9.
12 Stanley Cavell, Contesting Tears, epigraph.
13 Jonathan Lahey Dronsfield, 'The Condition of Film as Philosophy', Film and Philosophy, vol. 10 (2006), pp. 135–39.
14 Chris Darke, 'Review of On Film', Philosophers' Magazine (1st quarter, 2003), p 57. This reviewer then went on to accuse me of failing explicitly to employ a concept (mise-en-sc{e-grave}ne) without which he felt that an 'auteur' approach would make no sense. He didn't stop to consider whether that concept's absence might render his first accusation null and void.
15 Cavell, Contesting Tears, pp. 8–9.
16 This point was central to one of the anonymous readers' reports Routledge commissioned when the idea of a second edition of this book was mooted.
17 Steven Schneider, 'Review of On Film', American Philosophical Association Newsletter (June 2002).
18 cf. Darke, 'Review of On Film'
19 This paragraph summarizes a version of a line of thought laid out in Paisley Livingston, 'Theses on Cinema as Philosophy', in TTC, pp. 11–13.
20 As Noel Carroll claims, in his Theorizing the Moving Image (Cambridge University Press: Cambridge, 1996).

6 PRECRIME, PRECOGNITION AND THE PRE-REFLECTIVE COGITO

1 Dick's short story 'Minority Report' was first published in 1956; all later page references are keyed to its appearance in the collection Minority Report (Gollancz: London, 2002).
2 Matthew, 5, 27–28.
3 Jean-Paul Sartre, Being and Nothingness, trans. H. Barnes (Routledge: London, 1958).
4 Dick, Minority Report, p. 3
5 It may be worth noting that Spielberg has reportedly secured a dozen Moviolas (mechanical rather than digital editing devices), together with the necessary spare parts and technical support, in order to guarantee their availability for the foreseeable future, in the face of the now almost universal Hollywood preference for digital editing. Such reluctance to work with a digital version of his film camera's images even in the editing process suggests little appetite or respect on his part for digital means of capturing or creating them in the first place. Cf. Walter Murch, In the Blink of an Eye, second edition (Silman-James Press: Los Angeles, 2001), p. 79.

7 THE IMPERSONATION OF PERSONALITY

1 David Thomson, *The New Biographical Dictionary of Film*, fourth edition (Little, Brown: London, 2003).
2 Thomson, *The New Biographical Dictionary of Film*, p. 946.
3 Thomson, *The New Biographical Dictionary of Film*, pp. 225–26.
4 Thomson, *The New Biographical Dictionary of Film*, p. 192.
5 For more on this idea of 'modernism', to which I have already adverted more than once in this book, see the 'Introduction' to Stephen Mulhall, *Inheritance and Originality* (Oxford University Press: Oxford, 2001).
6 Cavell, *The World Viewed*, fn. 33.
7 Ideas expressed in 'The Fact of Television', in Cavell, *Themes Out of School*.
8 'The Fact of Television', in Cavell, *Themes Out of School*, pp. 257–58.
9 Thomson, *The New Biographical Dictionary of Film*, p. 226.

8 THE BURDEN OF SEX

1 Thomson, *The New Biographical Dictionary of Film*, p. 946.

FILMS DISCUSSED IN THIS BOOK

The Abyss (James Cameron, 1991)

Alien (Ridley Scott, 1979)

Alien[3] (David Fincher, 1992)

Alien Resurrection (Jean-Pierre Jeunet, 1997)

Alien vs Predator (Paul W.S. Anderson, 2004)

Aliens (James Cameron, 1986)

Amelie [*Le Fabuleux Destin d'Amélie Poulin*] (Jean-Pierre Jeunet, 2001)

Battleship Potemkin (Sergei Eisenstein, 1925)

Black Hawk Down (Ridley Scott, 2001)

Blade Runner (Ridley Scott, 1982)

The City of Lost Children (Marc Caro and Jean-Pierre Jeunet, 1995)

Delicatessen (Marc Caro and Jean-Pierre Jeunet, 1991)

Face/Off (John Woo, 1997)

Fight Club (David Fincher, 1999)

The Game (David Fincher, 1997)

Gladiator (Ridley Scott, 2000)

Kingdom of Heaven (Ridley Scott, 2005)

Minority Report (Steven Spielberg, 2002)

Mission: Impossible (Brian De Palma, 1996)

Mission: Impossible II (John Woo, 2000)

Mission: Impossible III (J.J. Abrams, 2006)

Notorious (Alfred Hitchcock, 1946)

Panic Room (David Fincher, 2002)

Paycheck (John Woo, 2003)

Se7en (David Fincher, 1995)

Snake Eyes (Brian De Palma, 1998)

Star Trek: The Wrath of Khan (Nicholas Meyer, 1982)

Terminator (James Cameron, 1986)

Terminator 2: Judgment Day (James Cameron, 1993)

Terminator 3: The Rise of the Machines (Jonathan Mostow, 2003)

The Untouchables (Brian De Palma, 1987)

Vanilla Sky (Cameron Crowe, 2001)

Zodiac (David Fincher, 2007)

BIBLIOGRAPHY

Andersen, N., 'Is Film the Alien Other to Philosophy?', in *Film and Philosophy*, vol. 9 (2005), pp. 1–11.

Baggini, J., 'Alien Ways of Thinking', in *Film and Philosophy*, vol. 9 (2005), pp. 12–23.

Carroll, N., *Theorizing the Moving Image* (Cambridge University Press: Cambridge, 1996).

Cavell, S., *The World Viewed*, expanded edition (Harvard University Press: Cambridge, Mass., 1971).

— *The Claim of Reason* (Oxford University Press: Oxford, 1979).

— *Pursuits of Happiness* (Harvard University Press: Cambridge, Mass., 1981).

— *Themes Out of School* (North Point Press: San Francisco, 1984).

— *Contesting Tears* (University of Chicago Press: Chicago, 1996).

Creed, B., '*Alien* and the Monstrous-feminine', in A. Kuhn (ed.), *Alien Zone* (Verso: London, 1990).

Darke, C., 'Review of *On Film*', in *Philosopher's Magazine* (1st quarter, 2003), p. 57.

Diamond, C., 'Anything but Argument?', in *The Realistic Spirit* (MIT Press: Cambridge, Mass., 1991).

Dick, P.K., *Minority Report* (Gollancz: London, 2002).

Dronsfield, Jonathan Lahey, 'The Condition of Film as Philosophy', in *Film and Philosophy*, vol. 10 (2006), pp. 135–50.

Dyer, R., *Seven* (BFI Publishing: London, 1999).

Livingston, P., 'Theses on Film as Philosophy', in M. Smith and T. Wartenberg (eds), *Thinking through Cinema* (Blackwell: Oxford, 2006).

Mulhall, S., *Inheritance and Originality* (Oxford University Press: Oxford, 2001).

— *On Film*, first edition (Routledge: London, 2002).

— 'Reply to Andersen and Baggini', in *Film and Philosophy*, vol. 9 (2005), pp. 24–29.

— 'Film as Philosophy: The Very Idea', in *Proceedings of the Aristotelian Society* volume CVII, part 3, 2007).

Murch, W., *In the Blink of an Eye*, second edition (Silman-James Press: Los Angeles, 2001).

Rothman, W. (ed.), *Cavell on Film* (SUNY Press: New York, 2005).

Sartre, J.P., *Being and Nothingness*, trans. H. Barnes (Routledge: London, 1958).

Schneider, S., 'Review of On Film', in *American Philosophical Association Newsletter* (June 2002).

Smith, M., 'Film Art, Argument and Ambiguity', in M. Smith and T. Wartenberg (eds), *Thinking through Cinema* (Blackwell: Oxford, 2006).

Smith, M. and Wartenberg, T. (eds), *Thinking through Cinema* (Blackwell: Oxford, 2006).

Swallow, J., *Dark Eye: The Films of David Fincher* (Reynolds and Hearn: Richmond, 2003).

Thomson, D., *The Alien Quartet* (Bloomsbury: London, 1998).

—— *The New Biographical Dictionary of Film*, fourth edition (Little, Brown: London, 2003).

Wartenberg, T., 'Beyond Mere Illustration', in M. Smith and T. Wartenberg (eds), *Thinking through Cinema* (Blackwell: Oxford, 2006).

Wittgenstein, L., *Philosophical Investigations*, trans. G.E.M. Anscombe (Blackwell: Oxford, 1953).

INDEX

Related titles from Routledge

Thinking on Screen: Film as Philosophy
Thomas E. Wartenberg

'This book is a powerful defense of the view that films can philosophize. Characterized by its clear and lively presentation, and by
its intertwining of philosophical argument with detailed discussion
of several important films, it will be of interest not just to those
studying philosophy and film but to everyone who believes in the
importance of film to our cognitive life.'

Berys Gaut, *University of St Andrews, UK*

Thinking On Screen: Film as Philosophy is an accessible and thought-provoking
examination of the way films raise and explore complex philosophical
ideas. Written in a clear and engaging style, Thomas Wartenberg examines
films' ability to discuss, and even criticize ideas that have intrigued and
puzzled philosophers over the centuries such as the nature of personhood,
the basis of morality, and epistemological skepticism.

Beginning with a demonstration of how specific forms of philosophical
discourse are presented cinematically, Wartenberg moves on to offer a systematic
account of the ways in which specific films undertake the task of philosophy.
Focusing on the films *The Man Who Shot Liberty Valance, Modern Times, The
Matrix, Eternal Sunshine of the Spotless Mind, The Third Man, The Flicker*, and
Empire, Wartenberg shows how these films express meaningful and pertinent philosophical ideas.

Thinking On Screen: Film as Philosophy is essential reading for students of
philosophy with an interest in film, aesthetics, and film theory. It will also
be of interest to film enthusiasts intrigued by the philosophical implications
of film.

ISBN 13: 978-0-415-77430-7 (hbk)
ISBN 13: 978-0-415-77431-4 (pbk)
ISBN 13: 978-0-203-03062-2 (ebk)

Available at all good bookshops
For ordering and further information please visit:
www.routledge.com

Talk to Her

Edited by Anne W. Eaton

Pedro Almodóvar is one of the most renowned film directors of recent years and *Talk to Her* is one of the most discussed and controversial of all his films. Dealing principally with the issue of rape, it offers profound insights into the nature of love and friendship whilst raising important philosophical and moral questions in unsettling and often paradoxical ways.

This is the first book to explore and address the philosophical aspects of Almodóvar's film. Opening with a helpful introduction that places the film in context, specially commissioned essays go on to examine the following topics:

- Gender and issues of rape and consent
- Virtue and the ethics of love and friendship
- The nature of dialogue and what 'talking to someone' involves
- The role of moral judgement and narrative of 'living a life'
- Art and morality

Including annotated sections of further reading at the end of each chapter and a biography of Almodóvar, *Talk to Her* is essential reading for students interested in philosophy and film as well as ethics and gender. It is also provides an accessible and informative insight into philosophy for those in related disciplines such as film studies, literature and religion.

Contributors: Robert B. Pippin, George M. Wilson, C.D.C Reeve, Cynthia Freeland, Noël Carroll, Anne W. Eaton.

ISBN 13: 978-0-415-77366-9 (hbk)
ISBN 13: 978-0-415-77367-6 (pbk)

Related titles from Routledge

The Thin Red Line
Edited by David Davies

The Thin Red Line is the third film from acclaimed director Terrence Malick, set during the struggle between American and Japanese forces for Guadalcanal in the South Pacific in World War Two. It is a powerful, enigmatic and complex film that raises important philosophical questions, ranging from the existential and phenomenological to the artistic and technical.

This is the first book to explore and address the philosophical aspects of Malick's film. Opening with a helpful introduction that places the film in context, seven specially commissioned essays go on to examine the following topics:

- the role of truth, immortality and 'calm' in the Thin Red Line
- the central place of Heidegger's thought in Malick's work, such as authenticity and being-towards-death
- metaphysics and the concept of rationality and community
- Malick's use of style and emotion to contrast the 'natural' world with the 'human' world
- The centrality of the themes of vision and touch in *The Thin Red Line*

Including annotated sections of further reading at the end of each chapter and a biography of Terrence Malick, *The Thin Red Line* is essential reading for students interested in philosophy and film or phenomenology and existentialism. It is also provides an accessible and informative insight into philosophy for those in related disciplines such as film studies, literature and religion.

Contributors: Amy Coplan, Simon Critchley, David Davies, Hubert Dreyfus, Camillo Prince, Iain Macdonald.

ISBN 13: 978-0-415-77364-5 (hbk)
ISBN 13: 978-0-415-77365-2 (pbk)

Available at all good bookshops
For ordering and further information please visit:
www.routledge.com